NEOLIBERALISM, PERSONHOOD, AND POSTSOCIALISM

T0304073

Neoliberalism, Personhood, and Postsocialism
Enterprising Selves in Changing Economies

Edited by
NICOLETTE MAKOVICKY
University of Oxford, UK

Routledge
Taylor & Francis Group
LONDON AND NEW YORK

First published 2014 by Ashgate Publishing

2 Park Square, Milton Park, Abingdon, Oxon OX14 4RN
711 Third Avenue, New York, NY 10017, USA

Routledge is an imprint of the Taylor & Francis Group, an informa business

First issued in paperback 2016

British Library Cataloguing in Publication Data
A catalogue record for this book is available from the British Library

The Library of Congress has cataloged the printed edition as follows:
Neoliberalism, personhood, and postsocialism : enterprising selves in changing economies / [edited] by Nicolette Makovicky.
    pages cm
 Includes bibliographical references and index.
 ISBN 978-1-4094-6787-8 (hardback) – ISBN 978-1-4094-6788-5 (ebook) –
 ISBN 978-1-4094-6789-2 (epub) 1. Post-communism – Europe, Eastern.
2. Neoliberalism – Europe, Eastern. 3. Former communist countries – Economic conditions. 4. Former communist countries – Social conditions. I. Makovicky, Nicolette.

 HN380.7.A8N46 2014
 320.51–dc23

                                                                            201303232

ISBN 978-1-4094-6787-8 (hbk)
ISBN 978-1-138-24700-0 (pbk)

Contents

List of Figures

Notes on Contributors

Aet Annist is Postdoctoral Research Fellow at the Department of Social and Cultural Anthropology at Tallinn University. She holds a PhD from University College London (2007) and has taught at several social sciences departments in Estonia. Dr Annist has published widely on the topics of development institutions and cultural heritage, but also on the juxtapositions between post-socialist changes in social mutuality and neo-liberal economy, new technologies of power, and identity. Her latest book *Otsides kogukonda sotsialismijärgses keskuskülas. Arenguantropoloogiline uurimus* (2011) explores the community-building initiatives of two British-funded participatory development programs in rural Estonia.

Zuzana Sekeráková Búriková works at the Faculty of Social Sciences at Masaryk University in Brno, the Czech Republic. She also has a part-time position at the Institute of Ethnology at Slovak Academy of Sciences in Bratislava, where she received her PhD in ethnology. She has a special interest in material culture, consumption and transnational domestic labour. Zuzana has published articles and book chapters on au pair migration, consumption and material culture, especially in relation to religion and the (post)socialist condition. With Daniel Miller as a co-author, she completed the book *Au Pair* (Polity, 2010) on the experience of Slovak au pairs and their host families in London. Her research has been funded by the Leverhulme Trust, GAČR and VEGA; she has previously held fellowships at the Institute for Social and Cultural Anthropology at Oxford University (2000–2001), the Department of Anthropology at University College London (2002–2003), and Institut für Wissenschaften vom Menschen in Vienna (2003).

Liviu Chelcea is Associate Professor and Head of the Department of Sociology and Social Work at the University of Bucharest. He holds a PhD in cultural anthropology (University of Michigan, 2004) and has researched the transformations of urban and family life in relation to the confiscation of housing by the socialist state. He has published articles on deindustrialization, informal economy, kinship, consumption in Romanian and contributed to international journals such as *Cultural Studies*, *Comparative Studies in Society and History*, and *International Journal of Urban and Regional Research*. His research has been funded by grants obtained from Ford Foundation, National Science Foundation, Wenner-Gren Foundation, and the CNCSIS. His latest book *Bucureştiul postindustrial: Memorie, dezindustriale şi regenerare urbana* (Polirom, 2008) deals with deindustrialization of Bucharest.

Gareth E. Hamilton is Assistant Professor in the Department of Social Anthropology at the University of Latvia, Riga. He previously tutored and lectured in the Anthropology Department, University of Durham, where he completed a PhD in Social Anthropology as part of the ESRC-funded project _Sociality and Rhetoric Culture in the Interpretation of Situations: An Anthropological Theory and its Application in East Germany_. Gareth has been published in _Social Anthropology_ and was guest editor and contributor to the _Durham Anthropology Journal_ Special Edition _Beyond Post-socialism: Creativity, Moral Resistance and Change in the Corners of Eurasia_, 17(1), 2010.

Maria Padrón Hernández completed her doctorate in Social Anthropology, School of Global Studies at the University of Gothenburg in December, 2012. Her research interests span the fields of economic and urban anthropology, morality, kinship, late and post-socialism and Latin America. She has undertaken long-term fieldwork in Mexico and Cuba. Maria lectures in Social Anthropology and Global Studies at the School of Global Studies and the Department of Psychology, Gothenburg University. In the summer of 2011, she was Linnaeus Palme visiting lecturer at the Universidad Nacional de Tucumán, Argentina. Maria currently works as a consultant at Contextio Ethnographic in Gothenburg.

Don Kalb is Professor of Social Anthropology at the Central European University, Budapest, and researcher at Utrecht University, the Netherlands. His current research focuses on problems of economic restructuring, culture, class, and citizenship in Eastern Europe. He has written several monographs including _Expanding Class: Power and Everyday Politics in Industrial Communities, The Netherlands, 1850–1950_ (Duke University Press, 1997) and _Globalization and Development: Themes and Concepts in Current Research_ (Kluwer, 2004). He (co-)edited the volumes _The Ends of Globalization. Bringing Society Back In_ (Rowman and Littlefield, 2000), _Critical Junctions: Pathways beyond the Cultural Turn_ (Berghahn Books, 2005), and _Headlines of Nation, Subtexts of Class: Working-Class Populism and the Return of the Repressed in Neoliberal Europe_ (Berghahn Books, 2011). Don Kalb is the founding editor of _FOCAAL, Journal of Global and Historical Anthropology_.

Jonathan L. Larson is Visiting Professor of Anthropology at the University of Iowa. He received his PhD in Anthropology from the University of Michigan, Ann Arbor, where he was the recipient of a Václav Havel Dissertation Award. His research is on the acquisition and practice of civic and civil criticism, the ethics of critical communities, and critical thinking as a problem of postsocialism. This has led him to write broadly about language, knowledge, and politics, particularly in recent Eastern European history. He is the author of the book _Critical Thinking in Slovakia after Socialism_ (University of Rochester Press, 2013). His research articles have appeared in the _Journal of Linguistic Anthropology, Critique of Anthropology_, and _Ethnos: Journal of Anthropology_, and _Europe-Asia Studies_.

Nicolette Makovicky is a Lecturer in Russian and Eastern European Studies at the School of Interdisciplinary Area Studies, University of Oxford. Her research considers the impact of socio-economic reforms and EU-integration on historically embedded modes of economic activity in Central Europe. She has a particular theoretical interest in processes of value creation, work ethics, entrepreneurialism, gender, and citizenship in post-socialist society. Nicolette has contributed to a wide range of edited volumes, as well as publishing in a number of journals such as *The Journal of Modern Craft*, *FOCAAL*, and *Journal of the Royal Anthropological Society*. She previously held a Junior Research Fellowship at Wolfson College, Oxford (2007–2010) and was an External Tutor in History of Design, Royal College of Art (2007–2011). She is the co-editor of *Economies of Favour after Socialism* (Oxford University Press, 2014).

Alina Petrovici is a consultant at SC CE SA and Research Fellow in the Department of Sociology at Babeş-Bolyai University. Her recently completed PhD was entitled *Transforming Neoliberal Corporate Environments. Human Resources Perspectives in Cluj, Romania* and was an organizational study focusing on corporate management and labour relations in a Romanian telecoms company, paying particular attention to the displays of power, resistance and submission amongst employees. Alina holds an MA in Sociology from Babeş-Bolyai University, and received training in research methods and statistical analysis at the University of Bologna and Fribourg University, Switzerland. She has previously undertaken research into regional development and resource management, and also worked as a Program Consultant for the Department of Social Work and Child Protection, Cluj.

Radu Umbres completed his doctorate in Social Anthropology at the Department of Anthropology, University College London in 2012 and is currently a post-doctoral researcher at the Institut Jean Nicod (CNRS-EHESS-ENS) in Paris, France. He holds an MSc in Sociology (University of Oxford), a BA in Sociology (University of Bucharest) and a BA in Economics (Bucharest Academy of Economic Studies). His research interests lie in understanding on folk theories of the social contract and their articulation in kinship, political and economic practices. He is co-author of *Migration and Entrepreneurship: Social Change in Rural Romania* (Lumen, 2006).

Acknowledgements

This volume started life as a conference panel at the 11th European Association of Anthropologists Biannual Conference in Maynooth, Ireland, with the name *The self as 'mini-corporation'? The fate of neoliberal models in the boom (and bust) economies of Central and Eastern Europe.* Anticipating limited interest in the subject, the organizers allocated us a modest teaching room off the main lecture theatre. However, as the session got underway, a constant stream of listeners filled the seats and all the available floor-space until we found ourselves turning people away. The theme had evidently struck a nerve with colleagues working in and beyond the region, and sparked a lively debate which has continued since.

I would like to thank Dimitris Dalakoglou, who was the discussant on the original conference panel, for his encouragement and enthusiasm for this project. The manuscript and many of the chapters benefited from comments and critique of senior colleagues at various times, we would like to thank Miloslav Bahna, Juraj Buzalka, Michael Carrithers, Peter Collins, Irina Culic, Ina Dietzsch, Susan Frekko, Stephen Gudeman, Irena Jenčová, Don Kalb, Daniel Miller, Norbert Petrovici, and Peter Phillimore, as well as the three anonymous reviewers recruited by Ashgate for their valuable input. As editor, I would like to extend my heartfelt thanks to Neil Jordan from Ashgate, who has provided support and advice at every stage from the initial proposal to the production of the finished book. Likewise, I would not have been able to complete and format the manuscript without the generous and enthusiastic help of my partner Nicolas Schaeffer.

Finally, like all other academic endeavours, book projects require funding, as well as the time and efforts of the contributors and the editor. Much of the work assembling and editing this volume was supported by an Arts and Humanities Research Council Early Career Fellowship (AH/I001891/1).

Me, Inc.? Untangling Neoliberalism, Personhood, and Postsocialism

Nicolette Makovicky

Economics are the method, but the objective is to change the soul –
Margaret Thatcher, Interview, *The Sunday Times*, 3 May 1981.

Introduction

In January 1990, just two months after the fall of the Berlin Wall and barely a week after the execution of the Romanian dictator Nicolae Ceaușescu, the Harvard economist Jeffrey Sachs presented the world with a new vision for Central and Eastern Europe. 'Businessmen, not economists, will determine the new technologies, organisational systems and management techniques that will be the source of Eastern Europe's reinvigoration' he wrote in his seminal article *What is to be done?* for *The Economist*. With his ironic appropriation of Lenin's 1901 manifesto title, Sachs invoked the spirit of revolution and instructed the politicians and economists of the former Eastern Bloc to 'reject any lingering ideas about a "third way"' in favour of 'western-style market economy' (1990: 1). Indeed, for Sachs, reform-minded economists and Western-oriented politicians were to be the midwives of the post-socialist transformation. The birth-mother of a new, democratic, capitalist Eurasia, however, would be the only agent ostensibly free of any ideological contamination: capital. To ensure a quick delivery, billions of dollars in Western aid in the form of loans, export credits, and technical assistance were injected into the limping economies of Central and Eastern Europe by USAID, the European Union, and Western Europe. By the mid-1990s, post-socialist transformation had itself becoming a booming industry supporting an army of fly-by-night development consultants and 'econolobbyists' (Wedel 1998), NGOs, planners, and academics, proffering solutions and predicting outcomes for their Eastern cousins.

In her recent monograph on privatization, managerial change and labour reform in Poland, Elizabeth Dunn notes that the successful adoption of a market economy 'requires changing the very foundation of what it means to be a person' (2004: 6). In line with Margaret Thatcher's statement that economics was the tool for a reform of the soul quoted above, the majority of the agents and architects of 'transition' believed that a reform of the socialist psyche would be an inevitable outcome of the dismantling of the institutional structures which had help create and sustain it. As Leszek Balcerowicz, Poland's first post-Communist minister of finance and an advocate of the 'shock therapy' approach to economic reform, remarked: 'Private market economy is the natural state of contemporary society' and the wiping away of state prohibitions 'always leads to the development of private enterprise' (Balcerowicz in Dunn 2004: 4). For libertarians promoting the therapeutic value of capital injection and deregulation human nature was 'always already' entrepreneurial. It was communist central planning which set unnatural strictures upon the natural propensity to 'truck, barter, and exchange one thing for another' to use the words of Adam Smith (1981: 117). Others went further, projecting the value-laden language of delinquency used to assess the discredited institutions of the socialist system wholesale on the subjects they had produced: passive individuals coddled by the paternalism of socialism, and characterized by pessimism, dissimulation, an attraction to populist demagogy, and a lack of civic virtues (Jowitt 1992). As Trenholme Junghans (2001) points out, these pathologies of the socialist mind-set grew out of a Cold War discursive regime which pitched the 'determined', totalitarian Other against a 'self-authoring', liberal-democratic Self. While projects of social, political and economic reform were thought to 'liberate the entrepreneurial energies and patterns of grass-roots association' which had been suppressed by socialism, they were also meant to 're-orient behavioural and conceptual repertoires' emphasizing 'the need for conversion, or radical self-reform' (2001: 384).

This volume makes the rise of this discourse of the 'enterprising' self (Rose 1996), and the technologies of self-government which have appeared in its wake, the subject of critical enquiry. Bringing together ethnographic research from across the former Soviet Bloc, the contributing authors explore sites and events which frame the formation of new subjectivities in newly marketized or marketizing societies. From coaching sessions in business-practice in the former East German city of Halle, to the effects of changing managerial strategies in a Romanian bank, the contributing authors illustrate the proselytizing of a rhetoric of responsibility, self-help, flexibility, and choice which characterizes the discourse of neo-liberal governmentality (McNay 2009), while bringing into view the lived experience of the economic, social, and cultural changes brought on by increasingly globalized flows of capital, labour, and commodities. Others focus on marginal capitalists and entrepreneurs working in the grey zone between the formal and informal economies, underscoring the co-existence and co-production of multiple forms of capital and systems of value in contexts as diverse as a Romanian village to a Cuba toying with the possibility of economic liberalization. They reveal the full complexity of the relationship between historically and socially embedded economic practices and the increasing influence of libertarian political and economic thought on public policy, institutional reform, and civil society initiatives.

Narratives of Transformation

By bringing together the study of 'neoliberalism' and that of 'postsocialism', this volume aims to create a dialogue between two, parallel narratives of global socio-economic change. One is the story of the transformation of Euro-American modernity from industrial capitalism to a regime of 'flexible accumulation' (Harvey 1987). The second is an attempt to describe and organize the heterogeneous experiences of economic and political liberalization in post-1989 Europe and the former Soviet Union. One of the assumptions underpinning the contributions to this book is that much can be gained from investigating the manner in which these narratives intersect and inform one another. Approaching specific instances of market socialist and post-socialist liberalization as variants of neo-liberal models of governance can provide a potent critique of old dichotomies and homologies inherent in the study of 'postsocialism', as well as throw light on problematic issues of contemporary capitalism itself. The conceptual work done by scholars of neoliberalism can benefit those with a critical eye on the post-socialist condition by opening up for a new engagement with discourses of 'market transition' as cultural process that look beyond questions of direction and development. Conversely, ethnographies of socialist and post-socialist society provide a useful counterpoint to claims of pervasive neo-liberalization, and throw a questioning light on the validity of Foucaultian notions of 'neo-liberal governmentality' in particular.

The problem of finding an adequate theoretical framework for dealing with large-scale socio-economic change has long been familiar to any scholar of the former Eastern Bloc. Throughout the 1990s, anthropologists voiced scepticism about the practice and literature of 'transitology' (Burawoy and Verdery 1999), detecting both economic determinism and a naive teleology in the linear narratives of progress spun by lobbyists, politicians, and policy-makers seeking to reform post-socialist Central and Eastern Europe. Chris Hann (2002) suggested that anthropology could supply the 'necessary corrective' to its deficits by offering insight into postsocialism as lived experience. Amongst anthropologists, 'postsocialism' itself won out over 'transition' as the chosen term of reference, emphasizing the need to assess the institutional legacies and cultural heritage of socialism within and beyond the borders of Europe (Humphrey 2002, Verdery 2002). The 'post' of 'postsocialism' implied a temporal shift in place of the more heavily politico-geographical emphasis of 'transition' discourse. Nevertheless, there has been no lack of discussion about the term's longevity and conceptual usefulness (Sampson 2002), Chris Hann going so far as to say that while postsocialism is 'useful as a general label', it has ultimately brought 'no theoretical advance' to the study of post-1989 Eurasia (2006: 5). Just as postsocialism continues to be bandied-about for lack of a better alternative, few anthropologists have been willing to engage textually with the nitty-gritty of policy change and fiscal reform which affected the lives and livelihoods of their subjects (although see Dunn 2004, Gille 2007, Collier 2011). Instead, ethnographies of 'postsocialism' are generally content with refereeing to these changes using generic and theoretically vague terms such as 'market reform' and 'capitalism'. As Katherine Verdery asserts '"capitalism" is a category that people go on using profitably, without qualms. So, while "postsocialism" is certainly a construct of the academy, it is not ours alone, and it does correspond to certain historical conditions "out there"' (2002: 12). What remains to be said, however, in order to gain an accurate understanding of the 'conditions "out there"' it is necessary to interrogate the nature of local capitalism (and thus postsocialism) itself, as well as nature of the capitalist world into which these countries and their citizens entered after 1989.

In short, the contributions in this volume follow Chris Hann's encouragement to 'take neo-liberalism seriously' (2006: 7) in their attempts to depict the effects of contemporary social change in what is still called the post-socialist world. The conventional re-telling of the history of neo-liberal political and economic philosophy will already be familiar to many readers. Against the waning success of post-War Keynesianism, neo-liberal economic thought gained prominence with the 'stagflation' and the deregulation of the international monetary markets in the 1970s. Combining neo-classical theories economics with free-market libertarianism, neo-liberal thinkers advocated the non-intervention of the state in markets in favour of a *laissez-faire* approach, and encouraged the minimization of state industry in favour of private enterprise in the belief that free-market competition supplied most efficient and rational mechanism for utility maximization, price efficiency, and resource allocation. Thatcherite neo-conservatism, Reaganomics, and the rise of IMF 'structural adjustment' programs as a novel political technology, were the direct outcome of a fusion of economic philosophy with a libertarian ideological paradigm which modelled both individual and state actors – as well as the relationship between them – on a market logic. Their legacy has been 30 years of 'technocratic, marketized, audit-oriented mode of governance' (Kingfisher and Maskovsky 2008), which has actively shrunk the state through the privatization of national assets and liberalization of public service provision, strengthened capital and employers vis-à-vis the labour force, and created a move from welfare to 'workfare' provisioning.

David Harvey's (2003, 2005) interpretation of neoliberalism as a political economy of capitalist expansion led by the interests of a global entrepreneurial class has been an influential – if much criticized – attempt at constructing a grand narrative chronicling the effects of neo-liberal policy implementation on a global scale. Neoliberalism, he contends, can be seen as a regime of 'accumulation by dispossession' (2005: 159) operating through an aggressive process of commodification, privatization, and re-distribution of resources in favour of 'vulture' capital. Following Harvey's lead, Katherine Verdery (2009) has suggested that studies of the post-socialist experience might provide a privileged critical standpoint from which to study and evaluate the effects of neoliberalism as the dominance of capital over labour. Coining the term 'fuzzy property' (2003) to describe the results of the meeting of classic, liberal notion of property with the complex, lived practices of community life, Verdery herself is representative of a strong tradition within contemporary anthropological writing which identifies the creation of new property objects and property regimes as a primary characteristic of the neo-liberalization of society (see collections such as Benda-Beckmann et al. 2009, Hann et al. 2003, Strathern and Hirsch 2005, Verdery and Humphrey 2004).

Much of this work – particularly on themes of human reproduction and biotechnology – intersects with another, equally influential, strand of scholarly thought on the subject of neoliberalism. Perhaps best represented by the work of Peter Miller and Nikolas Rose (Miller and Rose 2008, Rose 1996, 1999), it invokes the Foucaultian notion of 'bio-power' to re-conceptualize neoliberalism from a question of political economy to a problem of governance. Miller and Rose define 'neo-liberal governmentality' as the introduction of the market and market logic within the realms of the state itself: The imperative to run the state 'like a business' is transferred to the individual enabling government 'at a distance' through the technologies of targets, audits, risk management, and standards. Rose shows how neo-liberal political philosophy has articulated equally comfortably with the consumer society and with psychotherapeutic techniques, constituting the self as a domain of government through the cultivation of individual desires and emotions, while prescribing responsibility and prudence. It thus produces a 'new ethic of the active, choosing, responsible, autonomous individual obliged to be free, and to live life as if it were an outcome of free choice' (Miller and Rose 2008: 18). In short, the neo-liberal 'style' of government operates through the construction of particular socio-economic structures that induce desired behaviour in the individual, while making these appear to be entirely directed by the will of an autonomous subject.

The wide-reaching impact of Foucaultian approaches to contemporary government on the anthropological world is reflected in the birth of 'audit culture' as a new, legitimate field of ethnographic enquiry (Carrier and Miller 1998, Strathern 2000, Shore 2008, 2010), as well as a propensity to read neo-liberal policy-making as a force productive of a new, transnational politics of life (Ong 1999, 2007). For Aihwa Ong (2007), neoliberalism is characterized by a certain geographical and political promiscuity: neoliberal government is a free-floating, de-territorialized 'migratory technology of governing' (2007: 5) that creates new production, labour markets and 'flexible' citizens through 'techniques of calculative choice' (2006: 19). As a style of regulatory authority, neoliberalism interacts and co-exists with other political rationalities across social classes and states, and can be applied to territorially confined spaces to create fertile ground for the investment of transnational capital without impinging on state sovereignty. In so far as Ong's work suggests that the relation between features labelled 'socialist' and 'liberal', or 'market capitalist', is neither a straightforward question of chronology, nor the product of diametrically opposite political rationalities, it sits well within the remit of this volume – and, indeed, within the general anthropological critique of theories of teleological models of 'transition'. Yet, if she is correct in her assertion that neoliberalism as a tool of government is a flexible assemblage of practices that happily co-habit with other techniques and regimes of truth, the question becomes not only how far these are understood to reach, but how exactly this co-habitation is arranged, and to what degree are neo-liberal assemblages qualitatively different from their bedfellows.

The contributions to this volume add their voices to a growing number of critiques of neoliberalism as a 'style' of government emerging from the post-socialist context. Jonathan Larson, for example, highlights the importance of (Czecho)Slovakia's historical engagements with other forms of political and economic liberalism for the contemporary organization of personhood, warning against the danger of over-emphasizing the post-socialist rupture. He echoes Andrew Kipnis' warning to scholar not to assimilate the 'neo-liberal aspects of post-Soviet governing – the "shock therapy" of rapid privatization" – with a wide range of more ambiguous governing actions' (2008: 280), thus overstating their unique nature and their importance. In contrast, Aet Annist questions the degree to which ethnographers have tended to analyse the macro-level socio-economic and political conditions and the lived reality of the individual micro-level as reflections of one-another. In so doing, she joins a cohort of scholars questioning the formal affinities between socialist(-era) bio-politics and the ostensibly neo-liberal goal of producing 'self-mastering' subjects, and illustrating how 'forms' of governance are themselves subject to ideological interpretation on the part of their subjects and scholars alike (Matza 2009, Kipnis 2011, Collier 2011).

Indeed, whether understood as a macro-economic doctrine or an 'art of government', the recent rush to operationalize neoliberalism as an interpretive tool has not been without its detractors. As a conceptual cousin of 'globalization', the concept of neoliberalism has suffered the similar problems of scale, territory and theoretical ambiguity. Scholars from across the disciplines of anthropology, sociology and geography have emphasized the spatially uneven and contextually embedded nature of neo-liberal projects and processes, calling for the analysis of 'actually existing neoliberalism' (Brenner and Theodore 2002, Gledhill 2004), and paying attention to its 'spatialization' (Gupta and Ferguson 2002, Peck and Tickell 2002) and 'domestication' (Smith et al. 2010). Others have pointed to the conceptual weakening of the term that has come in the wake of its almost indiscriminate application across extremely diverse social, historical and political contexts (Clarke 2004, 2008, Ferguson 2010, Kingfisher and Maskovsky 2008). As an analytical category, John Clarke notes, neoliberalism suffers from 'promiscuity, omnipresence, and omnipotence' (2008: 135): its ability to co-habit with any number of theoretical perspectives has only fuelled a tendency label it the cause and effect of any number of socio-economic and political changes across the globe. James Ferguson levels his critique at its misappropriation as 'a sloppy synonym for capitalism itself, or as a kind of shorthand for the world economy and its inequalities' (2010: 171).

Despite its conceptual shortcomings, however, the contributions to this volume make judicious use of 'neoliberalism' to describe a particular technology of governance (and self-governance) implemented and expressed through the gradual economization of social and institutional life under the guise of post-socialist structural transformation. The fact remains that ethnographic approaches to neoliberalization of society have shown the potential to deliver social and intellectual critique of precisely the widening inequality between individuals, communities, and nations, but also the proliferation of exclusionary practices which have accompanied the rise of capital. Nowhere is this more potent than in studies of the effects of neo-liberal economic policy on post-socialist class-formation, identity politics, and nationalism: highlighting the problems of social inequality, working class marginalization, and elite formation, they connect the experiences of the individual with the constitution of collective identities through class, religion, and subculture (Creed 2011, Kalb and Halmai 2011, Kiedeckel 2007, Schröder and Vonderau 2009). This volume aims to contribute further to this tradition of critical scholarship by focusing on an area that has enjoyed relatively little attention from anthropologists of post-socialist Eurasia, namely the consequences of the rise of neo-liberal political and economic philosophy for the constitution of citizenship, subjectivity, and self-identity.

Narratives of Personhood

A steadily rising number of ethnographies from across Euro-America and East Asia have identified an ostensibly novel form of reflexive subjectivity, understood to be produced by industrial restructuring, rapid globalization, and the implementation of capital-friendly, neo-liberal policies. Today, the 'enterprising selves' of Miller and Rose's Britain are joined by 'flexible citizens' in Asia (Ong 1999, 2007), 'choosing subjects' from Poland (Dunn 2004), and Americans encouraged to run themselves as 'mini-corporations' (Martin 2000a, 2000b). Today's individuals are encouraged to 'view their lives and identities as a type of enterprise, understood as a relation to the self, based ultimately on a notion of incontestable economic interest' (McNay 2009: 56). As the entrepreneur of his or her own life, the individual is called to propel themselves forward through the continual exercise of life-style and consumer choices, while subjecting themselves to frequent de- and re-skilling exercises, 'personal development techniques', and self-audits in public and private life (Martin 2001, Hochschild 2008). In an environment where universal entitlements and jobs-for-life are disappearing in favour of 'flexible' employment and work-fare, neo-liberal subjects are seen as being encouraged to regard themselves not simply as property-owners and their owners of their labour power (as in the classical liberal tradition), but as a 'collection of assets that must be continually invested in, nurtured, managed, and developed' (Martin 2000: 582). In short, the individual is encouraged to understand themselves as a form of human capital, and act upon themselves as such.

Few have offered as evocative an example of the socio-cultural resonances of these developments as Emily Martin. Tracing the metaphorical connections made between the body, health, and society in America, she shows how popular imagery of reproduction and the immune system has shifted from a hierarchical, mechanistic model reflecting the 'form and function' of 'early twentieth-century Fordist mass-production' (1997: 544), to illustrations of the body as a complex, flexible, and self-regulating system akin to perceptions of global capital, manufacturing, and the market of 'flexible' capitalism. Indeed, the image of the 'flexible', 'self-regulating' immune system mirrors the ideal of the self-managed, innovative, and ambitious 'entreployee' created by contemporary management techniques (Martin 1992, 1994, 2000a). Pushing the analogy further, Martin suggests that the environment of accelerated change has contributed to the positive valuation of hyper-activity with creativity, energy, charisma, and successful enterprise (Martin 2007). Here, too, Martin exploits linguistic crossovers in the depictions of the mind and the global economy, pointing to references to 'manic capital' and 'depressive loses' that litter journalistic reporting of the stock market (2000b: 580) to underscore a loss of faith in the calculative rationality of the market and a growing acknowledgement of the role of emotion and impulse.

Martin's vivid evocation of the charismatic 'entreployee' as neo-liberal ideal haunts two of the contributions to this volume. Writing about managerial reform and changing work practices in a Romanian bank, Liviu Chelcea describes how the transformation of power within the workplace and a disciplining of the workforce is achieved through a variety of methods, from a new office lay-out and team-building courses, to merit-based pay and the introduction of 'charismatic' managers. Yet, most striking is a colonization of personal time by the corporation through long work hours, weekend course and compulsory training. As Chelcea shows, the bank is a 'greedy institution' whose voracious appetite for the employees' time results not only in their description of the privatization process through a temporal idiom, but a qualitative change in employees' experience of time itself. Alina Petrovici, on the other hand, spins the question of corporate governance through the prism of gender. She shows how power in the work environment is exercised by capitalizing on prevalent negative perceptions of the failings of the socialist employee, and how the performance of role of enterprising employee relies heavily on the belief in and acting-out of stereotypes of gendered behaviour. Striving to demonstrate 'male' characteristics such as efficiency and assertiveness, Petrovici concludes, leads female managers to internalize an ostensibly egalitarian discourse of self-improvement to the extent that they lose the ability to access avenues of negotiation and dialogue with both subordinates, and higher management.

These two chapters illustrate how the workplace provides an arena for the enactment of the self as human capital by promising autonomy and empowerment. Another arena is the marketplace. Writing on post-socialist Poland, Elizabeth Dunn notes that after 1989 novel practices of advertising worked to 'reconstruct desire, identity, class, and occupation' by linking 'marketization and personhood' (2004: 60). Indeed, the act of consumption became not only constitutive of individual subjectivity, but choosing itself became elevated to a social virtue: the individual 'choice-making entrepreneur of him or herself ... consumes products in order to act upon his or her qualities' and 'becomes an engine of economic growth' (2004: 128). The right to consumer choice thus became coupled with a 'duty to consume' (Berdahl 2005: 238). At the same time, consumption promised to make the individual governable: the exercise of choice as self-actualization is taken to reflect a unity of intention and action rendering an individual 'knowable'. As the 'non-substitutable and irreducible atom of interest' (2008: 291) in market-driven society, the individual is governed through the 'organized proliferation of individual difference in an economized matrix' (McNay 2009: 56) which multiply social differences, rather than levelling them. In short, consumption became the crux of a new set of disciplinary techniques modelled on the competitive marketplace. In fact, all over post-socialist Eurasia the 'duty to choose' and the 'duty to consume' are now part of the performance of citizenship as spaces and acts of consumption have expanded to include areas previously covered by public provisioning, such as education, housing, and health insurance. The reluctance or inability to exercise consumer choice becomes characteristic of 'faulty' citizens, marked out by their seeming inability to behave as rational, autonomous, self-regulating actors in a competitive marketplace (Bauman 2005).

Unsurprisingly, the post-socialist subject has all too often been presented as just such a 'faulty' citizen by policy makers, non-governmental actors, and academics alike. Known collectively as 'transition losers', such individuals are presented as indelibly marked by socialist paternalism because if their age or lack of (re-) education, a predicament evident in their inability to find employment in the new economy, an attraction to political populism, and a penchant for clientelism, and corruption (Klicperova-Baker 1999, Sztompka 1996, Vainshtein 1994). Their pathology is assumed to be a product of life under a totalitarian regime which brought about the destruction of social linkages, and was responsible for the growth of informal networks established to serve the narrow, self-directed ends of a population living within a defective political and economic system (Hann 1985, Kideckel 1993, Ledeneva 1998). Neo-liberal rhetorics of 'enterprise' and 'self-help' are thus indelibly linked to the belief in liberalization as a moral corrective to the defects of the 'socialist' persona. Indeed, the chapters by Larson, Chelcea, Hamilton, Petrovici, and Sekeráková Búriková, all illustrate how the habit of labelling personality traits as 'socialist' or 'capitalist' has found its way into development discourse, into the workplace, and into popular culture, and become an effective tool in the (self-) governance of the individual (Dunn 2004). Not only have words such as 'choice', 'responsibility', or 'dependent', and 'inflexible' gained a new conceptual dimension along with novel constructions of personhood, but models of the ideal post-socialist agent as neo-liberal subject continue to be constructed as part of a double image with their historical ('socialist') counterpart.

The pitfalls of this classificatory schema are not difficult to spot: while 'flexibility' and 'choice' celebrated as a desirable trait of the contemporary, liberal subject, not all kinds of flexibility in professional and personal life are seen as legitimate, effectively denying the comparability and validity of life experiences gained prior to 1989. The de-legitimization of previous social values and lifestyles take centre-stage in Zuzana Sekeráková Búriková's chapter on the migratory experience of Slovak au-pairs in London. In the context of rapid neo-liberalization, the old certainties of life delivered by the Czechoslovak socialist regime have faded and have become tainted with the discourse of backwardness. Not only do young people no longer conceive of such a life as possible, they no longer see it as desirable for their careers and their personal development. Yet, as Gareth Hamilton shows in this volume, one should not assume that such classifications and value-judgements on behaviour and life-choices are fixed. His ethnography of professional training and coaching, amongst self-employed in the east German city of Halle shows that while commercial enterprise (and the entrepreneur) continue to be interpreted through the prism of the West/East German divide, these interpretations are made on shifting ideological and cultural ground. The lines are no longer drawn between 'socialist' or 'capitalist', 'East' or 'West', but at the much vaguer boundary between 'good' and 'bad' entrepreneurs. Stereotypes of *Wessie* (Western) and *Ossie* (Eastern) personal characteristics and their value have become fluid, exemplified by the emergence of the hybrid, entrepreneurial *Wossie*, described by Hamilton as an assemblage structured by the standards and broad ideological practices of neo-liberal policy, and the continuing legacy and tensions of the East-West relationship.

Hamilton offers perhaps the most striking example of the notion of the 'enterprising self' in his description of the German neologism *Ich AG* (Me PLC.) coined by policy-makers wishing to promote self-employment and private enterprise as a solution to long-term unemployment, and universally reviled for its apparent reduction of the person 'to the linguistic level of a stock-market' (Hamilton ibid.). As is evident throughout this volume, the very terminology of the neo-liberal discourse of the self is instrumental to programs of reform and self-reform. It is precisely this role of language as the vehicle for the organization of knowledge and self-authorship, which is taken up by Jonathan Larson in his chapter on Slovak classroom-based English language training. While essay-writing might initially seem an unlikely candidate for ethnographic deliberations on the subject of neoliberalism, Larson effectively uses the question of authorship to consider one of the classic issues of liberal thought and the anthropological literature, namely the value of (private) property. Unpacking the teaching of essay-writing, he examines how instruction contains multiple (and sometimes conflicting) ideologies of knowledge, argument, and authorship. Larson uses this example to critique the perception of neoliberalism as a flexible 'assemblage' of entrepreneurial forms and practices replicated across the globe, arguing instead for the historical and contextual analysis of the genealogy of apparently novel, 'neo-liberal' ideas. His fellow contributor on Slovakia, Sekeráková Búriková, voices a similarly critical attitude to the neoliberal discourse as an idiom for the expression of self-identity. Problematizing narratives of migration as self-improvement and self-investment offered by Slovak au-pairs, she reveals how their decisions to migrate do indeed relate to a wish to gain greater self-possession through experience, but that this wish for increased agency relates far more to the complexity of their domestic and romantic relations, than their position in the labour market. Rather than signalling the hegemonic nature power of neo-liberal discourse in the post-socialist, Slovak context, Sekeráková Búriková argues, narratives of empowerment become the framework for describe au-pairing as a rite of passage to maturity.

Narratives of Enterprise

In each their own way, both Larson's, Sekeráková Búriková's and Hamilton's contributions draw attention to the crux of neo-liberal political and economic philosophy: possessive individualism and its enactment through the concept of 'enterprise'. As seen above, 'enterprise' and 'entrepreneurship' have recently outgrown their conventional association with business ventures and commerce, to signify a broader meaning of initiative, action, and agency. Yet, while there has been plenty of willingness to expand the notion of 'enterprise' to any activity related to the self, undertaken in the spirit of rational calculation, little effort has been put into a deeper epistemological engagement with the term. The close linguistic, conceptual, and ideological relationship between the 'enterprising' individual, economic rationality, and the practice of commercial entrepreneurship, suggests there exists a great deal of conceptual baggage which as yet remains to be unpacked. It also highlights the need to focus more attention to the notion of *homo oeconomicus,* which all too often is simply billed as the economists' (faulty) counter-image to the anthropological concepts of personhood. Indeed, while the alleged transparency of 'choice' and the encouragement openly declare one's interests in the name of civil society invites us to take the actions of the individual at face-value, the fundamental liberal tenet of the freedom of the individual to pursue his (or her) interests ultimately precludes their direct government (McNay 2009). For the anthropologist, such an observation re-opens theoretical questions about the notion of agency, rationality, and morality in contemporary society. What constitutes legitimate activity in the eyes of government, the community, and the individual, as well as in the models of the ethnographer?

These questions are central to the contributions of Radu Umbres and Maria Padrón Hernández on the intersection of informal economy, business, and making a living in Romania and Cuba, respectively. Umbres' micro-ethnography of the small-time entrepreneur Mihai seeking to re-establish his business as a builder after a failed migration to Greece, bears the hallmarks of classic rural anthropology, focusing on the importance of factors such as trust, mutuality, and kinship networks for the successful conduct of enterprise in a small community. The collective and collaborative nature of house building sets the home apart from other commodities, and creates a situation in which the market does not necessarily mediate successfully between the norms of the rural collective and the entrepreneurial self-interest. Umbres shows how Mihai negotiates this troubled relationship by eschewing the use of legal contracts and instead cultivating extensive social relations with potential clients in order to secure orders and payments. He uses his observations as a baseline to ask some novel and provoking questions about the nature of village life as an incubator of individualism both during and after socialism, suggesting the need to acknowledge alternative performances of 'flexibility' and 'enterprise' at the margins of the market as an integral part of contemporary neoliberalization, rather than as its counter-image. Hernández' ethnography of Cubans 'inventing' a living under severely constrained economic circumstance also questions the relationship between enterprising behaviour and structures of governance, as well as the influence of global structures of power and economy on Cuban life. Comparing the terminology of development studies and the literature on neo-liberal personhood, she highlights the similarity between strategies of improvization developed under the pressures of poverty and those traits of 'flexibility' celebrated as characteristic of the 'enterprising' self. Hernández compels us to consider how enterprise engages with normative categories of informal and formal economic practices on the ground, as well as in the literature. In the final instance, her chapter asks whether there is an essential practical, moral, or social difference between enterprising to prosper, and enterprising to survive.

Hernández' chapter is perhaps most forceful in exposing the linguistic and conceptual ambiguity of the notion of the 'enterprising self' as used in contemporary literature. In fact, the contributors to this volume identify no less than three possible interpretations of this 'enterprising self': the enterprising character (as in the classic, charismatic 'self-made' man), those able and willing to adapt to the changing socio-economic circumstances of the globalized economy (the 'flexible' citizen), and those who live at the margins and enterprise to survive. While all cases, the endangered species appears to be the Fordist (and/or state-socialist) employee, the relationship of these various 'enterprising' selves to various modes of governance (and to each other) remains unclear. What is certain, however, is that their co-existence questions the apparent 'novelty' of the 'enterprising self' and its assumed link to the neo-liberal condition, thus suggesting areas for further theoretical elaboration. Aet Annist takes up this challenge in her chapter on enterprise in rural Estonia. Her ethnography documents how a new competitive environment fostered by neoliberal policies has led to rapid economic stratification and social atomization in two villages adversely affected by the demise of collectivized agriculture. Despite efforts to encourage the cultivation of aspirations towards the constitution of an 'active', 'self-regulatory' citizenry in the village, Annist shows how endemic poverty and pervasive mistrust in the community has undermined the solidarity which is a precondition for local social and commercial enterprise. In fact, Annist finds more evidence of entrepreneurial behaviour in the village's Soviet socialist past than in its current state. She suggests that it might be useful to consider the 'entrepreneurial self' a phenomenon that can be more or less central in the planned and official arrangements of the State, more or less common, and even more or less legal, yet never completely absent – regardless of its ideological flavour.

A related question is posed by Nicolette Makovicky the final chapter of this book. She traces the parallel development of new forms of commercialization of local culture and new modes of civic engagement in the Polish-Czech borderland, and illustrates how local notions of enterprise as a 'typically Górale' trait intersect and inform the production of 'enterprising' political and economic subjects. Those willing and able to engage with the bureaucratic demands of regional and European funding structures have contributed to an explosive growth of civic and commercial associations which support novel forms of territorial belonging which draw on the area's Austro-Hungarian imperial heritage and myths of Górale migratory pastoralism. As in the case of Hamilton's *Ossies* and *Wessies*, these actors make playful use of established cultural stereotypes of the Górale as 'entrepreneurial' to explicate both their success and their goal of asserting their minority identity. The enactment of 'enterprising' citizenship thus facilitates and becomes equated with the performance of Górale identity, but simultaneously produces new inequalities in the community by creating localized elites privileged by their ability to establish and maintain trust, social ties, and working relationships with public administrators and other not-for-profit organizations. As in Annist's case of community demise in Estonia, empowerment for the few is here accompanied by the exclusion of others. Illustrating how models of personhood implicit within the bureaucratic structures of contemporary governance become appropriated at the level of the community and the individual, Makovicky's chapter illustrates the need for more ethnographically informed approaches to the study of the consequences of neo-liberal policy-making for populations of the former Eastern Bloc and beyond.

References

Bauman, Z. 2005. *Work, Consumerism and the New Poor*. Maidenhead: Open University Press.

Benda-Beckmann, F. von, Benda-Beckmann, K. von and Wiber, M. 2009. *Changing Properties of Property*. Oxford and New York: Berghahn Books.

Berdahl, D. 2005. The Spirit of Capitalism and the Boundaries of Citizenship in post-Wall Germany. *Comparative Studies in Society and History*, 47(2): 235–51.

Brenner, N. and Theodore, N. 2002. Cities and Geographies of "Actually Existing Neoliberalism". *Antipode*, 34(3): 349–79.

Burawoy, M. and Verdery, K. 1999. *Uncertain Transitions: Ethnographies of Change in the Post-socialist World*. Lanham: Rowman and Littlefield.

Carrier, J. and Miller, D. 1998. *Virtualism: A New Political Economy*. Oxford: Berg Books.

Clarke, J. 2008. Living with/in and without neoliberalism. *FOCAAL*, 51: 153–247.

Collier, S. 2011. *Post-Soviet Social. Neoliberalism, Social Modernity, Biopolitics*. Princeton and Oxford: Princeton University Press.

Creed, G. 2011. *Masquerade and Postsocialism. Ritual and Cultural Dispossession in Bulgaria*. Bloomington and Indianapolis: Indiana University Press.

Dunn, E. 2004. *Privatizing Poland. Baby Food, Big Business, and the Remaking of Labour*. Ithaca: Cornell University Press.

Ferguson, J. 2002. Spatializing States: Toward an Ethnography of Neoliberal Government. *American Ethnologist*, 29(4): 981–1002.

Ferguson, J. 2010. The Uses of Neoliberalism. *Antipode*, 41(s1): 166–84.

Gille, Z. 2009. The Tale of the Toxic Paprika. The Hungarian taste of Euro-globalization, in *Food and Everyday Life in the Post-socialist World*, edited by M. Caldwell. Bloomington and Indianapolis: University of Indiana Press, 57–77.

Gledhill, J. 2004. Neoliberalism, in *A Companion to the Anthropology of Politics*, edited by D. Nugent and J. Vincent. Oxford: Blackwell Publishing, 332–48.

Hann, C. 1985. *A Village without Solidarity. Polish Peasants in Years of Crisis.* New Haven: Yale University Press.

Hann, C. 2002. Farewell to the socialist 'Other', in *Postsocialism: Ideals, Ideologies and Practices in Eurasia*, edited by C. Hann. London and New York: Routledge, 1–11.

Hann, C. 2003. *The Postsocialist Agrarian Question: Property Relations and the Rural Condition.* Münster: Lit Verlag.

Hann, C. 2006. *"Not the Horse we Wanted!". Postsocialism, Neoliberalism, and Eurasia.* Münster: Lit Verlag.

Harvey, D. 1987. Flexible accumulation through urbanization: reflections on 'postmodernism' in the American city. *Antipode*, 19(3): 260–86.

Harvey, D. 2003. *The New Imperialism.* Oxford: Oxford University Press.

Harvey, D. 2005. *A Brief History of Neoliberalism.* Oxford: Oxford University Press.

Hochschild, A. 2008. Through the Crack of the Time Bind: From Market Management to Family Management. *Anthropology of Work Review*, 28(1): 1–8.

Humphrey, C. 2002. Does the category 'postsocialist' still make sense?, in *Postsocialism: Ideals, Ideologies and Practices in Eurasia*, edited by C. Hann. London and New York: Routledge, 12–15.

Jowitt, K. 1992. *New World Disorder: The Leninist Extinction.* Berkeley and Los Angeles: University of California Press.

Junghans, T. 2001. Marketing Selves. Constructing Civil Society and Selfhood in Post-socialist Hungary. *Critique of Anthropology*, 21(4): 383–400.

Kalb, D. and Halmai, G. 2011. *Headlines of Nation, Subtexts of Class: Working Class Populism and the Return of the Repressed in Neoliberal Europe.* Oxford and New York: Berghahn Books.

Kideckel, D. 1993. *The Solitude of Collectivism: Romanian Villagers to the Revolution and Beyond.* Ithaca: Cornell University Press.

Kideckel, D. 2008. *Getting By in Postsocialist Romania: Labour, the Body and Working Class Culture.* Bloomington: Indiana University Press.

Kingfisher, C. and Maskovsky, J. 2008. Introduction. The Limits of Neoliberalism. *Critique of Anthropology*, 28(2): 115–26.

Kipnis, A. 2008. Audit Cultures: Neoliberal governmentality, socialist legacy, or technologies of governing? *American Ethnologist*, 35(2): 275–89.

Kipnis, A. 2011. *Governing Educational Desire: Culture, Politics, and Schooling in China.* Chicago: University of Chicago Press.

Klicperova-Baker, M. 1999. *Post-communist Syndrome.* Budapest: The Open Society Institute.

Ledeneva, A. 1998. *Russia's Economy of Favours: Blat, Networking and Informal Exchange.* Cambridge: Cambridge University Press.

Matza, T. 2009. Moscow's Echo: Technologies of the Self, Publics, and Politics on the Russian Talk Show. *Current Anthropology*, 24(3) 489–522.

Martin, E. 1992. The end of the body? *American Ethnologist*, 19(1): 121–40.

Martin, E. 1994. *Flexible Bodies: Tracking Immunity in American Culture.* Boston: Beacon Press.

Martin, E. 2000a. Flexible Survivors. *Cultural Values*, 4(4) 512–17.

Martin, E. 2000b Mind-Body Problems. *American Ethnologist*, 27(3): 569–90.

Martin, E. 2007. *Bipolar Expeditions. Mania and Depression in American Culture.* Princeton and Oxford: Princeton University Press.

McNay, L. 2009. Self as Enterprise. Dilemmas of Control and Resistance in Foucault's *The Birth of Biopolitics. Theory, Culture and Society*, 26(6): 55–77.

Miller, P. and Rose, N. 2008. *Governing the Present. Administering Economic, Social and Personal Life.* Cambridge: Polity Press.

Ong, A. 1999. *Flexible Citizenship: The Cultural Logics of Transnationality.* Durham, NC: Duke University Press.

Ong, A. 2006. *Neoliberalism as Exception: Mutations in Citizenship and sovereignty.* Durham, NC: Duke University Press.

Ong, A. 2007. Neoliberalism as Mobile Technology. *Transactions of the Institute of British Geographers*, 32(1): 3–8.

Rose, N. 1996. *Inventing Our Selves: Psychology, Power, and Personhood.* Cambridge: Cambridge University Press.

Sachs, J. 1990. What is to be done? *The Economist* [Online, January 13] Available at: http://www.economist.com/node/13002085 [Accessed 24 April 2012].

Schröder, I. and Vonderau, A. 2009. *Changing Economies and Changing Identities in Postsocialist Eastern Europe.* Münster: Lit Verlag.

Stenning, A., Smith, A., Rochovska, A. and Szwątek, D. 2010. *Domesticating Neoliberalism: Spaces of Economic Practice and Social Reproduction in Post-socialist Cities.* Oxford: Wiley.

Sharad, C. and Verdery, K. 2009. Thinking between the Posts: Postcolonialism, Postsocialism, and Ethnography after the Cold War. *Comparative Studies in Society and History*, 51(1): 6–34.

Shore, C. 2008. Audit Culture and Illiberal Governance. *Anthropological Theory*, 8(3): 278–98.

Shore, C. 2010. Beyond the Multiversity: Neoliberalism and the Rise of the Schizophrenic University. *Social Anthropology*, 18(1): 15–29.

Smith, A. 1981. An inquiry into the nature and causes of the wealth of nations, in *Glasgow Edition of the Works and Correspondence of Adam Smith vol. II*, edited by R.H. Campbell and A.S. Skinner. Glasgow: Liberty Press.

Strathern, M. 2000. *Audit Cultures. Anthropological studies in Accountability, Ethics, and the Academy.* London: Routledge.

Strathern, M. and Hirsch, E. 2004. *Transactions and Creations: Property Debates and the Stimulus of Melanesia.* Oxford and New York: Berghahn Books.

Sztompka, P. 1996. Looking back: The year 1989 as a cultural and civilizational break. *Communist and Post-Communist Studies*, 29(2): 115–29.

Vainshtein, G. 1994. Totalitarian public consciousness and in a post-totalitarian society: The Russian case in the general context of post-communist developments. *Communist and Post-Communist Studies*, 27(3): 247–59.

Verdery, K. 2002. Whither post-socialism?, in *Postsocialism: Ideals, Ideologies and Practices in Eurasia*, edited by C. Hann. London and New York: Routledge, 15–21.

Verdery, K. 2003. *The Vanishing Hectare: Property and Value in Post-socialist Transylvania*. Ithaca: Cornell University Press.

Verdery, K. and Humphrey, C. 2004. *Property in Question. Value Transformation in the Global Economy*. Oxford: Berg Publishers.

Wedel, J. 1998. *Collision and Collusion: The Strange Case of Western Aid to Eastern Europe, 1989–1998*. New York: St. Martin's Press.

Chapter 1

Selling, Yet Still Social: Consociational Personhood Among the Self-Employed in Eastern Germany

Gareth E. Hamilton

Introduction

Dear readers!

Difficult times produce courageous people. A comforting message because we live in difficult times: careers disappear, jobs cut, and factories close almost overnight.

Brave people however do not let themselves be dismayed. They trust their strength, creativity, ability to perform and decide to set up their own business. That's what I call courageous. If you keep this book to hand, you're on the right path! (Opoczynski 2006: 9)[1]

This introduction to a guide to starting a business from one of Germany's state broadcaster's consumer-rights/financial advice programmes seems a message for our times. Although the book is from 2006, similar situations abound today, and the notion of setting up businesses has spread to British universities which encourage commercial 'entrepreneurship' among academics. Before hearing those exhortations, and of course researching individual start-up businesspeople, the thought had not particularly crossed my mind. My family were all employees. This sets me off badly for major business success, according to the biographies of major businesspersons as analyzed by Villette and Vuillermot (2009: 73–4). In their analysis of life histories of high-ranking entrepreneurs, owning large companies such as Ikea, Wal-Mart and AXA, their *curricula vitae* share common points:

Raised in a business family
Exceptional education compared to generational contemporaries
Early personal introduction to business practices
Benefitting from competitive advantages in comparison to others, and

---

1   All translations from non-English texts are by the author of this chapter.

A mentor who intercedes, like some *deus ex machina*, at decisive junctures.
(Villette and Vuillermot 2009: 73–4)

This chapter's subjects, people living in the area of the former German Democratic
Republic with its former state socialist, economic and personal individualism-
disapproving system, are likely to have been thus 'unfortunately' placed too.
Further, eastern Germans have also been faced with multiple economic and
social crises, such as unemployment brought about by the closing of former and
now apparently inefficient state enterprises, and depopulation as people move
westwards for work. Despite – or because of this – however, great rhetorical effort
is made to encourage them to get onto Opoczynski's 'right path' towards self-
employment. As there is so much effort made to persuade and to mould persons
to fit on this path, my analyses are based on that part of anthropological theory
which deals squarely with persuasion as a social tool: rhetoric culture theory. I
follow here mostly Carrithers' (2005a, 2005b) formulation of culture as containing
common items, understood by persons together, which form tools 'used by people
on one another, to persuade and convince, and so to move the social situation from
one state to another' (Carrithers 2005b: 581). These are placed into narratives,
stories, which are used to persuade. Besides Carrithers, I will also make reference
to Fernandez's conception of pronominalism (2010), the strategic use of pronouns
in such processes of persuasion. Alongside this, in narratives, metaphors are a
further strong rhetorical tool.

No less important is its focus on the interaction of the meta with the micro by
allowing us to analyse how narratives at different levels mingle, how cultural items
come together and replicate and metamorphose. It does so by allowing us to trace
the development of the narratives, of the trails of cultural items, of inferences and
interactions – from far and wide both temporally and geographically. Carrithers
notes 'for ethnographers, [it] sets a high standard of achievement' in that merely
describing structures is not sufficient, but we are required 'to go beyond that to
their skilled use in one situation or another' (2005b: 582). However, as will be seen
below, there are so many sources of persuasion, and so many potential receivers
of such messages, that the idea reveals linkages between the abstract and the more
traditionally ethnographic. Further, the pure volume of persuasion requires a multi-
level approach. Therefore in this chapter, I will demonstrate how and in which
multiple circumstances this persuasion, and the reaction to it, takes place. I will
show how government, the press and universities try to mould eastern Germans
into so-called 'business types' who can succeed in the modern economic climate.
Based on analysis of entrepreneurship manuals and mass media magazines for a
wider German audience I show how this becomes linked to individual persons
and their morality. I demonstrate, however, that in an eastern German context,
the message is adapted to account for the importance eastern Germans place on
sociality. Further, based on my attendance at various courses designed for potential
and new start-ups, I highlight that while eastern Germans may tacitly accept the
need for self-employment, there still remains a certain potential for criticism of its

practices when these conflict with eastern German social values. However, it is first necessary to consider the precise space into which this rhetorical effort flows.

Plugins Narratively Assembled into 'mini-corporations'?

The variety of 'business' Villette and Vuillermot refer to is the self-managing, entrepreneurial version not prevalent in planned economies. In 1990 there were relatively few persons in eastern Germany who had experience of self-employment, although it was not totally absent. In 1988, there were 181,700 full-time self-employed persons in the GDR (Pickel 1992: 78–89). However, 'difficult times' in the pan-German economy and the job market were one of the reasons for a 2003 root-and-branch reform of the welfare system due to persistent (costly) high-level unemployment. This infamous programme became known as the *Hartz* reforms, a word which was liberally peppered through the German daily press, especially due to *Hartz*-IV, the fourth measure in the programme concerning the alteration and reduction in magnitude of unemployment benefits. '*Hartz*-II', the second measure itself provided a further neologism in its official nickname, '*Ich AG*', perhaps best translated as 'Me PLC', or 'Me Inc'. It enabled the long-term unemployed to receive a bonus besides their normal unemployment benefit in order to set-up their own, individual, business. A government brochure published to promote it does so by highlighting potential for 'unlocking start-up potential in those who before had neither the courage nor the chance to realise their own business idea' (BWA 2004: 27).

It appears that a certain type of person is being identified as the target of the encouragement offered in that particular case. This person has two characteristics: firstly, having had no chance to become self-employed, and secondly, lacking the necessary courageousness. The second of these characteristics is emotional and further carries a certain moral tone. Or rather, the overall message is 'not courageous enough *yet*', as the programme will allow this characteristic to be overcome. This focus on persons, and of their characteristics, is one which is quite common in the printed and online material in Germany on the topic of becoming a businessperson. In the book mentioned above, one of the noticeable sections of the first chapter entitled 'Core question: are you the type for independence?', is itself titled 'to set up a business means changing yourself' (Opoczynski 2006: 23). Much of the material I gathered is not specifically related to eastern Germany, but produced for the whole of the Federal Republic. And it seems that Opoczynski is quite adamant that Germans in general are in need of deep personal change – and changes take place in narrative space through time. The persons he would like them to become more like are apparently fearless Americans. After asking his readers if 'we in "old Europe" are mostly "scaredy-cats" (*Angsthasen*)?', he affirms that 'we' are. 'Only' 29 per cent of Americans, in contrast, believe that a business should not be setup when a risk of failure exists (ibid.: 11). Clearly, being the metaphorical 'scaredy-cat' is something which one should change away from, while holding onto hopes of a positive forward narrative. Fear should be expunged from our minds as we narrativise forward, imagining the business careers stretching before ourselves.

It would be patently unfair given a discussion of risks to accuse the writer of blithely ignoring the negative aspects of becoming self-employed or of joining the mega-wealthy. He does attempt to disabuse his readers of the notion that entrepreneurship is an easy option, with a bullet point list of how the 'reality' stands in opposition to the 'aspiration' (ibid.: 17–19). However, the message remains compellingly pro-risk and pro-entrepreneurship, the British getting an honourable mention for having amongst their number more 'optimists' than 'pessimists' in comparison to Germans (ibid.: 12). The reader is shown a narrative of stages 'identified by scholarship' which begin with 'lack of perspective' in a position of employment, followed by a transformation, via stages of 'preparation', 'acting', and 'perpetuation' (ibid.: 24–5). This narrative ends with the optimistically over-toned 'arrival at the goal', where 'earlier problems are forgotten and the new identity as an independent person has become part of the individual personality' (ibid.: 25).

The above narrative was presented in a section entitled 'To set up a business means changing oneself' (ibid.: 23). A story is told of a certain type of person who has negative personal characteristics and practices. Through the unfolding of the narrative, this person loses these negative aspects while simultaneously gaining the positive personal characteristics and practices of a positive type: a positive ending. The person themselves has changed. The message, in short, is that this process of positive change is one the reader is able to emulate, with positive results to follow. For example, the front cover of Opoczynski's book shows a nameless, but shirted, man – obviously a 'businessman' – on the front cover. Another book in the genre, entitled *Am I the business type? Judge, use and optimise personal characteristics* (Schön 2008) shows a suited, blouse-wearing and pensive woman sitting in a blurred out location. Still recognizably 'business-like', the blurred, bland anonymity provide by its 'anyplace' nature gives it great imaginative potential for the creation of a blank narrative canvas which allows a reader to imagine themselves sitting in such a location.

Schön claims there is a dearth of books of the 'how-to' type on the market. Rather, she suggests, the real need is for a 'what to be' volume instead. Notably, she uses an acrostic, a list formed from the initial letters of the German words for 'turnover and success' as the headings for various sections in her book, and on the back cover. This list, although it has a number of items which relate to practical issues, such as having developed a business plan, is to a large extent a set of characteristics which are being ascribed to a successful person. The book, in short, promises to give the reader the necessary knowledge to gain these characteristics. Despite the old adage about using covers to judge books, it is a key location for the reader browsing a shelf, and also for analysis. From a rhetoric culture point of view, in such lists, the person is to a large extent a character, who is placed into the change narrative as mentioned above. There are a number of interesting points which the list thus raises. Firstly, this sense of characteristics to be adopted is reminiscent of the 'plug-in' person which Latour (2005) has proffered based on actor-network theory and on the model of the assemblage. This sense of collecting parts to make effective wholes he likens to 'discreet *pellets*, or, to borrow from cyberspace, *patches* and *applets*, whose precise origin can be 'Googled' before they are downloaded and saved one by one' (Latour 2005: 207, original emphasis). Humphrey argues against his general view that individuals cannot be said to exist in themselves, and asks in response, if there is no individual in existence then 'who does the composing, Googling and saving, and why?' (2008: 365).

Despite Humphrey's critique, I believe in this case there is still value within the notion of parts of a whole. It is, for example, very much in alignment with Emily Martin's conception of 'mini-corporations' (2000, 2007). Martin suggests that individuals are encouraged to think of themselves, through the teaching and adoption of neoliberal economic principles, as an entity 'oriented primarily to its own interests in global flows of capital' rather than 'citizens, oriented to the interests of the nation' (2007: 42). In this, they should think of themselves as 'collections of assets that must be continually invested in, nurtured, managed, and developed' (2000: 582). In Schön's book, these bullet-points are almost like shopping lists, or the tick-boxes of modern 'audit culture' (Strathern 2000) – but they actually are not, or at least, not *yet*. It should not be overlooked that aside from the 'how to and how to be', the significant purpose of these texts is to *persuade* the reader to become self-employed. The list style is a means of making self-employment and the things necessary to engage in it seem a manageable task. However, whether one could indeed be persuaded that these things are able to be ticked off, and that the changes which such books suggest are both possible and desirable, in light of the difficulties self-employment can produce, is a different question altogether. It would represent a considerable achievement if anyone did have all these positive characteristics. If it is necessary to make myriad changes in order to gain the required 'turnover and success' by assuming the said characteristics, for many persons these changes could easily represent a task which sounds discouraging in its intensity. This poses a further question. If it is necessary to change into a different type of person, is this particular model of a self-employed person morally desirable?

It may be a linguistic coincidence, but *Ich AG* embodies this sense of person-as-corporation in its name. This was widely derided, being given the dubious honour of '*Unwort des Jahres*' ('anti-word of the year') by the Society for the German Language who described it a 'reduction of individuals to [something] on the linguistic level of a stock market' (GdDS 2002). Even the otherwise business-friendly and liberal, weekly wide-circulation *Stern* magazine – from which, much more below – noted its name could potentially 'sound like selfishness and stock-market lasciviousness' (Röhrig and Halbauer 2003). These criticisms of the *Ich AG* concept were federal German criticisms. But what about the east? Firstly, the resurrected 'Monday demonstrations' (taking place on the iconic day of the week on which the mass protests against the GDR regime took place in 1989) against the 2003 Hartz reforms still taking place weekly during my fieldwork in 2008–09 highlight ongoing dissatisfaction amongst the public with state actions. The taking up of this iconic piece of eastern German culture of demonstration at injustice, and here specifically against the removal (or at least significant weakening) of an important tenet of social protection, is an example of the expression of what eastern German socialist Engler has called the 'eastern German idiom' (2004: 13ff.). In general, Engler suggests that eastern Germans are vocal in criticizing actions they see as furthering individual self-interest, and/or placing self-interest above solidarity with other members of society. While *Hartz*-IV constituted an erosion of social protection, *Hartz*-II, *Ich AG*, and similar schemes were easily portrayable as encouraging self-interest. These appeared in contrast to memories of work in the GDR, where factories or the larger *Kombinate* were, in comparison to the individual *Ich AG*, multiplexes 'of both work and social life where people not only toiled but engaged and enjoyed collective leisure pursuits laid like a "corona" around them' (ibid.: 116). Further, as reunification with the west, and the actions of western managers, were seen as responsible for the removal of this style of working and socializing (as well as the introduction of self-serving individualism), Engler's idea of an East German 'idiom' easily becomes associated with the west, or rather *against* the West, itself. The fact remains, however, that it is in the individual – or the image of the individual – where much of the work to portray the self-employed person as worthy of emulation occurs. Below, I will show how this particular aspect of eastern German culture gets taken up rhetorically. In encouraging East Germans to become self-employed, certain aspects of individualist discourse are strategically employed and others avoided. However, before dealing with eastern Germany in particular, and as a means of comparison, it is necessary to show how this is done at a pan-German (and western-leaning) level.

Personalization of the Businessperson

At a national German level, a common rhetorical tool used by authors to render businesspersons attractive characters to be emulated, involves a shifting from the indefinite person to the definite. Until this point, the focus on 'the businessperson' was in the inchoate third person. The businessperson is defined by certain characteristics, and a 'he' or 'she'. However, an interesting use of pronominals a shift to the definite person occurs in Schön's acrostic-using text. With Schumpeterian overtones, the necessary abstract characteristics are shown via individual, named and successful persons in general. In Schön's particular case, she herself receives the treatment in her introductory chapter where the reader learns of her family life in a business environment. While noting that she sometimes felt that her parents' business was an additional 'corporate sibling', the author is no longer merely a voice which instructs, but transformed into a person who has a history and a narrative. In the terminology of Schütz (1962, 1967), the writer of the book becomes more than mere 'contemporary', someone not known personally, but by their social type or function. Rather, she takes on the form of a public consociate, as a person or persons 'who are known intimately' and whose life and 'one's fate is bound up with' (Carrithers 2000: 365). Further, it is necessary to think of the strategic use of pronouns (Fernandez 2010) here. Alongside Schön's photograph on the back cover, by giving us biographical information and being able to cast herself as an 'I', she makes herself into someone with whom we can empathize.

In Schön's case, 'the author' becomes a 'she', but not only an inchoate 'she'. Rather it is a public version of 'Carmen Schön': a businessperson, but still a real person, capable of sociality. A (metaphoric) business sister shows that she has emotions. In an intersubjective, if public, sense she becomes a temporary consociate, suggesting that by emulating her example will not render us atomized individuals. Another book, *Desire to do Business?* calls upon the reader to 'inspire yourself by the experience of 15 Belgian business creators!' (de Bray 2007). The impression given there is generally unsurprisingly positive, given that people portrayed wrote their own stories. Here too, the link between narrative and the inspiration to become a businessperson is explicitly expressed. The same characteristics are shared by a promotional bookmark from a Saxony-Anhalt regional government campaign to encourage people to start-up businesses. It uses personalization alongside a very visual representation of the change from students/ researchers into the 'business type': half of the image is the person a laboratory coat, the other in a suit with an arrow wrapped around to show the transformation. Clearly, wearing a suit means business.

However, it is the title of the Belgian book *Desire to do Business?*, and the question embedded within the title, which raises a vital question about this variety of advertising and texts. Is it necessary to have a 'desire to do business' as a precondition of being in a situation where one is looking for a book called *Desire to do Business?* It, and the German examples referred to above, were certainly available in bookshops and likely to be found by someone searching for *a* book on becoming self-employed. To become a member of its audience by buying the text, or lending it from a library, a person would need to actively take steps to do so, signalling the presence of an already incubated idea or desire to become an entrepreneur. As we shall see below, another book about German entrepreneurs, which contains nothing but stories of the successful, provides an interesting link between these relatively limited circulation titles for those who actively seek them out, and mass-circulation publications.

Personalized Businesspersons in Public

The book which links these entrepreneur guidebooks to a larger audience is entitled *Gründergeschichten* (Osterkorn et al. 2007) ('Start-up Stories'), a compendium of the business histories of the winners of the *Deutscher Gründerpreis*, or 'German start-up prize'. Awarded annually to different businesspersons, the prize is organized by ZDF (Germany's second state television channel), who also published the first book mentioned in this chapter, alongside the Sparkasse banking group, Porsche, and *Stern* magazine. Presented in *Gründergeschichten*, the detailed business and life histories of the winners are also printed in *Stern*, which had an average weekly circulation of 995,780 in the quarter in which the 2008 winners appeared (Q2 2008), and was thus probably (as in my case) where most readers discover the competition. Alongside newer start-ups, the competition includes a prize for 'life-time achievement, or 'life's work', and internationally-famous German businessmen feature among the winners of this award since its inception in 1997. In 2008, the winner was Berthold Leibinger, of Trumpf Engineering (Flemming and Pielow 2008). Notable in the article's heading was the focus on invention, innovation, and Trumpf's expansion: 'he began as an apprentice, now he owns the firm', his 'revolutionary invention', 'made into a world concern' (ibid.: 86). In this way, a life's narrative, combined with a business story of expansion, is told at a fast pace.

His family life is mentioned, but a humorous anecdote about how he told his father he would use his above-average intelligence to have to work at a less-than-average rate is tempered by stating he has no hobbies, and citing Leibinger: 'when normal people solve a crossword, I prefer to think about a technical problem' (ibid.: 87). The firm, though a large corporation, is part of him or perhaps the inverse. Or perhaps he is the (once mini, now certainly not) corporation: 'Wherever he goes – he has travelled 80 times alone to Asia – he is Trumpf' (ibid.: 88). The dimensions are large, and focused on growth. Another winner had €2M to invest from an earlier business failure (Gronwald 2008: 94–5), circumstances somewhat removed from that of most people. Given this lack of similarity between these extremely rich and successful, and a less wealthy majority, it is valid to question whether examples of large corporate expansions headed by such people are the key to persuading persons to engage in entrepreneurship. Would Liebinger and his seemingly focused, and if not slightly eccentric, behaviour as be a model of the ideal person for an eastern German audience in particular? Would such an individual not be a target for the eastern German idiom? A further example from the German press stable provides an interesting source of comparison.

Personalized Businesspersons in Public, Eastern-style

Although almost 20 years may have passed since German reunification, 'East' remains a employable category for the media, presumably because they regard it both as important and understandable by their readers. The major German Sunday *Bild am Sonntag* tabloid features a weekly poll on a question with a 'yes/ no' answer. Alongside male or female, ages, education and, despite, representing approximately 20 per cent of the population, the 'West' is represented as a category alongside the 'East'. This latter group has, according to another newspaper, a 'central organ' (Staud 2000: 41): the weekly news/lifestyle magazine, *SUPERIllu*, with a circulation of 453,106 in Q2/2008. Its content focuses on eastern, still-performing GDR-era, stars, discussions of the GDR past, and the beauty of the eastern landscape and its cultural heritage. Its penetration in the former Eastern German regions represents a much higher rate than its sister magazine *Stern*. Given the incompatibility between the socialist personality of the past, which many of the readers might be said to have experience of, the *SUPERIllu* is surprisingly extremely pro-entrepreneurship. Indeed, it too runs its own annual competition for start-ups, sponsored by the federal development bank, and regularly features eastern businesspersons, praising them for their actions. The competition's winners are portrayed in the same format as those in *Stern*, detailing their life stories, on multiple occasions as the competition progresses. However, despite these apparent similarities, there are some crucial differences.

Firstly, these differences are detectable in the style of language used. Whereas there is a certain raciness in the *Stern* examples, the *SUPERIllu* feels more homely and less showy. Furthermore, the focus of the detail highlighted is likewise subtly different. In the issue from 19/2008, alongside an ongoing series of interviews with still-performing GDR-era, rock band Die Puhdys, there appears an article titled 'Great ideas! We are looking for more' (n.d. 2008b: 20–21). Here, business success stories of eastern Germans are presented to encourage entrants into the annual competition, and into self-employment. There is scant mention of money in the story of one smiling lady who set up a fitness business for the over-50s. Rather, her motivations to start the business were described as coming from her own experience of being an over-50 who wanted to keep fit. Posing beside a *papier-mâché* giraffe (her logo), she claims, 'I'll not get rich, but it is fun for everyone!' (ibid.: 20–21). Another example features two more women who were long-term unemployed, despite practical qualifications (common in eastern Germany). They turned their hobby into a business, making felt toys, saying: 'It is going super! We can live from it' (ibid.: 20–21). These are micro-narratives of success, like those viewed in *Stern*. Here, however, the tone is of provisioning and not expansion, augmented by the accompanying picture of them smiling, holding two felt rabbits kissing one another. A 20 per cent increase in one featured firm's profits is tempered by its occurrence after a management buyout which saved the firm from the 'danger' of takeover by western Germans and Americans. These narratives display a distinct thread of ending personal employment, or avoiding it happening to others; any hint of barefaced capitalist expansion is neutralized.

Issue 17/2009 recounts how a family bought a former state cooked-meats concern, maintaining 450 jobs. The writers suggest there was much courage and much communal effort involved, with 30 former workers helping out in difficult days keeping the firm alive and growing. The owner is reported as saying: 'we slogged away day and night. Everyone got stuck in. We could only have done it in that way'. Rhetorically, the original German uses a particle verb with a '*mit-*' prefix to added to '*anpacken*' ([n.d.] 2009: 8). This '*mit*' participle is often used by eastern Germans in situations where others likely would not. Issue 45/2008 further highlights the community's importance, in an article on 42-year-old Volker Seifert, a village baker who, using traditional recipes, became Saxony's 'bakery king' ([n.d.] 2008a: 24–5). News of a new, larger factory is tempered by highlighting the social space in the new premises, featuring a physiotherapist's room and modern canteen.

There is a distinct narrative echo of the socially important 'multiplexes', the 'corona' *Kombinate* Engler describes as typical of the GDR. Seifert enjoys playing his part in the region, and states that if he had accepted a recent €16M western buyout, it would have 'put our workers up into the air. I couldn't do that to them and their families!'. Reminiscent of the importance placed on the communal before the individual, the bakery king's reticence to accept the buy-out despite his achievements is praised. He is cited as claiming that he remains grounded, with the writer confirming that he has indeed 'remained on the ground'. In these examples, there are various clear narrative echoes of the GDR past: communal working, deep social workplace linkages, rejection of uncontrolled capitalism and personal excess. The narratives are also clearly linked with the social values which were expressed by eastern Germans when referring to western Germans. Indeed, expansion of personal wealth seems to have been acceptable when staving off threatened western expansion. Engler's 'east German idiom' seems always in the background. Despite this, capitalist expansion is present in the articles, and the message is neoliberal in its overtones. Might easterners actually accept these principles? Given purchasing the publication is naturally voluntary, and circulation figures remain steady, the suggestion must be that their presentation does not offend to an extent that readership is affected.

It seems from this image, with the on-going promotion of start-ups in its pages, and the annual competition, that members of the eastern German *SUPERIllu*-reading public are thought to believe it is good to become individual owners of the means of production, make money, expand and better individuals' situations. These stories make good persons out of bravery, hard work, and unflappability. However, reticence and good quality are important, and it is paramount that an entrepreneur improves others' circumstances through his business practice. Furthermore, eastern interests should be favoured. This message contains two meta-themes: capitalist success is encouraged, but while doing it, one should work hard and not exceeding accepted norms. Secondly, these imperatives are thought to resemble the characteristics which eastern Germans are said to have gained during the GDR. In general, *SUPERIllu* feels remarkably in tune, or sensitive, to what they can publish for their public. If it can be regarded as a form of para-ethnography (Holmes and Marcus 2005) recognizing that both anthropologists and marketers use focus groups for at least some similar ends, then some inference can be taken firstly from the fact that *SUPERIllu* organizes readers' panels, which aim to give their readers a consultative voice in the editing process. It seems that *SUPERIllu* wishes to find out and thus remain aligned to its general readership's views. Evidence that it manages to do so came two weeks after the article on the 'bakery king' appeared in *SUPERIllu*, a reader's letter was published about him. Its writer 'does not begrudge such capitalists their success' due to their tax paying and social responsibility among other things. This is in stark contrast to the 'turbocapitalists' who '[Seifert] could tear strips off' (Rotekirch 2008: 18). I do not know if this letter was itself was pretested in the group 'pre-screened to meet specific client criteria' as apparently some marketers do (Sunderland and Denny 2007: 175), but, we do know that readers seem to like what is presented within its pages.

Assemblages from East and West

In some senses, as stated above, the positivity in the *SUPERIllu* position as regards this once alien and capitalist activity can be viewed as surprising. However, there are certain factors which actually render it less so. Firstly, it is interesting to note that the (now former, as of 2011) long-term editor of the publication, Jochen Wolff, hails from the West, having grown up in Bavaria (a fact that many people I spoke to during fieldwork were unaware of). He is quoted as having published a string of 'I-did-it-this-way-stories' because of his desire to 'show the people that one can be successful in this country' (Staud 2000: 41, also Boyer 2001: 4). The author of the article which quotes him also notes the possibility that his policy of treating eastern Germans with 'respect, love and understanding' might sound patronizing. And while the author notes that *SUPERIllu* might be seen as being replete with 'ideal-world stories', Wolff calls such items 'courage giving', which is not so far removed at all from the task of entrepreneurship manuals such as those shown above. In some senses, however, *SUPERIllu* could not be other than 'courage giving', because that is what it wants to achieve.

The magazine, as the article's author claims, may be 'central organ of the east'. Yet, he also suggests that no other publication 'does more for German unity' by further leading 'easterners into the new country' (Staud 2000: 41). It is clear that the 'situation' in eastern Germany has been changed by events which brought about this 'new country'. Carrithers has analysed an example from a 1994 biography where a woman, Petra, 'sets out some moral conceptual landmarks for herself and for her family' at reunification, where 'concern for one another's interests, devotion to one another, consideration, uprightness' are deemed as still important in 'the new setting' of the FRG (2000: 377). New, and adapted, moral positions may have to be adapted, however, what is seen as the basic moral stance of the GDR is kept. The *SUPERIllu* position on entrepreneurship is rather in the same vein. It is mostly 'new country' but also a bit of 'central organ'. The wider situation and its characters are too.

Wolff is western, but the article highlights 'easternness' in his accent and his views on music, for example. One might argue that Wolff is a *Wossi*, a combination of *Ossi* and *Wessi*. While Berdahl sees the *Wossi* as 'an Ossi who takes on exaggerated characteristics of Wessis' (1999: 181), I think that we can rather see this as a term for a particular synergy, or combination of characteristics. For example, in emic usage, the writer of an 2009 (Eastern German)[2] edition of a *Born In* ... series of books, which attempts to summarize a generalized life course for persons born in the year in the title, uses it to describe those born in 1980 but who later (and seemingly without much difficulty) became normal citizens of the Federal Republic. One of its sections, detailing the collective post-*Wende* experience, is entitled 'Out of "Ossis" become "Wossis"' (Ludeck 2009: 40–49). The Petra whom Carrithers has written of, and to whom I referred above, showed some synergizing of this nature, but not enough time had passed in 1994 to for her to have become a *Wossi*.

The *Stern* competition mentioned above also had a prize for school-based companies. Two out of the ten were in the east, as might be expected purely on population ratios. It might seem that eastern young people take their rightful, statistically-aligned place in the new individualistic Germany. However, I have also witnessed the eastern-German-idiom-imbued criticisms of the west and its capitalism as viewed above expressed among young, technologically-literate computer users, among others. Even the young can express the views more in keeping with the GDR period in terms of solidarity, while others win business competitions. I have met even met those with successful Internet-based businesses who successfully sell to the west, but can criticize what they perceive as its ways of behaving. Even with this mixing to create *Wossis*, it should not be forgotten that while Petra, the 1980 cohort, and the school prize-winners, would be eastern *Wossis*. Wolff, in contrast, is a *western Wossi*. If the post-reunification Federal Republic is anything on the *Wossi* scale – even western persons have complained about changes that unification brought (cf. Biller 2009, also Boyer 2006) – it is more Wolff-like, significantly more western *Wossi* than eastern.

The relative size of the populations, the means of reunification where federal law was supreme, suggests that any latent desire to use the word hybridity is not the most appropriate. As a better term to describe self-employment in the new Federal Republic, I prefer the notion of 'assemblage', as in Collier and Ong's conception of 'global assemblages' (2005). In this case, the Latourian-inspired notion of assembling can be of use. Collier and Ong adapt the idea of Latour's 'immutable mobiles' (1987: 227) to suggest that 'immutable' standards and broad ideological practices are placed into different, and differing, places within the world. These are global, in that they are 'broadly encompassing, seamless, and mobile' but also assemblages which 'impl[y] heterogeneous, contingent, unstable, partial, and situated' (Collier and Ong 2005: 12). This 'suggests inherent tensions' (ibid.) because they have to be combined into assemblages in local conditions. Generally, the same things are required, and the same risks are required to be taken (if at different intensities). Thus, as eastern Germany has, on a federal level, the same regulatory/financial system as the rest, entrepreneurship and self-employment policy cannot be particularly different there, local government notwithstanding. But this does not mean that how enterprise is dealt with and conceived by those

---

2   In this series, the years until 1986 exist in two versions for east and west, after which it seems the series editors think it is time to combine them into one.

involved must be the same in the east and west. Neither must the same view of
the people involved be held by those persons themselves, or by others. In this
vein, I do not renege on my view that assemblages are inappropriate models in
understanding personhood. However, in *metaphorical* terms, the assemblage is a
useful tool in helping to envisage how neoliberal economic practices are applied
in eastern Germany.

The assemblage, taken as a metaphor, shows that – at least at the public level
as represented by *SUPERIllu* – it is something which can have a certain amount
of eastern-ness assembled along with it. While broadly the same as anywhere
else, eastern German-ness only finds its place where the standards, laws, and neoliberal practices allow them leeway. While the eastern view of self-employment
and entrepreneurship in *SUPERIllu* does appear to have such an assemblage
character, is it the case *in situ*? How does this actually appear at the cutting face
of entrepreneurship as taught in 'real life' coincide? A reader's letter can criticize
'turbocapitalists', but it will be editorially chosen by the publication or modified.
What occurs when people are permitted to speak out? From attending various
voluntary seminars and talks for entrepreneurs in my fieldwork site of Halle,
and one in Hanover in the west, along with interviews with course organizers,
leaders and participants as part of broader fieldwork, I would suggest that there is
a similarly assembled mixture of standard (western) messages mixed with eastern-
ness when there is opportunity for it to budge in. Below, it will be possible to view
what happens when the message meets those addressed.

The Assemblages in Formation

While Hanover is a prosperous city, Halle has suffered significant depopulation
since reunification and also high unemployment. Before going on to contrast them
– and there are many contrasts due to their eastern and western locations – it is
important to first consider the similarities between events in Halle and Hanover.
There was focus in both places on the great effort needed to succeed, and to keep
going – that is, on tenacity. There was hope that expansion would occur, but the
reality that failure is possible was raised. Like the eastern business coach, the
Hanover teacher advised shunning fast cars as the embodiment of businessperson-
hood. Alongside this reticence of image, there was highlighting of networking,
which is always seen as essential, as well as marketing and gaining customers.
Further, as tax and business law is mostly federal, and any content on legal issues
was similar in both places. The differences between the courses, however, were
in terms of the atmosphere, in tone and participant reaction. It is thus time to
introduce some eastern aspects into the assemblage.

Remaining with the subject of financial law, one particular seminar in Halle
on the complexities of the tax system – led by an accountant and organized
by one of the state-sponsored coaches – revealed one characteristic, held to
be particularly East German. This is that easterners were used to being led by

Figure 1.1   'Setting up a business – finally my own boss'

the hand during the GDR era, and did not like to make their own decisions. According to an eastern entrepreneurship coach with whom I spoke, this still applies. In the course on tax, the coach even explained how, in very detailed and practical terms, to purchase the software required – down to the level of going into the shop, and what to say, and in what tone. Although the course was informal and friendly, the participants remained reticent. This did not mean they were silent, but, for example, when asked to introduce themselves they provided very simple self-descriptions, which were quick and far from elaborate. The course leader in Hanover met with no hesitation when she asked her audience of 12 to introduce themselves their plans and ideas. Even the few who seemed shy were relatively comfortable in so doing as these goals were placed on a large piece of paper at the front of the room (see Figure 1.1).

I witnessed this sense of eastern reticence elsewhere. I have mentioned above that eastern Germans have been regarded as being lacking in characteristics and abilities needed to succeed in self-employment, especially the variety of items featured in the lists above. Noting this had rankled, I was shocked when this was even thematized by a different course leader during his session in Halle. During the session on 'the key to success in marketing', this Dutch businessman who lived in Saxony-Anhalt asked for volunteers to introduce themselves and their businesses. He had described a well-known technique for successful introductions, the 'elevator method'; so-called as such a short period is all that is available to present oneself and business to someone. This is a shorter version of the panegyric narrative texts as encountered above in *Stern* and *SUPERIllu*. The difference here is that it is produced by the main protagonist in that text in the 'I' form, and 'live'. However, when asked to practise this, no-one out of the even larger group agreed. To use him as a para-ethnographer, during an interview this seminar convenor noted that it is particularly hard to get anyone to volunteer to do so, but in the east even more rare. He had informed participants that eastern Germans are particularly 'bad' at 'selling themselves' and their talent, further perceived deficiencies of reticent eastern Germans. At that point, there had been some murmurs of discontentment from around the room, but the coach who organized the event, and the leader of the town's entrepreneurship bureau who was also present, told me during an interview that she agreed.

When I discussed this event with her, she explained the term 'selling oneself' carries ambiguous connotations in the East German context, suggesting that an 'overselling' or perhaps 'miss-selling' of one's abilities and competences was being advocated. The phrase (and practice) was associated with dishonest western businesspersons who had come to Halle after reunification, and were perceived as having deceived locals by inflating their own competences. Referring to the phrase of selling oneself, she described them as having '*really* sold themselves'. In rhetoric culture theory, this idea of 'selling oneself' can be described as a cultural item which, despite semantic similitude, has the potential to allow eastern and western listeners to place it into very different narratives. Even if the experiences of Berdahl's (1999: 170–73) informants shows how unpleasant this selling could be, and the strength of the displeased reaction thereto, the passing of time and changing circumstances have allowed a tacit acceptance of the need to present oneself better to develop in this situation in Halle.

Despite the entrepreneurship bureau leader's acceptance of 'selling oneself', that someone who professionally 'sells' this message displays a concern for honesty in dealings with others is significant. Can similar evidence be seen from the floor of these events, over and above faltering introductions and disgruntled murmurs? During interviews with two participants of this particular course – a lawyer, there to improve her business, and someone who considered becoming a freelance graphic designer – I asked if they had tried practising elevator introductions. And indeed they had, and found it useful. No doubt, today it is practical and useful advice, but still we see assembled into this some sense of eastern values. The graphic designer recognized it was difficult, she could see eastern reticence in herself and her brother; it would be difficult to internalize the imperative to 'sell oneself'. But family and friends could provide practice opportunities, because with them 'nothing could go wrong'. Away from the public gaze, it could be perfected and honed. The lawyer in turn surprised herself with her own ability to manage it. But she told me that Westerners would be much more boastful about their achievements, and pointed out that course participants' refusals to introduce themselves resulted from the feeling that it is somehow almost indecent in the east to show that one has what it takes to succeed. Further, people, and customers, appreciate the reticence, and this was visible during the courses themselves.

At the beginning of this chapter I mentioned that my university offers free courses to encourage entrepreneurship, and the local universities in Halle did likewise, as part of a wider programme of support under the name *Univations*. In terms of expansion and gaining new customers, the leader of one of these courses on intellectual property protection was quite clear that as a lawyer her services were in most cases quite unnecessary, with no visible touting for business. Similarly, at the course mentioned above in Halle on tax and accounting, the instructor was quite adamant that participants had no actual need of her services, and that they could do all their own bookkeeping. But this seemed to gain her customers, and several people came up to her voluntarily at the end to request the very thing. Her strong personality, competence yet reticence, mirroring the presentation of entrepreneurs in *SUPERIllu*, seemed much more likely to cause her services to be used. The course led by the Dutch management consultant mentioned above was notably different. He sent out his details afterwards, even after covering his slides with name and logo. I wondered if a malfunction with the PowerPoint presentation, and a promise to distribute it later, was not some ruse to harvest email addresses from these potential customers! Even if not, the opportunity to offer his services was not missed, and repeated at the course's conclusion. He 'sold himself' quite well, and could present the narrative of his personal and business development with ease.

A further example, again highlighting the theme of personal integrity and honesty as in that of the municipal official, occurred during a course on advertising. The instructor, a 'postdoc' from the town's main university, provided the participants with examples of negative advertising as examples of innovative thinking. In one case, a long-established hairdressing salon retaliated against a new cut-price competitor opposite, when it advertised itself as adept at rescuing people from cheap haircuts (referring to the presumed poor quality services of the latter). In another, a business accepted other firm's vouchers (to save on printing costs and gain customers). After keenly giving examples of negative advertising which were meant to be emulated one hand went up. A young lady asked, with much incredulity, if such practices were acceptable, or even permitted? During the session, it was also suggested that it was a good idea to set prices high because the general public misjudge product prices, something to take advantage of. However, a local felt product maker told me that while she could earn higher prices for her products in Berlin, especially among the western tourists at markets in Potsdam, she kept her prices at almost break-even level in Halle because she felt sympathy for those persons there who otherwise could not afford them.

This could be interpreted as elaborate and contrived warehouse clearance combined with 'mouth propaganda' advertising. However, the social networks of such customers likely contain those on similar incomes rather than higher-paying customers. If anything, it was likely to be in the importance of 'love and humanity', the virtues she attributed to a local café-patisserie she recommended to me. For her, the attention to detail and care when choosing the ingredients for their cakes, and their manufacture, made their elevated prices worthwhile. From her talk of customers being able to 'purchase some spirituality', of care and attention from the heart, alongside these products, and from watching her demonstration of felt making, I believe she showed a similar level of careful thoroughness, which quietly emphasizes her own product pricing policy even further. Unlike the possibly staged and twee kissing bunnies in the *SUPERIllu* display of her felt-making professional colleagues, her tone was one of genuine caring.

I do not wish to suggest that East German businesspersons are 'soft' in a way which is unsuccessful. The success on a pan-German level of Rotkäppchen sparkling wine, formerly a nationalized firm, but which became Germany's largest manufacturer after a management buyout, is a sign of capability. Given the importance placed on being social and social thinking in the examples above, there is an inversion here of the Balinese personhood suggested by Geertz (1966). While this Balinese example is one where people show an outward lack of emotionality, in eastern Germany, outward caring is the key. In the face of neoliberal capitalism what might thus be called 'consociational personhood' is needed. While we see a neoliberal, 'Me Inc'.-style business personhood celebrated throughout the start-up literature and the examples from the *Stern* competitions, publications like the *SUPERIllu* move towards an image of the entrepreneur which is far more consociational. However, from ethnographic evidence it is clear that consociational personhood is not merely some empty notion, even if it is being used for reasons somewhat removed from its imagined origins in GDR sociality.

References

Berdahl, D. 1999. *Where the World Ended: Re-unification and Identity in the German Borderland*. Berkeley, Los Angeles and London: University of California Press.

Biller, M. 2009. Deutsche deprimierende Republik. *Frankfurter Allgemeine Sonntagszeitung*, 22 March 2009, 27.

Boyer, D. 2001. Media Markets, Mediating Labours, and the Branding of East German Culture at 'Super Illu'. *Social Text 68*, 19(3): 9–33.

Boyer, D. 2006. Ostalgie and the Politics of the Future in Eastern Germany. *Public Culture*, 18(2): 379–89.

Carrithers, M. 2000. Hedgehogs, foxes, and persons: Resistance and moral creativity in East Germany and South India, in *Being Humans: Anthropological Universality and Particularity in Transdisciplinary Perspectives*, edited by N. Roughley. Berlin & New York: Walter de Gruyter, pp. 356–78.

Carrithers, M. 2005a. Anthropology as a Moral Science of Possibilities. *Current Anthropology*, 46(3): 433–56.

Carrithers, M. 2005b. Why Anthropologists Should Study Rhetoric. *Journal of the Royal Anthropological Institute*, 11(3): 577–83.

Carrithers, M. 2008. From Inchoate Pronouns to Proper Nouns: A Theory Fragment with 9/11, Gertrude Stein, and an East German Ethnography. *History and Anthropology*, 19(2): 161–86.

Collier, S.J. and Ong, A. 2005. Global assemblages, anthropological problems, in *Global Assemblages: Technology, Politics and Ethics as Anthropological Problems*, edited by S.J. Collier and A. Ong. Oxford, Blackwell, pp. 3–20.

de Bray, C. 2007. *Envie d'entreprendre?: Déclics*. Liège: edipro.

Engler, W. 2004. *Die Ostdeutschen als Avantgarde*. Berlin: Aufbau.

Fernandez, J.W. 2010. Pronominalism. *History and Anthropology*, 21(1): 63–71.

Flemming, B. and Pielow, S. 2008. Leibinger ist Trumpf. *Stern*. 17 June 2008, 86–9.

Geertz, C. 1966. *Person, Time, and Conduct in Bali: An Essay in Cultural Analysis*. New Haven, CT: Southeast Asia Studies, Yale University.

Gesellschaft zur deutschen Sprache (2002). *'Unwort des Jahres 2002', Unwort des Jahres: Informationen zu einer Sprachkritischen Aktion* [Online] Available at: www.unwoerterdesjahres.org/2002.htm [Last accessed 7 August 2007].

Gronwald, S. 2008. Zwei Männer unter Strom. *Stern*. 17 June 2008, 94–5.

Hamilton, G.E. (2012). Plural gifting of singular importance: mass-gifts and sociality among precarious product promoters in eastern Germany. *Social Anthropology*, 20(2): 145–60.

Hartz IV: Menschen in Arbeit bringen. Berlin: Bundesministerium für Wirtschaft und Arbeit 2004.

Holmes, D.G. and George E.M. 2005. Cultures of Expertise and the Management of Globalization: Towards the Re-Functioning of Ethnography, in *Global Assemblages: Technology, Politics and Ethics as Anthropological Problems*, edited by S.J. Collier and A. Ong. Oxford: Blackwell, pp. 236–52.

Humphrey, C. 2008. Reassembling individual subjects. *Anthropological Theory*, 8(4): 357–80.

Latour, B. 1987. *Science in Action: How to Follow Scientists and Engineers through Society*. Cambridge, MA: Harvard University Press.

Latour, B. 2005. *Reassembling the Social: An Introduction to Actor-Network-Theory*. Oxford: Clarendon Press.

Ludeck, N. 2009. *Wir vom Jahrgang 1980: Kindheit und Jugend (Aufgewachsen in der DDR)*. Gudensberg-Gleichen: Wartberg Verlag.

Martin, E. 2000. Mind-Body problems. *American Ethnologist*, 27(3): 569–90.

Martin, E. 2007. *Bipolar Expeditions: Mania and Depression in American Culture*. Oxford and Princeton: Princeton University Press.

[n.a.]. 2008a. Mühlenbäckerei Stangengrün: Vom kleinen Dorfbäcker zum Backkönig von Sachsen. *SUPERIllu*. 30 October 2008, 24–5.

[n.a.]. 2008b. Tolle Ideen! Wir suchen mehr davon. *SUPERIllu*. 30 April 2008, 20–21.

[n.a.] 2009. In Radeberg geht's um die Wurst. *SUPERIllu*. 16 April 2009, 8.

Opoczynski, M. 2006. *ZDF WISO: Existenzgründung*. Frankfurt and New York: Campus Verlag.

Osterkorn, Thomas, et al. 2007. *Gründergeschichten: Vom Abenteuer, ein Unternehmen aufzubauen*. Frankfurt/Main: Campus Verlag.

Pickel, A. 1992. *Radical Transitions: The Survival and Revival of Entrepreneurship in the GDR*. Boulder: Westview Press.

Röhrig, J. and Halbauer, A.G. 2003. Was taugt die Ich-AG? *Stern* [Online 4 February]. Available at http://www.stren.de/wirtschaft/arbeit-karriere/arbeit/arbeit-was-taugt-die-ich-ag-503480.html [accessed 5 August 2007].

Rotekirch, S. 2008. *Beispielhaft* (Reader's letter). *SUPERIllu*. 30 October 2008, 18.

Schütz, A. 1962. *Collected Papers 1: The Problem of Social Reality*. The Hague: Martinus Nijhoff.

Schütz, A. 1967. *The Phenomenology of the Social World*. Evanston, IL: Northwestern University Press.

Staud, T. 2000. Das Zentralorgan des Ostens. *Die Zeit*, 41 [Online 5 October]. Available at http://www.zeit.de/2000/41/Das_Zentralorgan_des_Ostens [accessed 5 August 2007].

Strathern, M. 2000. *Audit Cultures: Anthropological Studies in Accountability, Ethics and the Academy*. London: Routledge.

Sunderland, P.L. and Denny, R.M.T. 2007. *Doing Anthropology in Consumer Research*. Walnut Creek, CA: Left Coast Press.

Villette, M. and Vuillermot, C. 2009. *From Predators to Icons: Exposing the Myth of the Business Hero*. Ithaca & London: Cornell University Press.

Chapter 2

Work-Discipline and Temporal Structures in a Multinational Bank in Romania

Liviu Chelcea

Introduction: Post-socialism meets Flexible Accumulation

During the 1990s, the people of the post-socialist countries gradually entered a new universe of labour very different from what they were used to during state-socialism. For one thing, statistics show that post-socialists work longer hours than the rest of Europeans. According to 2010 EU data, all post-socialist countries – except for the Baltic States – rank above the EU 27 average for the number of people who work more than 40 hours a week.[1] Similarly, 2007 EU figures showed that 12 out of the 16 countries ranking higher than the EU average for the percentage of population with long working hours (48+ hours per week) are post-socialist. Romania ranked first in the entire European Union. Greece apart, it was followed, in descending order, by eight ex-socialist countries: Poland, Bulgaria, Hungary, the Czech Republic and so on (Parent-Thirion et al. 2007: 18). For highly skilled service-sector employees, the situation is similar. Romania ranked again first again and the Czech Republic third of all EU member states.[2] Of the 13 countries ranking above the EU 27 average in respect of overwork by skilled service-sector employees, seven are post-socialist.

Besides the sheer number of hours, the intensity, discipline and porousness of daily work have also changed since the end of socialism. Recent decades have facilitated the regional and global circulation of experts and consultants, as well as of various forms of discipline, work habits, and time structures to many parts of the world, including, after 1989, post-socialist countries (Appadurai 1996). Kept at a safe distance by state socialism (Verdery 1996), corporate investments and corporate culture have during the last 20 years penetrated the economic, administrative and media landscapes of the ex-socialist countries. To the extent

---

1   According to the European Working Conditions Survey 2010, available at http://www.eurofound.europa.eu/surveys/smt/ewcs/ewcs2010_02_02.htm, accessed on 25 December 2011. Personal analysis.

2   According to European Working Conditions Survey 2010, available at http://www.eurofound.europa.eu/surveys/smt/ewcs/ewcs2010_02_02.htm, accessed on 25 December 2011. Personal analysis.

that a transnational corporate capitalist class is conceivable (Sklair 2000), such investments generate local groups with new work disciplines new time structures and, ultimately, new personas (Dunn 2004). As Elizabeth Dunn (2004: 7) puts it, 'these "doctrines of flexibility" – and demands that both workers and firms become "self-regulating selves" – mark the advent of a fundamentally new form of power in postsocialist Eastern Europe'.

In this chapter I attempt to understand the temporal transformations that accompany the transition from socialist to multinational corporate work practices.[3] The study focuses on high-skilled labour – more precisely, on banking sector employees. How did people discard their older daily routines and time-sense, and how did they acquire flexible selves and skills, and a new time-sense? My aim is not to explain why the post-socialist labour force works longer hours; rather, I focus on the 'how' questions of these labour transformations. In order to answer these questions, in 2005 and 2006 I carried out in-depth, semi-structured interviews with top-level, and also with non-managerial personnel employees of a multinational bank (Q Bank – a fictional name) that has been operating in Romania since the early 2000s.[4]

The individuals whom I studied were on the way to becoming members of the transnational capitalist corporate class (Sklair 2000). Among that group, one finds people similar to my interviewees, i.e., owners and controllers of transnational corporations and their local affiliates. The people whom I studied fit that category in several respects. Their work contacts are linked to global or regional markets

───────────

3   This research was part of the 'Dioscuri Research Project: Eastern Enlargement – Western Enlargement. Cultural Encounters in the European Economy and Society after the Accession'. The project was funded within the European Commission's 6th Framework Program. Project coordination was provided by the Centre for Policy Studies of the Central European University, Budapest. The project was supported by the Principal Researcher based at the Institute for Human Sciences in Vienna and was carried out between 2004 and 2007. I would like to thank Violeta Zentai, Janos Matyas Kovacs (project coordinators) and Vintilă Mihăilescu (country coordination) for organizing the research activities. Many thanks to Diana Mihăloiu, who acted as a research assistant. Narcis Tulbure closely read the article and offered useful comments. I would also like to thank Patty Mullally and Jonathan Larson. Finally, I would like to thank Nicolette Makovicky and Dimitrios Dalakoglou for organizing the panel 'The self as "mini-corporation"? The fate of neo-liberal models of personhood in the boom (and bust) economies of Central and Eastern Europe' at EASA 2010 in Maynooth, Ireland.

4   The interviewees were seven middle managers, five members of the human resources department and a few employees who had worked for the bank prior to privatization. The interviews were carried out *in situ*. Due to their time constraints, I could interview the managers only once, while I had repeated conversations with human resources department employees. The interviews with the managers contained questions about their daily routine, their previous workplaces and how their life changed over time. The conversations with the human resources people and the 'old-timers' provided valuable information about the changes to the company after privatization.

through their headquarter-based supervisors and the nature of the financial sector. All interviewees graduated during the late 1990s and early 2000s with MBAs offered in Romania through cooperation with American, Canadian, and French business schools. They read similar national and international editions of the same business magazines. Moreover, their lifestyles, residential and holiday aspirations are internally similar, and rather different from many other groups in Romanian society.

These new work habits and new senses of time emerged as a key area of transformation triggered by their gradual affiliation with the transnational corporate class.[5] The following section, therefore, places this case study within the literature on work and time under the flexible accumulation regime. After that, I provide a condensed overview of the post-privatization transformations of the bank, emphasizing the devaluation of older skills and the championing of 'seller' skills, individualization, the stimulation of entrepreneurialism and the importance of charismatic actions on the part of expat workers and managers. The chapter then continues with a detailed description of the new time-sense created after privatization. In that section, among other transformations, I point to a new time regime, which might be called 'virtual time'. It is created by organizational pressure, overwork, and the postponement of personal plans to an indefinite future.

Transformations of Self, Work and Time in the Flexible Accumulation Regime

The transformations that I describe below have been analysed in other ethnographic contexts within the theoretical framework of a regime of flexible accumulation (Harvey 1990, Gorz 1999). Since the 1970s and 1980s, large-scale companies have set out to increase profit and decrease turnover time by speeding up, among other things, the processes of labour. This has led to significant changes in the organization of economy, culture, space and time, both in the core and periphery of the world system. The entire world of work has been redefined in order to facilitate this process. For the current economy and culture, the 'accelerated destruction and reconstruction of workers' skills' (Harvey 1990: 230) have been central. Flexibility has become a true organizational religion. As Harvey describes

---

5   There are some valuable ethnographies of labor processes during state socialism (Burawoy and Lukács, 1992; Creed, 1998; Humphrey, 1983/1998 ; Lampland, 1995; Verdery, 1996). They were carried out in agricultural and industrial settings and they usually emphasized the specificity of labor during state socialism. This specificity was many times related to the mechanism of shortage economy. The present study describes a process of global economic and cultural integration, one of the key dimensions of the post-socialist period. It also covers a rather substantial gap in the post-socialist literature about the transformations of time and work in the growing service sector of post-socialist countries.

it, 'workers, instead of acquiring a skill for life, can now look forward to at least one if not multiple bouts of de-skilling and re-skilling in a lifetime' (Harvey 1990: 229–30; see also Martin in Kirschner 1999: 266 on this point).

Because of the changes and instabilities in the new nature of companies, jobs and work cultures, people have begun to think of themselves as 'entrepreneurs', seeing 'the individual as an entrepreneur of his own life' (McNay 2009: 62; Kasmir 2001). Emily Martin has argued that this has led to greater individualization, in the sense that individuals' organizational commitment is no longer intense and long-lasting, as it would have been during the period of large bureaucratic, vertically integrated organizations (Harvey 1990). Instead of 'organization men' (White 1956), this new economic design has turned individuals into 'minicorporations', i.e. sites for resource accumulation of education, houses, savings, stocks, children, valuable insurances etc. (Martin in Kirschner 1999: 267).

Along with the entrepreneurial imperative, new forms of labour requiring flexibility and multitasking have emerged. The maximization of bodily and mental potential, and the exercise autonomy and choice, have become important cultural values in post-Fordist economies (Martin in Kirschner 1999: 267–9, Rose 1998: 161). Such values are objectified into a variety of practices in the corporate world, such as 'personal development' techniques, an increase in the use of stimulant drugs, coaching sessions paid for by companies, as well as rapid, magical procedures aimed at delivering instant happiness, efficiency and skills. Jonathan Larson (2002, 2008), for instance, observing a workshop on CV writing in Slovakia, described how résumé construction maps and translates a person into neoliberal categories, that are transparent, accountable, and suitable for verification by would-be employers. Other objectifications of neoliberal subjectivity are condensed in mini training courses, teambuilding activities, time management techniques (Larsson and Sanne 2005), or even family 'audits' (Hochschild 2008).

These corporate cultural practices are delivered by various 'experts in subjectivity', such as organizational psychologists and management consultants, who help the intensification of labour and re-skilling of the labour force, delivering flexible and entrepreneurial individuals to a flexible economy (Rose 1998: 161). Such practices all share a mediation function between organizational objectives and personal goals; as Nikolas Rose (1998: 161) put it: 'Expertise plays the role of relay between objectives that are economically desirable and those that are personally seductive, teaching the arts of self-realization that will enhance employees as individuals as well as workers. Economic success, career progress, and personal development intersect in this new expertise of autonomous subjectivity'.

Key among these transformations has been the experience of time. As Amy Todd reminds us, 'time has always been a salient dimension of work culture' (2009: 50), but the regime of flexible accumulation brought new temporal structures (Rubin 2007: 8). These include project time (Shih 2004); intermittent or zero physical presence in the company on the part of nomads, independents, team workers and homeworkers; extended and erratic periods of working; flex-time (Worthington 2006: 21–51); the reversal of work time in the global service sector; the 'time famine' for knowledge workers (Perlow 1999; Vuckovic 1999); or buying time with self-medication when productivity imperatives dictate that there is 'no time to be sick' (Vuckovic 1999).

All these studies indicate that the contemporary workplace in many parts of the world functions according to new and accelerated rhythms, paces, routines and schedules (Rosa 2003: 11–12, Rubin 2007: 2). Surprisingly perhaps, the multiplication and fragmentation of work and time for the post-socialist workforce may be fruitfully understood through E.P. Thompson's (1967) classic work on the emergence of early capitalism. Thompson describes the slow process of disciplining the workforce and instilling a sense of routine and daily schedule. According to him, ex-peasants turned industrial workers had a hard time adjusting to the discipline of fixed working hours. Reviewing several anthropological works about the perception of time, he defined the non-commodified, non-standardized form of time as task-oriented, i.e. dependent upon particular practical events rather than uniform measurements of time. He also noted that, in task-oriented communities, there seems to be least demarcation between 'work' and 'life'. In such situations, 'social intercourse and labour are intermingled – the working-day lengthens or contracts according to the task – and there is no great sense of conflict between labour and "passing the time of the day". […] To men accustomed to labour timed by the clock, this attitude to labour appears to be wasteful and lacking urgency' (Thompson 1967: 60).

Recent reconsiderations of E.P. Thompson's thesis have argued that time-discipline may be experienced in a variety of ways (Sauter 2007: 687). While Thompson described the transition from an agrarian to an industrial economy, however, the argument may be fruitfully used for the transition from socialism to a flexible accumulation regime, even if socialist societies were themselves industrial. Because of its structural shortage and hoarding practices, work during socialism was a combination of task-oriented time and clock time (Dunn 2004: 16, Kornai 1992, Müller 1997: 544, Verdery 1996: 42–5). Socialist-era work culture was an alternation of idleness and task-oriented frenzy. As Katherine Verdery (1996: 43) put it, 'hoarding made for unpredictable delivery of inputs, which caused irregular production rhythms, with periods of slackness giving way to periods of frantic activity ('storming') when a delivery of materials finally enabled effort towards meeting the production goals'. After Q Bank's privatization, the management attempted to eliminate the idleness and generally succeeded in instilling a new, constant and intensified work rhythm. I will describe these transformations in detail, but first I will give an overview of the transformations prompted by the purchase of Q Bank by the European bank.

Privatization, Flexibilization, and New Persons

Before I present the post-privatization time-sense and work culture, let me briefly sketch the ways in which this bank was transformed after the European bank purchased it. Due to political parasitism during the early 1990s, the bank went bankrupt. The liabilities accumulated on behalf of the Romanian state prior to privatization were close to 1 billion dollars. While preparing for privatization, the losses were nationalized, i.e. transferred to the public debt. Q Bank (a fictive name) purchased and reorganized the operations of the virtually bankrupt bank. A predictable trend was the search for profitability or, using Janos Kornai's concepts (1992), the transition from a seller's market to a buyer's market. This meant many things. One was the rescaling of number and location of the banks' branches. During the post-1989 period, the bank extended its branch network throughout the country quite substantially, in many cases irrespective of the profits these branch offices were generating. While loss-making branches were shut down, new ones opened, especially in Bucharest, where some 20–30 branches served the large market of the capital city. This recalibration of the network has remained an on-going process, in the sense that each branch has to produce yearly a certain profit, depending on the number of its employees.

The geographical rescaling of branches was accompanied by the downsizing of the internal workforce. The number of employees decreased from about 9–10,000 to about 4,900. The current management argues that, prior to privatization, there was excess labour, an argument in which there may be some truth. Katherine Verdery (1996: 42) has suggested that state companies during and shortly after socialism, 'learned to hoard materials and labour, overstating both their material requirements for production and their investment needs'. Outsourcing, too, reduced the number of employees. It was prompted by a general trend among companies in Romania, but also adopted as a strategy to avoid requests for bribes from various state institutions during controls.

The restructuring of labour routines also facilitated the firing of employees. According to several interviewees, the labour routine prior to privatization was based on simple, rigidly defined skills: some people simply stamped the receipts, others wrote their registration numbers into a notebook, and so on. By the standards of 'parent' bank labour culture, the job assignments were too fragmented and too mono-task. The post-privatization human relations department employees whom I interviewed described these jobs as 'artificial' and the persons occupying them as 'untrained' or 'lacking any skills'. As a result, the new management engaged in an 'accelerated destruction' of prior skills, followed by the concentration of tasks and a reskilling of the workforce. Each new employee was supposed to master and perform most operations previously assigned to different employees. The concentration and reskilling overlapped temporarily with the imposition of computer literacy, a process that made prior labour routines and jobs obsolete. The agglutination of previously divided skills was accompanied by the compression and intensification of labour for each job.

To give just one example, that of front-desk clerks: labour intensification meant an increase in the number of invoices from 80 to 100 a day. Their work also became multitask: they faced multiple tasks ranging from register keeping and stamping receipts to the emotional work of counselling.

Another form of reskilling that accompanied the transition from the seller's to the buyer's market was the inculcation of what the interviewees describe as a 'sales mentality' or a 'capitalist stance'.[6] The new management used three main methods of sales-oriented reskilling. The most important was training. Sales and customer service courses (i.e., teaching the speech and posture patterns required for interactions with clients) were, and still are, mandatory for all employees in every country where Q bank operates. They last for one month. Immediately after privatization, these courses were delivered by international trainers sent over from the bank's headquarters. Besides these mandatory courses, training programs are a permanent concern of the management. Each yearly operational budget contains a substantial amount for such activities.

Charismatic action, a frequent form of legitimacy in the world of finance (Preda 2009), combined with bureaucratic domination also facilitated the unmaking of the older organization and the creation of a corporate culture shared across countries. One example was the arrival at the Romanian branch of Q Bank of 50 to 60 expats from non-Romanian branches, both from the 'parent' country and elsewhere. Labelled officially by the management as 'seeds of change', these expats were placed at various hierarchical levels in order to radiate proper labour skills to the local workers. When asked why these people had to be expats, one interviewee said that it was costly time-wise to identify role-model employees from inside the Romanian branches and that foreigners had more credibility. Another such charisma-led action was the implementation of a top-down organization change led by a foreign CEO.

The human resources department, directly answering to the CEO, had a quite substantial role in these changes. It took a very energetic stance, overseeing everything related to personnel: recruitment, compensation and benefits, teambuilding, training and the personal development of the employees. The human resources department engaged in a very large-scale operation to screen and monitor their employees, firing some and recruiting new ones. Upon obtaining a job, the new recruits entered a process of institutional socialization. This took the form of transmitting to newcomers the message of the Mission/Vision/Values document, a programmatic statement of the bank's aims. According to our interviewees, the newcomers go through an express socialization, named 'induction training', which lasts for two days. During this period, the human resources department trainers introduce the newcomers to the program, the code of conduct, the collective labour contract and various internal procedures. Then there is a longer period of informal learning, which takes about six months, during which, as one interviewee put it:

---

6   See Kaczmarczyk and Lewicki (2007), but Birgit Müller (1999) for a review of several similar cases from East Central Europe.

you get to know the structure of the organization, whom you are supposed to work with, whom you have to contact in order to get a pen, whom you have to talk to in order to solve a daily problem, how you are supposed to relate to each person – all these take time and can only be learned after we had contacts and common assignments with certain people.

Pay changed too, with privatization, in the sense that for those who continued to work it increased significantly. A short discussion of this topic is useful, because pay is not just about monetary value. It also indexes how power is administered and how employees' sociability functions inside the organization. Pay was an instrument of individualization, as two examples make clear. The human resources department attempted to weaken the strong sense of universal entitlement to bonuses existing before privatization by fostering an entrepreneurial self. Because Q Bank inherited quite a strong labour union from the pre-privatization era, as one interviewee explained, there was a strong pressure for the payment of equal bonuses to all employees. The post-privatization management, however, only granted bonuses for achievement and performance, rewarding those who over-performed and ignoring those who had average results. The union asked the management to eliminate the achievement bonus system and award everyone a flat amount at Easter and Christmas. Deploying the language of objectivity and science, the management, according to one HR employee, explained that not everybody can work the same, invoking Gauss's curve. Very few people get distributed to the extremes; the vast majority fall into the middle, which means achieving the 'according to job description' grade. After about three or four years of disputes the union and the workforce accepted the new entrepreneurial, differential system.

Because of the individualization pressures from the management, remuneration also became something of an 'open secret' inside the organization. It came as a cultural shock to the European management that its insistence on the confidentiality of remuneration levels was constantly disregarded. Confidentiality with regard to earnings is an important taboo in Western economic culture. One interviewee spoke at some length about this, saying that 'one cultural thing that foreigners do not understand it is why Romanians tell each other what they earn. Irrespective of what the management does, and of the fact that the collective work contract stipulates that you get fired if you reveal what you earn, employees do it. It simply does not work!' Silence about pay is a power technique, in the sense that it helps pacify the labour force. Earnings are a vehicle for potential commentary on and opposition to management practices, because they allow an easy comparison of employees with their peers. Silence about them means eliminating frustration among people who do the same work, but get paid differently. Employees, on the other hand, resist the practice of individualization and gagging by making pay a political element in the bank's life. Pay, whether high or low, is a vehicle of social commentary. If the level is perceived to be too low, by disclosing it people demonstrate that there is a huge conspiracy against them and point the finger at whomever they deem guilty for that. If, on the other hand, pay is high, then people begin to brag about it. This might be the core mechanism in a larger network of 'classified' knowledge about pay used in the internal economic and political struggle.[7]

The Post-privatization Time-sense

The new post-privatization time culture came as surprise to many of the former employees. One older interviewee, who had worked in the bank since 1981, said that 'people were not used to working in such a way. As regards volume, time and dedication ... those who worked at the state bank had no chance of adapting. Practically speaking, [before privatization] they were doing four hours' worth of work in an eight-hour workday. The rest was a cup of coffee now and then ... you know, other stuff'. The issue of the differences between socialist-era work-discipline and intensity and that of private/foreign companies came out in another interview, when someone remembered his experience at his first job, just before the fall of communism. He described how his first day of work came as a big shock:

> When I first went to the research institution where I worked, they left me alone, like a wild plant, for a month. For a month nobody told me anything [...]. I was getting there in the morning, reading the sports dailies for about two hours, I smoked, I drank a couple of coffees, around lunch I went out to eat. Then we came back, then the day was over.

He became bored and instead of reading the newspaper he began to read an English language book and a computer book. That got him into trouble because the next day he ended up having to sort out a large pile of files. He left them on the desk and the next day resumed his previous activity of reading the newspaper. 'Everybody was happy!' By contrast, he said, the first two weeks at Q were an intensive 'induction training'. He was introduced to the company, he met a lot of people and attended training programs. His first day was a rather long interaction with the human resources department, who presented the company and the organizational chart to him. He perceived all this as an intensification of time, as things moving faster, as a 'huge change of speed' – whereas in the socialist-era company things moved in a 'perpetual first gear', as he phrased it. When asked to describe a typical workday for him, he said it lasts from 8 am to at least 7 pm, but might go on

---

7 Although I did not find this in my interviews, Narcis Tulbure (personal communication) states that open secrecy regarding wages and bonuses is common to most Romanian banks. Moreover, people are aware even of the pay of their counterparts from other banks. All this knowledge is then used as leverage in the negotiations with the human resources departments.

longer. Two Saturdays a month he has to go to the office – and occasionally on Sundays too. His description of his schedule abounded in small time units: he used hours and minutes to describe his daily routine, rather than longer and vaguer units such as 'morning', 'afternoon' or 'evening'. This is similar to historical studies of the emergence of capitalism and the redefinition of time (Dohrn-van Rossum and Dunlap 1996), which demonstrate that the dynamism of capital-related activities produced a higher standardization of time keeping.

Aside from the compression and intensification of labour, the post-privatization office layout further separates 'work' and 'life', eliminating the conditions conducive to idleness and non-work-related interactions. It is organized as an open space without walls and cubicles – except for a few people in higher positions – a meeting room and the kitchen. The office floor seemed very quiet; nobody seemed to be talking to one another. The individual desks are located far enough apart so that you have to speak in a loud voice to communicate with a neighbour. In order to talk to somebody, you have to stand up and walk to that person's desk. Such interactional activities were transferred to common-area spaces, where one could not spend too much time because access to them was card-based (which means that they are verified by the management).[8]

This mixture of overwork, clear separation of work from life, and time shortage leads to several time transformations. One is the emergence of a time regime that might be called 'virtual time'. One interviewee said:

> I don't really get to socialize … there are office colleagues whom I speak to about many work-related issues. There are also college friends that I see more often, but that's about it. When I came to Bucharest [to work for Q], I told myself that I would get to see a lot of friends and that it would be great – we would have time to do plenty of things together. We see each other once every three months, for an hour at the most, because we are busy and tired.

This future-oriented virtual time may reach a point where one is left with nothing but work, which occupies most of the time (like the person who stays at the office for 11 hours). Other desires and time plans are pushed into a vividly imagined, but indefinite and potentially unrealizable future. Living in virtual time is the opposite of what Oili-Helena Ylijoki (2010) has called instant living: ignoring the future and focusing on the present. It is more like 'inconspicuous consumption' – the imagined future use of already made purchases by people who have enough money, but insufficient leisure time (Sullivan and Gershuny 2004: 79).

---

8   Although the data that I gathered do not suggest this, Narcis Tulbure (personal communication) suggests that the social void projected by spatial tactics of the management is actually filled by employees' sociality. He argues that in various banking offices there is an intense system of mutual observation and communication through SMS, internet, social media and non-verbal sign codes. He suggests that actually open-layout offices are very dense socially.

Another transformation of temporal structures can be seen in the increased value of time and the emergence of time hyper-consciousness. One interviewee explained: 'I don't know if this is something to be proud of, but I began to value leisure time much more. Before that I could afford [to waste time], not going at the pace that I do now. I indulged in time-wasting, watched a soccer game or just wasted time in general'. Linked to the redefinition of the value of time, another transformation of the temporal regime lies in the intensification of time planning. One interviewee described how he plans his free time in much more detail. He moved from indefinite 'relaxation time', time which 'appears to have no destination' (Heintz 2002: 150) to clearly defined, task-oriented free time. Before he worked in Q Bank, his relaxation time was casual and elastic: 'Things were not so condensed ... I was hanging out, listening to music, chatting with friends, maybe playing bridge ... stuff like that'. Lately, he said, his free time has been no longer casual and spontaneous, but rather planned: 'Having much less free time, I try to condense it into very clearly defined time. If I manage to put together two hours, I have a very clear goal, like going to the theatre. I plan them the same way that I planned meeting you: I write down in my agenda what time I am going to the theatre and I have a very clear plan of action'.

The reorganization of labour routines leads sometimes to conflict and other times to blending organizational time with personal time. From this point of view, the bank may be regarded as a 'greedy institution' (Coser 1978: 101–5; see Burchielli et al. 2008 for the use of this concept for firms), which, in this context means that it demands loyalty and attempts to weaken links to other institutions and groups, mainly family and friends.[9] This may be best noticed in the case of job-related activities such as training programs or teambuilding. One interviewee described the initial excitement of new recruits when they enrol in training programs. At first people attend such training programs on Saturday and Sunday, because they are anxious to learn new things in order to be sure that they continue to work at the bank. However, in about a year, the employees begin to avoid weekends and pressure the managers to move the training programs to working days. The only activities left for weekends are teambuilding activities.

Organizational time and personal time meet in another area, that of teambuilding and mandatory socialization outside the physical boundaries of the organization but within its social ambit. One interviewee explained how she began to hate restaurants in another corporate job that she had before Q Bank, where, instead of extra money, the employees received invitations to restaurants from the company. Initially, this seemed extraordinary to her, because, as an ordinary person in Romania, one went there once or twice a year. Although at the time she was working 12 hours daily (7.30 am to 7.30 pm), the company took employees out for teambuilding activities after work. She explained that she would rather

---

9   Weak or non-existent family ties are sometimes sought after by the human resources companies who hire people. Single women are preferred, moreover, during interviews such women are asked about future pregnancy plans.

have gone home or brought family members to the teambuilding meetings, but she was not allowed to. She also soon realized that teambuilding meetings held in restaurants were not leisure, in the sense that one could not bracket off the discipline of work. Here is how she described it:

> It was not like going out with friends. When you go out in a business situation you keep on self-censoring yourself. It's not like you can drink until you drop or talk nonsense or let yourself go. There you talk business again, you have to eat moderately, to drink as little as possible – preferably not at all.

She said that this is taken for granted. She said that you observed the same rules that you did at the office. Such meetings were part of the company's policy and you could only have excused yourself once or twice, because the pressure was huge. Moreover, she pointed to the idea of surveillance during such meetings when she said that one's behaviour in an informal, extra-work environment reveals one's 'real' self. If one is not aware of that and gets drunk, it can seriously affect one's career.

Teambuilding activities seem to be an intermediate area between work and life, situated closer to the former. Employees get a sense of proper behaviour and self-restraint, while the Q Bank's human resources managers get a better sense of their employee's personality. The human resources department attempts to channel conflict into cooperation and harmonize individuals' energies, actions which are highly resonant with the organization's objectives and with the idea of self-regulation in individuals. I asked each interviewee about their teambuilding experience and learned that the success formula is that of moderate physical effort. One may get a sense of this from the following account by one interviewee:

> Bankers are office people, they are not extreme action-oriented individuals. If you ask them what kind of teambuilding they want, a physical or less physical one, they will answer 'a less physical one', mainly because they are afraid that they will not cope with it. Actually, they like a more physical one, precisely because they sit all day long in the office. So, the best kind is one that seems very physical, but is actually simple, which means that they prefer an outdoor exercise. They want to feel like they've done something they never did before and that they were up to it, but it should not be very difficult, because if it is too difficult they really cannot do it, because they do not have super-muscles – myself included.

I asked interviewees whether people can actually relax during the teambuilding retreats. The answers emphasized the role of familiarity in determining whether one enjoys such trips. One of them said that the first time one attends, one is extremely tense. He said that employees feel as if everybody is watching them. Two days later, by Sunday, people begin to loosen up. By the bus trip home, people start to feel sorry they are leaving. On their next trip, they begin to relax by Saturday, and on the third trip they relax from boarding the outbound bus. He also said that what surprised him the first time he attended a teambuilding session was that everybody was assigned to work with people whom they had never had any interaction with more serious than saying 'Hi, how are you?' Mandatory mixing actually generates surprises about fellow workers. He told the story of an older, rather oversized lady who was supposed to slide downhill hanging on a rope and succeeded in doing so. Everybody changed their opinion of her, taking into account her efforts. He said that getting another angle on people is actually a more general experience during such exercises.

Another human resources department interviewee mentioned that it is increasingly difficult to find new exercises to carry out during the teambuilding activities. People get to know them. Another observation about teambuilding was that, unlike their counterparts from other parts of the world, Q bank employees (and Romanian employees in similar structural positions in general) prefer non-natural settings for their retreats. Instead of outdoor camps, they insist on going to luxury hotels and eating fancy food.

Conclusions

In this chapter I have analysed how work-discipline and time-sense changed when a socialist/post-socialist managerial and work culture was replaced by multinational corporate management techniques. These transformations were narrated by interviewees in terms of human improvement through efficiency, flexibility, transparency, and a fair reward for hard work. During their integration in the multinational corporation, the ex-socialist workforce came to share traits, subjectivities, and aspirations similar to their counterparts from other flexible accumulation economies. They reskilled themselves through various training programs imposed by the bank, faced individualization techniques orchestrated by the management, and subjected themselves to subtle disciplining actions.

The new forms of corporate work-discipline generated a new, fast-paced time-sense. The socialist alternation of idleness with overwork has been evened out in favour of a steadier, accelerated rhythm of work. Post-privatization management techniques made the bank a 'greedy' firm (Coser 1978: 101–5, see Burchielli et al. 2008), creating insatiable demands for its employees' time. Organizational time invaded personal time through prolonged office hours, but also through activities such as teambuilding trips and training sessions, scheduled outside the regular work program and at weekends. Under these circumstances, employees postponed some personal plans, developed over-planned time-accounting strategies for leisure time and diminish their temporal investments in the maintenance of social relations with friends and sometimes families. These deferred personal plans and social engagements and incipient forms of workaholism lead to what might be called 'virtual time', i.e. the intensive elaboration and subsequent relocation of various personal plans to an indefinite future.

Finally, taking into account the literature on other countries where flexible and entrepreneurial selves became ways of life, one would expect the emergence of various forms of resistance among such employees. Debates about work–life balance, downshifting, 'sabbatical' leave, flexibilization of work hours and attempts to avoid unpaid supplementary work hours emerged as forms of resistance to the flexible accumulation regime. To the extent that I met resistance to the new managerial techniques, it tended to be oblique rather than overt. Alina Petrovici, who studied similar issues in another company noticed that managerial abuses are experienced with frustration and desperation, but the only strategies that employee use (exit from the firm, ironies, backstage jokes) are inherently individual and non-threatening to the management (Petrovici 2010: 164).

The situation regarding confidentiality about pay, described above, would be a good example of such oblique resistance. The recent crisis has made resistance an even less salient issue in Romania. At a more general level, the dialectic between discipline and resistance at Q bank seems to suggest that in economies recently incorporated into the flexible accumulation organization, there seems to be a significant time lag between the anticipative appreciation of the assets offered by accession to the transnational capitalist corporate class and the cognitive representation of its liabilities.

References

Appadurai, A. 1996. *Modernity at Large: Cultural Dimensions of Globalization.* Twin Cities: University of Minnesota Press.

Burawoy, M. and Lukács, J. 1992. *The Radiant Past: Ideology and Reality in Hungary's Road to Capitalism.* Chicago: University of Chicago Press.

Burchielli, R., Bartram T. and Thanacoody R. 2008. Work-Family Balance or Greedy Organizations? *Relations industrielles/Industrial Relations*, 63(1): 108–33.

Coser, L. 1974. *Greedy Institutions: Patterns of Undivided Commitment.* New York: Free Press.

Creed, G. 1998. *Domesticating Revolution: From Socialist Revolution to Ambivalent Transition in a Bulgarian Village.* Philadelphia: Pennsylvania State University.

Dohrn-van Rossum, G. and Thomas D. 1996. *History of the Hour: Clocks and Modern Temporal Orders.* Chicago: University of Chicago Press.

Dunn, E. 2004. *Privatizing Poland: Baby Food, Big Business and the Remaking of Labor.* Ithaca: Cornell University Press.

Gorz, A. 1999. *Reclaiming Work: Beyond the Wage-Based Society.* Cambridge: Polity Press.

Harvey, D. 1990. *The Condition of Postmodernity: An Enquiry into the Origins of Cultural Change.* Oxford: Blackwell.

Heintz, M. 2002. *Changes in Work Ethic in Postsocialist Romania.* PhD thesis. University of Cambridge. [Online]. Available at http://tinyurl.com/dxjoog7 [accessed 17 March 2013].

Hochschild, A. 2008. Through the Crack of the Time Bind: From Market Management to Family Management. *Anthropology of Work Review*, 28(1): 1–8.

Humphrey, C. (1983) *Marx Went Away, but Karl Stayed Behind.* Ann Arbor: University of Michigan Press.

Kaczmarczyk, P. and Lewicki, M. 2007. *'Lost in Transformation'. Cultural Encounters in Multinational Corporations Investing in Central and Eastern Europe.* Unpublished manuscript.

Kasmir S. 2001 Corporation, Self, and Enterprise at the Saturn Automobile Plant. *Anthropology of Work Review*, 22(4): 8–12.

Kirschner, S. 1999 From Flexible Bodies to Fluid Minds: An Interview with Emily Martin. *Ethos*, 27(3): 247–82.

Kornai, J. 1992. *The Socialist System: The Political Economy of Communism.* Princeton: Princeton University Press.

Lampland, M. 1995. *The Object of Labor: Commodification in Socialist Hungary.* Chicago: University of Chicago Press.

Larson, J. 2002. Selling Oneself, Selling the Nation: Translating Slovaks for the Eyes of Europe. *Anthropology of Eastern Europe Review*, 20(2): 37–41.

Larson, J. 2008. Ambiguous Transparency: Résumé Fetishism in a Slovak Workshop. *Ethnos*, 73(2): 189–216.

Larsson, J. and Sanne, C. 2005. Self-Help Books on Avoiding Time Shortage. *Time and Society*, 14(2–3): 213–30.

McNay, L. 2009. Self as Enterprise. *Theory, Culture and Society* 26(6): 55–77.

Müller, B. 1997. Du travailleur socialiste à 'l'homme nouveau' dans l'économie de marché. *Ethnologie Française*, 27(4): 543–51.

Müller, B (1999) Calculus et croyances: La mission civilisatrice d'une multinationale en Europe de l'Est. *Ethnologie Française*, 29(4): 543–48.

Parent-Thirion, A., Fernández, M., Hurley, J. and Vermeylen, G. 2007. *Fourth European Working Conditions Survey.* Luxemburg: Office for Official Publications of the European Communities.

Perlow, L. 1999. The Time Famine: Toward a Sociology of Work Time. *Administrative Science Quarterly*, 44(1): 57–81.

Petrovici, A. 2010. *Transforming Neoliberal Corporate Environments: Human Resources Perspectives in Postsocialist Cluj.* PhD dissertation, Babeş-Bolyai University, Department of Sociology.

Preda, A. 2009. *Framing Finance: The Boundaries of Markets and Modern Capitalism.* Chicago: University of Chicago Press.

Rosa, H. 2003. Social Acceleration: Ethical and Political Consequences of a Desynchronized High-Speed Society. *Constellations*, 10(1): 3–33.

Rose, N. 1998. *Inventing Our Selves: Psychology, Power and Personhood.* Cambridge: University of Cambridge Press.

Rubin, B. 2007. Time-Work Discipline in the 21st Century, in *Workplace Temporalities*, edited by B. Rubin. Amsterdam: Elsevier.

Sauter, M. 2007. Clockwatchers and Stargazers: Time Discipline in Early Modern England. *American Historical Review*, 112(3): 685–709.

Shih, J. 2004. Project Time in Silicon Valley. *Qualitative Sociology*, 27(2): 223–45.
Sklair, L.2000. The Transnational Capitalist Class and the Discourse of Globalization. *Cambridge Review of International Affairs*, 14(1): 67–85.
Sullivan, O. and Ghershuny, J. 2004. Inconspicuous Consumption: Work-Rich, Time-Poor in the Liberal Market Economy. *Journal of Consumer Research*, 4(1): 79–100.
Thompson, E.P. 1967. Time, Work-Discipline and Industrial Capitalism. *Past and Present* 38: 56–97.
Todd, A. 2009. From Polychronicity to Multitasking: The Warp of Time Across Disciplinary Boundaries. *Anthropology of Work Review*, 30(2): 49–54.
Verdery, K. 1996. *What Was Socialism and What Comes Next*. Princeton: Princeton University Press.
Vuckovic, N. 1999. Fast Relief: Buying Time with Medications. *Medical Anthropology Quarterly*, 13(1): 51–68.
White, H.W. 1956. *The Organization Man*. New York: Simon and Schuster.
Worthington J. 2006. *Reinventing the Workplace*. Amsterdam: Elsevier.
Ylijoki, O-H. 2010. Future Orientations in Episodic Labor: Short-term Academics as a Case in Point. *Time and Society*, 19(3): 365–86.

Chapter 3

Using Gender in Neoliberal Business: Reinterpretations of Female Utility in a Romanian Company

Alina Petrovici

Introduction

Neoliberal models of management emphasize entrepreneurship, self-development and inspiring leadership, accentuating more and more the need for 'soft' personal and interpersonal management skills. They therefore welcome traits and qualities conventionally understood as 'feminine', as particularly useful in an adaptive post-Fordist economy where professionalism and technical know-how alone are unable to provide positive engagement with subordinates. This tendency of incorporating previous critiques, specific to neoliberal managerial discourse and technique (Boltanski and Chiapello 2005), appears to be an opportunity for redressing the balance of unjust gendered practices, offering women the possibility of surpassing the glass-ceiling and widening their professional areas. Nonetheless, I consider that gender divisions are kept in place despite the new rhetoric; while empowerment and self-identification of women occurs only insofar as it benefits business. Excellent examples of neoliberal self-regulation, female managers conform to authoritarian methods previously conceived as 'masculine' and ruthlessly enhance control and domination. Moreover, as traditional gender divisions are maintained, women internalize the egalitarian neoliberal discourse of self-improvement and efficiency, striving to be veritable entrepreneurs of themselves despite the fact that they are still employed in feminized niches.

In this chapter I reshape Mojab and Gorman's (2003: 25) argument that 'empowerment and learning of workers themselves occurs, if it occurs at all, only as a by-product to organizational growth and profitability'. In the same fashion, I argue that the empowerment and self-identification of women in the neoliberal organization occurs only insofar this benefits business. I base my argument on a three-year ethnographic research project conducted on a construction company located in Cluj-Napoca, Romania; company for which I used the pseudonym Construct Energy. As my site revealed, business owners commodify women and men alike, as capitalist resources. Yet, neoliberal practices in the firm are not gender neutral, despite a strong gender equality narrative, supported by the individualizing meritocratic explanations of worth (Stobbe 2005). The tools of this redefinition of gender are somehow new and unexpected; traditional gender normalcy is reshaped through corporate expectations and practices framed in the leadership discourse. Management has been known as a masculine fief organized by masculine values. And consequently, women are encouraged to display – and they are subsequently promoted if they succeed in portraying – somewhat 'manly' characteristics, expected to prove beneficial to the business. I regard these non-discriminative practices which dismantle the glass-ceiling as an actual commodification process of using the 'valuable' female employee as objects to further enhance control. It may be falsely envisioned as a process of change in the traditional gender asymmetries of power, a change towards a more equitable and non-discriminative distribution in the gendered division of labour. As opposed to the literature on the 'glass ceiling' gender problem or the vertical diminished mobility (Arulampalam, Booth, and Bryan 2007, McDowell, Singell, and Ziliak 1999, Morgan 1998), women in Construct Energy do not encounter the discriminative practice of reduced promotion to senior or middle level positions. Even if it is true that a vast majority of management positions with women in charge can be found in departments formed mostly of women employees, we can still describe a notable example to the contrary, where a woman controls entire departments of male engineer employees and she is considered by the owners one of the best senior managers of the firm. We find this context to support Rudman and Phelan's (2008) feminization trends fostering cooperation and positive motivation consigned to lower and middle management positions, while top executive positions emphasize mostly agentic qualities such as ruthlessness, competitiveness and decisiveness (Boyce and Herd 2003). Also, specific feminine attributes become a plus for women who are reconstructing female identities to accommodate positions of responsibility that were previously owned by men and where we have, at present, a blank slate as to what constitutes 'appropriate behaviour' (i.e. for women managers).

My research site supports both arguments: that of a gendered division of labour, with subordinate, administrative desk work as the realm of either women or the non-typical male, and that of a more uncommon leap to management jobs for the neoliberal 'right' women, competent but also genuine 'iron fists'. However, as a particular governmentality, neoliberalism compels women to dedicate themselves to their work irrespective of its nature, whether subordinate or managerial, whether traditionally female or male jobs. They are entrepreneurs of the self in trying to be acknowledged and appreciated for their work. The concept of 'entreployee' used by Pongratz and Voß (2003) is useful here to point to this self-entrepreneurial individual who actively self-motivates, self-controls, rationalizes and self-commercializes his/her working capacities to adapt to a post-Taylorist world. This move to 'entreployment' is likely to produce winners and losers depending on various types of resources (socio-demographic, personality traits) to cope with the increased demands of self-control, self-rationalization and self-commercialization. As true entrepreneurs of the self, women have to remould themselves to bear some 'manly' attributes, for entrepreneurship is a masculine construction, concerned with self-interested assertiveness and an expectation of higher visibility when it comes to management positions loaded with the leadership narrative, where managerial women develop managing styles similar to those of men (Wajcman, 1998).

I argue that patriarchal managers of Construct Energy prescribe women's behaviour so that they can be considered for managerial positions or so that they can be acknowledged as valuable employees. Female behaviour, in turn, suffers a self-regulation, a process of normalization to correspond with such expectations of men in power. The most penetrating discourses actually in place are those of neoliberal commitment to managerial efficiency, productivity and cost reduction, which are most commonly linked to masculine potentialities. Female employees displaying characteristics usually attributed to men easily distinguish themselves and can benefit from the 'fast track', being regarded as having greater potential for promotion. As previously stated, the researched firm allowed the observation that the important gender discriminatory practice of diminished seniority for women is actually not the case. Male owners encourage all the managers in the firm to be tough and expressly demand long hours and 'results' from their employees. Those more willing and, also, more able to impose very strict control and to strongly demand submission are women managers. Moreover, women with top and middle managerial jobs borrow a dominant manner of speaking and behaving, previously conceived as typically male, coupled with a tendency to accentuate feminine traits by way of dress code and an obvious concern with beauty, a transformation documented also for women working in other neoliberalizing contexts, such as the financial system (McDowell 1997) and the academic milieu (Allen, Massey, and Cochrane 1998, Massey 1995). One can witness 'sovereign power' in the way these women themselves normalize behaviour and act as they imagine a 'real manager' should, which is still as extremely masculine, 'lean, mean, aggressive, goal oriented, efficient, competitive, profit maximizing entities' (Alexiou 2010: 12). In what follows, I explore the way femininity is performed in Construct Energy and the manner in which neoliberal discourse has transformed organizational traditional gender divisions, in unexpected ways.

Site and Method

This chapter is based on an ethnographic exploration of the lived experiences of employees from a large Romanian company operating in the construction of infrastructure sites. I have used pseudonyms for the company (Construct Energy) and the employees involved. The company comprises two core departments involved in the main activity of the firm: a production department of more than 100 low-skilled and semi-skilled workers and a technical department containing mainly male engineers. In addition, there are a few exclusively female departments, consisting of accountants, auction consultants, public relations, secretaries, legal employees and human resources specialists.

Gendered division of labour is an important fault line in the everyday organizational practices of our site company. While one can easily notice the high percentage of women among the professionals, the disproportionate number of women in some of the professions is still visibly present, the sexual divisions of labour being 'interwoven with and mutually supportive of divisions of power and authority among women and men' (Messner 2002: 10). Therefore, as far as field work is concerned, there are only men in the 'production department', involving low skill and manual labour. Also, the engineering domain positions women in support and data centralizing; while accounting, human resources, public relations and contracting and acquisitions are female arenas. Amongst women, those occupying management positions, the glass-ceiling victors, rapidly conform to the 'tough' manager role. Therefore, organizations do not have to change to accommodate women in new leading roles and non-traditional jobs; instead, women adapt to fit into roles that have been designed for men (Puwar 2004). In Construct Energy women are successful managers, even presented as examples to male counterparts, who are sometimes less authoritative due to male bonding that entails more horizontal relations.

Ethnography allowed me to investigate how both common employees and managerial staff interpret their work environment; hence, as a researcher, I could grow an understanding of what is central, distinctive and enduring about the organization (Albert and Whetten 1985). The co-participant observation started at the beginning of 2007, as an employee in the HR department, and covered the period between January 2007 and January 2010; it presupposed working mostly with management for recruiting projects and yearly evaluations of work performance. I gathered field material and assembled a 'thick description' (Geertz 1973) to allow the first step in my interpretation of the corporate culture. After leaving the company at the beginning of 2010, I undertook 20 interviews with former colleagues; I used a semi-structured interview format asking about changes in hierarchical structures, tasks performed and time requirements, interactions with colleagues and superiors. The interviews allowed a reformulation of some of the gendered issues previously observed and a possibility of asking about any new developments occurring in the firm. The undertaken case study derives from my perspective as an insider in a growing company, offering services to important multinationals, a company with a strong commitment to work and the neoliberal ideals of human development and self-determination, valuing loyalty and dedication in both male and female employees, often described in connection to time availability. The most valued traits of an employee in this neoliberal environment proved to be extra-hours availability, authoritativeness, determination and, also, skills of sociability. I was especially interested in the logic of power relations and the ways these relations created and recreated a gendered space.

Transforming Femininity to Suit Established Gender Prescriptions

Managers and employees alike see femininity and masculinity as natural states, associated with women and men, respectively. Behaviour is permanently influenced by perceptions of feminine or masculine features; men usually act in a gentlemanly fashion towards women, while both parties share an appreciation of the fact that their 'innate' differences are acknowledged and respected. Women are seen as more 'family-oriented', more emotional, less 'profession-oriented' or less active and competitive (the CEO in particular and many male and female colleagues agreed on that). Accordingly, in Construct Energy, the most visible discrimination places women in positions requiring patience and conscientiousness, in a similar vein to the operation of Fordist capitalism (Kalb 1997, 2005). This choice is driven by perceptions that women are less agentic than men and therefore not suited for prestigious, male-dominated occupations (Rudman and Phelan 2008). Consequently, women engineers fill support positions, centralize field data and ensure communication between field engineers and managers, between client staff and the company's own technical staff. The literature on this topic also offers an insight into the required behaviour of women in semi-technical jobs who would have to 'actively disconfirm the female gender stereotype by acting more like men'(Wiley 1985). Nevertheless, women working in engineering jobs are disadvantaged because of negative stereotyping and, in this respect, little has changed from the beginning of the Fordist era (Kalb 2005).

These positions are considered suitable for a woman both by their male counterparts and the women themselves. And that happens even if these jobs imply lower salaries and more routine, exhausting work in front of the computer. Male engineers enjoy a certain freedom because being away from company headquarters allows small breaks from work. This is not a woman engineer's prerogative, though, as they are glued to their desks, answering to different simultaneous requests from either colleagues or client companies. A frequent complaint made by all women employees points to the absurd number of tasks that makes them 'postpone even going to the bathroom'. Nevertheless, most of the time, they are strictly controlling themselves, being careful not to convey negative impressions and attract unwanted attention from supervisors and managers. Their submissive behaviour benefits a strong corporal discipline, which keeps women employees working at their desks for hours on end, without breaks.

The past's feminized qualities, such as 'nimble fingers', positioned women in poorly paid manufacturing jobs that required a great deal of attention and routine work, where assertive and energetic manliness was not employed (Calàs and Smircich 1993, Kelan 2008). Today one can observe that the labour market still uses feminized skills, based on traditional patriarchal stereotypes of women, and which places women in jobs that bear the same mark of diminished status. Accounting represents a predominantly feminized form of work because it uses female patience and perseverance. Because of its immobility and repetitive work, male employees in Construct Energy have often expressed a proud 'incapacity' to perform this job: 'I couldn't possibly do this, I don't know how you do it', 'I'd go mad, really', 'I did something similar for one day, but I really don't want any … I can't sit in front of the computer all day like you girls do' (M, 28, engineer and M, 33, engineer).

According to traditional stereotypes women are not only better at dexterous and enduring routine, they are also better at communicating and the natural embodiment of beauty and cleanliness. Therefore, another important feminine job is that of Public Relations (PR) manager, with subordinate female secretaries, assistant managers, and receptionists. The PR middle manager, a former assistant for the CEO, manages a relatively large department, which also includes the cleaning personnel. Because the image of a company has to do with cleanliness also, the CEO decided that 'the person responsible for the image of the firm should also control the cleaners'. The whole department was formed as an interactional, communicative department, ensuring administrative support for the rest of the firm. Managers and employees alike – many women too – agree that certain jobs are 'made' for women because of their 'natural' qualities, but these jobs are usually not so well situated on the status ladder and enjoy smaller incomes.

The normalcy of the well-established gender prescriptions indicates everybody's place in the division of labour. Nevertheless, the new neoliberal discourse, following the specific logic of incorporating the previous critiques only halfway, performed some interesting adjustments to the traditional gender narratives. Fordist capitalism was attacked for its patriarchal parlance and also for practices that reinforced/recreated the traditional gender divisions in the labour market. In opposition, the new neoliberal discourse portrayed women as the new ideal workers of the future flexible economy, possessing the 'right skills'. This narrative assumes that organizations would seek a multitask worker, valuing instinct and intuition as much as rationality and analytic capacity, someone 'who can be tough but also tender, focused but friendly, and people who can cope with these necessary contradictions' (Handy 1994: 179). Many of the new skills, supposedly sought after by the new flat and flexible organization, are strongly feminine-gendered, which is problematic in itself, as it still constrains women employees in adequate niches while closing other opportunities for them. But more importantly, this conceptualization proves ineffective in practice following the unexpected modalities of male responses to the newly desirable qualities. Men themselves appropriate the new working positions by either mimicking female traits or underscoring their utility. Some of the male managers pride themselves on being empathetic, having good listening skills or being good communicators. Their masculine qualities being firmly established and undisputed, they found that they could only gain from parading their 'soft' side: 'I feel when something is wrong, if one of them has a problem … we discuss, they can always come to me and speak openly. I am quite good with these communication issues. A good manager can also talk to his people, right?!' (M, 33, technical department manager). Conforming to the new soft skill requirements is not a very common phenomenon among male managers, but it helps some provide an image of a 'people's man' or being 'good with people'. These are, perversely, 'valued' commodities in the firm – and declared as such, as they are seen as equivalents of being a 'people manipulator', or 'convincing employees of anything'(F, 32, legal department middle manager); in short, the firm can use their talents for soft coercion.

Nonetheless, women employees, either in administrative positions or management ones, do respond to the neoliberal imperatives of the firm while reinterpreting their gender roles within the confines of the new power discourse; but these roles still suit the traditional prescribed hierarchies. They are all entrepreneurs of themselves; the recruiting process is envisioned to hire mostly people 'who know what they want', who are ambitious, driven and assertive. Therefore, these are more likely to fit the role of self-reliable, self-taught employee. We witness women becoming the veritable embodiment of the successful entrepreneur in permanent search of bettering oneself, a person used to corporal and mental discipline and having a durable relationship with conformity. Within the firm, the neoliberal qualities demanded of a motivated self-made woman are taught and thence enhanced. As assistant manager, a young woman works as part-time secretary for four of the six top management directors, part informational base for the colleagues, and part PR assistant for the PR manager. She is disciplined and handles a lot of tasks with very different expectations: 'I am working myself into the ground ... today is a horrible day. I am everybody's subordinate'. But she receives compassion as a powerful self-made woman: 'Ehh, I can do this, I am strong. If only they weren't so stressed out ... Oh, well ... ' (F, 27, directors' assistant). The other two directors have their own assistants, but this is only a pompous way of naming a secretary who can also be assigned many other routine, administrative tasks. Even if the work they are supposed to do is usually undemanding, with many tasks assigned on the spur of the moment at a passing idea of the manager, still, when recruiting for an assistant manager, the expectations of the managers have always been extremely high. Sometimes they express disappointment for what the labour market offers, being intent on finding 'someone really good, a smart girl who can help me with everything' (M, 35, development director). Their idea of an assistant always and naturally portrays a woman, typically beautiful or at least pleasant looking, somebody with good communicational skills, always accommodating and polite, a nice presence to have around. They usually laugh with the recruiting specialist when discussing job requirements, hidden connotations implied, alluding to the fact that the assistant should be 'at least pretty'. Also, good assistants are required to possess other traits which somehow go beyond those merely ascribed to feminine women in general. Those highly valued are ambitious, determined, very organized and self-motivated, impressive problem solving abilities, efficient work and the right values of expediency and pragmatism. Beauty alone in a woman employee is not something to be desired because there is an overarching belief that women can combine physical attractiveness with the right desirable personality traits, so that they can be valuable in more than just one way. Even at reception, where two young girls greet clients and guests, the PR manager has chosen girls who are beautiful but also assertive. In addition to beauty, a job prerequisite, management expects a receptionist or a secretary to appear to 'know what she wants', which complements an attractive girl and makes her interesting, seemingly smart: 'We want someone who can deal with anything unexpected. Someone who is quick to act in any circumstance' (F, 29, PR manager).

At the other end of the corporate ladder, the ideal woman to be hired in the most important positions in the firm would combine beauty with intelligence and volition with the capacity to enforce submission. These neoliberal managerial women are actually expected to display characteristics habitually attributed to men, which is a change from the usual expectations from women limited to looks and sociability skills, used mainly to attract and entertain clients. As far as top management views on women employees are concerned, there are two types of women who are most likely to follow two different paths in career related choices, corresponding to two different types of work stimuli: reward systems and job responsibility. 'I think that some women are more suited – and they like more – a life dedicated to family, more old-fashioned' (M, 40, CEO). This first category generally portrays the feminine woman, infused with motherly emotions, who is – to a great extent – much more family conscious. On the other hand, the image of another kind of woman creates different behavioural expectations from all the other women in general. The second type has what are traditionally known as more masculine characteristics, being determined, capable of leading others with an 'iron fist' approach, professionally driven to a high degree, motivated for long hours at work, pragmatically setting family aside to pursue career ambitions. In this firm women employees are expected to be or to become this workaholic, imposing model set by the owners' vision and confirmed by a few of those named in power positions. The majority not fitting this pattern are confined to subaltern positions, regardless of professional knowledge and abilities.

The women chosen for managerial roles have accepted the role of demanding supervisor that has been bestowed on them, even if they acted differently before belonging to management. All of the women managers are in their late twenties and early thirties, being promoted after a few years of 'proving themselves' (Romanian language: *'s-au dovedit'*), which is a generic term for working longer hours than the rest of the firm and appearing interested in providing new ideas for organizing or bettering work activities. A continuous 'involvement' and 'dedication' brought these women the favour of a position that requires sacrifices in order to preserve their post. Those most committed to the neoliberal model of a selfmade person do not perceive their jobs as a sacrifice, though. They have internalized the necessity of being a model to the other employees under their supervision and strongly believe in the neoliberal work ideal they profess: 'I believe that when at work we should do our best and only think about work. Other things are irrelevant because we have a responsibility here, alright?' (F, 29, financial director).

This is a relatively common, typical utterance of a female manager. Women are more advantaged by the requirement to become an authoritarian female, displaying traditionally gendered male traits, than by a similar possible requirement to become a producer or practitioner in hard science domains, for example. Allen et al. (1998) note that women working in financial corporations benefit 'the more aggressive, laddish culture of the City … easier to subvert than that of the abstract, more instrumental masculine culture of high-tech spaces' (1998: 99). In Construct Energy it also seems that women appear to be able to define a new managerial identity for themselves within the parameters of a dominant form of masculinity or by subverting the masculine codes to their own advantage. Women managers often reprimand employees, either male or female, using harsh criticism and veiled threats of dismissal. There are frequent dismissive phrases such as 'I don't want to hear it', 'I want it done right away', 'This is the last time I'm telling you this' and 'I want it on my desk now' (used by all middle and senior women managers and heard at least once from each of them). The most important woman director in the company, the technical development director, uses very rigid conversational phrases, sentences reduced to a few words ('Why?', 'When?', 'How long does it take?' mark her strive for efficiency and managerial distance); she also controls the interaction with her inflexible tone and fixed stare. Therefore, this stark dominant style of leading makes them even more feared than their male counterparts.

As the neoliberal project brought enterprising masculinity to the fore, women have learnt of the valorized assertive masculine qualities and made claims to the same legitimacy of ascending to male positions by reinterpreting, subverting or simply replicating the desirable. Managerial owners have grasped the potential of this newly developing female 'resource' and smooth their path by accepting even stronger definitions of managerial power, as it also reflects their preferred 'iron fist' choices. Therefore, the masculine culture needing subversion is in this case subverted and transformed at the same time. The position of women managers is tough and demanding, not at all in accordance with the typical female projection of shyness and cautiousness. And that is because they have been promoted on the basis of being the exact opposites of the flat and flexible organization's ideal worker traits.

Strong Women, Even Stronger Managers

The company's top management includes two women and five men. The financial director comes from a traditionally female domain; the firm never had a male employee in accounting, which made the promotion of a woman to a top position unavoidable. The other female director graduated from the Technical Institute and occupied at first a secretarial position, when the firm was in its first years. After that she moved to an engineering job and then acceded to middle and top management, respectively. Also, the firm has many women middle managers, clearly favouring their perceived qualities. Even at a time when the traditional masculinities of managerial work are subject to a lot of debate and criticism in society, many of them are reintroduced in a different guise. 'An individual constantly involved in demanding project work will be just as separated from her/his family life and emotions as managers and entrepreneurs have always been', Lindgren and Packendorff (2006: 11) remarked, identifying project work as the new disguise maintaining previous masculine managerial habits. Through female employees these masculine practices and traits find new ground. Project work functions like a veil of short term efficiency which helps perpetuate criticized models of masculine authority; female empowerment functions to revive such masculine models for women's professional advancement. Previous masculine traits of important dominant positions become the prerogative of successful women trying to adapt to this masculinity-imbued world.

Nevertheless, women managers are confident that feminine characteristics can only add value in what is a habitually male business environment. They perversely retain the most basic feminine traits linked to clothing and use of makeup, but they knowingly utilize the means that have been so highly pervasive and efficacious in men's managerial work. Women managers in the company take pleasure in their new roles of managing others, being the success stories of a booming capitalist enterprise, highly praised by the owners. Managing others is mainly seen as a control activity, a disciplining of troops. The appropriate and expected behaviour for women in positions of power proves to be the one most effective in past experience, that which attains submission and enforces fearful discipline, and is also associated with centralizing, decision-making powers. Highly appreciated for their tough attitude, women managers strive to become better managerial performers and in doing so they imitate and perfect the masculine overbearing attitude. Their actions as managers of women, unlike those of men, are not hampered by the socialization constraints operating in men. The barriers implied in the male supervisor – female subordinate relationship, imposed by socializing boys to be gentlemanly to 'fragile' girls, have completely disappeared when women are given authority over other women. Consequently, there is a benefit for the firm, which is strongly intent on keeping every employee in line, ensuring discipline, long hours, permanent and fast flow of completed tasks.

Yelling at employees, slamming the door, storming into subordinates' offices and exploding with anger are common behaviours of women managers in the firm. The following excerpt demonstrates how the angry behaviour of a female manager can cause frustration but also disciplines and brings conformity. The tone of voice of the manager is extremely rough and annoyed; she is convinced she is right and the girls in accounting try fruitlessly to argue their point of view and show the impossibility of the director's demands:

> 'I told you to finish that and I expected you to have finished it; … we are not discussing this! So what if there were other tasks?! Don't tell me about it! You learn to prioritize and you can finish everything in time! … Girls, you leave when you finish, understood?! You could have done it already!'
> 'But Rada, please understand us. It was impossible to finish, you sent us that verification for the X account at 10 and that took like 2 hours. We can't finish everything when we have new things all the time!'
>
> 'It's your own fault you don't know how to prioritize and organize! I do not care how you do it! I want results and to see you want to get involved, not just wait for 5.30 to go home! This shows your involvement!'

'Rada, you know I stayed until 6.30 yesterday and 7 the day before! And we usually stay more ... ' (in a crying, upset voice)

'I wasn't talking about you, not everybody is putting in the same effort!' (F, 29, financial director, daily reprimanding routine in accounting department)

Occasions for such outbursts are even eagerly sought and to this type of manager, these opportunities present themselves even when employees have tried their best to please her. Furthermore, each minor detail of work can become an opportunity to prove to the CEO or to his most loyal people in the firm that subordinates are vigorously reprimanded and they, as managers, are treating each minor transgression by resorting to strong-arm methods, without flinching in the face of signs of insubordination or lack of efficiency. Complying with these kinds of owners' expectations towards managers, the women in power became even tougher than men. The most feared of them exemplify the transformation occurring in the company's gendered power. The technical development director, the financial director, the legal department middle manager and the auction department middle manager are such examples of the use gendered traits to contradict gender stereotypes and succeed in a capitalist, male regulated business environment. Specific masculine characteristics displayed in capitalist working milieus, such as ambition, self-confidence and a domineering style, have been borrowed by women so that they might be considered for power positions. The specific type of ruthlessness women employ is valued within the firm and called either decisiveness or leadership; it comes to demonstrate that the power acquired was also deserved. The behaviour that would be unacceptable from a male manager becomes accepted when it comes to women mistreating other women. One of the female technical directors treats all employees in the same manner, objectifying employees. She considers that business can profit most from permanently changing employees, as soon as they are tired or too relaxed: 'This crisis is good. We can bring new, cheaper people in the firm. We now get rid of those too cozy ... who are slacking. It's an opportunity to change those less dedicated with new blood' (F, 32, technical development director).

The tone of discussions between managerial women and subordinates are more distant than the relations fostered in men's departments where managers are men and employees both male and female. The manager of the legal department used to indicate her esteem for two of the male managers who have very good relations with their subordinates, being even quite close and friendly towards employees; this fact meant for her that people trusted them and could easily be influenced by them, which finally benefited the business. Even though she actually admires this style of working she cannot pride herself with the same trust from employees in the firm. Neither can the other important female occupied positions. Many of them are either despised or feared, which implies people are careful not to express any personal vexation towards the firm in their midst.

Disproportionate work requirements are pervasive all over the firm, in male as well as female-run departments. Nevertheless, male managers' reactions to the diminished completion of work or the partial finalization of a multitude of tasks are usually more contextual and aware of the circumstances and pressures existent in work. One of the technical middle managers told me that he verifies engineers' routes and he knows how long they could take to reach a specific field work site. He acknowledged the disproportion between what higher management expected of them and what was actually possible. 'I was that field engineer myself', he argues, 'I know how many hours they are on the road. I cannot be absurd' (M, 30, communications middle manager). These male middle managers are portrayed by their employees as more humane because they seem to listen to them, even if they cannot change the situational labour relations or the absurd time requirements. Women, though, tend to be very tense about their participation in management and attentive to the role they are playing as a body of management, which is thought of as completely separate and above the body of employees. The CEO himself is careful to remind each manager whose side they should be on: 'You are one of management, not a mediator, not at all a worker'. Therefore, all managers try to conform to these expectations and put a lot of pressure on workers to perform at maximum capacity for the longest time possible. Nevertheless, men usually try to have manly conversations with the discontent employees and explain that there are no other alternatives due to a number of factors – the market, the competition, high expenses with the work force, and so on. Women, on the other hand, are leaders who prefer coercion, threats and admonitions. This extreme behaviour, which proves completely opposed to the professed neoliberal model of a managerial integrator and inspiring motivator, is influenced also by the age distribution of managers.

All women managers in the firm are very young, in their twenties and early thirties; even if good professionals in their line of work, they have not been in a position of power before and are trying very hard to integrate the strong neoliberal messages received from the owner and CEO of the firm with the actual daily conflicting situations they encounter. They were promoted after only a few years in the company, which made them quite proud of their early success, which is attributed to merit, when they mention 'hard work', 'dedication' and 'being appreciated'. When facing opposition they aggressively rush into a quarrelsome inflexible retaliation so as not to betray the trust bestowed on them. I have reproduced below an extract which captures a violent argument between the financial female director and the HR specialist, which ended with the director slamming the door, furious at having been defied:

> 'I demanded something; you must have done it by now! I am the one in charge, after all!'

> 'Yes, and that is your final argument! You cannot bring real arguments; only that you are the boss! No matter how absurd your demands are we must comply because you said so!?'

'You cannot tell me I'm absurd! We'll settle this with the CEO!'

'Yes, please do, we should go to the CEO and tell him about it! Let's go now!'

This type of response to an abusive female manager is so rare that other individuals enjoy it as a personal victory. Nevertheless, subordinate frustrations do not form a common ground for a collective reaction because everybody grasps that these dictatorial managers also have powerful backup, as the CEO has promoted this particular kind of woman understanding the force they embody, as he openly admitted: 'We need to let people know we can discipline well. She is good at that too' (CEO about the young female financial director, who was also considered very capable as an economist). As tools of both disciplining and overworking employees, they are presented as models of efficient managers to the other managers in the firm. More determined to succeed than most of their male counterparts, women appear to be a managerial reserve army for the employer. Motivated for long hours, loyal and dutiful, women strive to prove their worth, to be recognized as self-made, independent and strong-willed. They make great examples of the neoliberal entrepreneur of the self. The employer can use them as an example to the male managers who are not sufficiently tough and demanding. The firm does not particularly promote the proliferated neoliberal ideals of managers being coaches with good communication and listening skills; therefore, this new typology of woman matches its needs more conveniently than male managers chosen from the ranks of engineers, who may be too much 'one of the guys'. Male bonding is not necessarily desirable, especially in the case of managers, because it is seen as possibly fostering perilous transgressions from the discipline of work.

In addition, women are more careful when perceiving a possible threat to their position or the CEO's image of them. Violent reactions are commonplace, with no refrain from fury: 'Never ever go over my head again [to the CEO], do you hear?! When you have a problem with one of my subordinates you come directly to me, you understand!' (F, 32, technical development director). This observation is not new because in other studies female protagonists in firms are frequently described as 'mavericks, even more ruthless and determined than their male counterparts' (Bruni, Gherardi, and Poggio 2005: 13). But generally these descriptions better suit women from families of entrepreneurs, those designated heirs, flanked by a male spouse or relative (Bruni et al. 2005). In our case, only one middle manager woman has relatives in the ownership of the firm. Her position in middle management is clearly different due to her family relations. Informally, she is part of top management and her opinions have considerable weight; she always profits from the power afforded by high ranking relatives. Some of the other women who were promoted to management were some of her favourite employees. She hired some of these women to fit her own model of the perfect manager; she often expresses satisfaction vis-à-vis her choices, pointing to her fine 'nose' for spotting the 'right' people. The women recruited by her became top and middle managers, therefore confirming her initial intuitions about their tenacity and dedication to work: 'Yes,

I chose them well, as one can see, even before we had a HR department!' (F, 32, legal department middle manager). Therefore, those hired by her, namely the financial director, the auctioning middle manager, the human resources middle manager, were all following the same pattern: determined, workaholic, ambitious and giving off a feeling of efficiency and urgency.

The Female Body as a Corporate Issue

Even if women employees spend a lot of time at work, top management nonetheless considers them a potential liability because of family demands. As the company employs mostly young people, it is a rather common phenomenon to have women either pregnant or on maternity leave in almost every department. Generally, the median female age in the firm is under 30 and an insignificant number amongst them have children. Many women, though, see maternity leave as a break from the company's stressful environment. As the world financial crisis hit the firm in 2009, women already on maternity leave had a second pregnancy allowing them to prolong staying at home for another two years; three departmental middle managers at the end of their maternity leaves announced in the first half of 2010 that they were pregnant again, two of which were from the accounting department and one from acquisitions. The latter was actually expected to return to work and surprised everyone with what was perceived as a 'lack of loyalty to the firm'. Male engineers enjoyed making a sarcastic joke of this situation: 'When they [top management] awaited her with open arms ... imagine she outmanoeuvred them! It's just unbelievable!' (M, 30, engineer). Second pregnancies while on maternity leave are considered schemes and tactics and are attributed to malevolence towards the firm. While colleagues congratulate the respective women for 'knowing what's important for them', 'for getting on with their lives unperturbed', top management meditates on these women's lack of predictability and the fact that they 'cannot be counted on' (Romanian: *'nu te poţi baza pe ele'*). The PR middle manager, amusingly translated the management's change of heart towards young mothers in the company having a second child after being absent for two years: 'This only proves she does not love us anymore!' (F, 29). Her mocking concern points to very real problems that take shape around women employees' life choices. A period of absence of one or two years can run the risk of losing one's position, despite labour laws stipulating obligatory re-admission of a woman returning from maternity leave to precisely the same job.

Nevertheless, such a binding legal requirement does not translate into practice because that particular period is not perceived as a natural absence, but as an exercise of freedom impossible for the firm to regulate. Moreover, maternity leave is perversely used by the company as means of comparing women and their loyalty towards the firm according to how late in the pregnancy they still come into the office, how rapidly they return to work after having a child, how much extra time they spend at work despite having an infant at home.

The company, through its top management, has also made clear a view of those who resign and move to other workplaces: that they could not 'adapt' or keep up the pace, or were traitors, so were 'not so valuable' after all – nothing to be missed. However, women leaving the firm only temporarily, for two years, are still seen as employees and trigger mixed feelings. On the one hand, being backed up by the Labour Code law, they 'force' the employer to take them back; on the other hand, they are valuable workers who obeyed the imposed rules, which increased their salaries and position, which in turn afforded them the possibility of considering children. Somehow resented for being able to leave at their will, somehow adding value by their return, these women have to struggle again to regain lost trust and reconfirm their position. This usually implies either sacrificing time by staying late or seeming very dedicated, which means disciplining others, suggesting new ideas, and striving to develop better management plans. It takes some degree of effort on their part to re-establish themselves in the managerial positions that they left. The economic director came back after only a year and a half and somebody else occupied her position. The replacement, some years younger than her, admitted that the most natural thing would have been for the economic director on maternity leave to immediately reassume the position, but 'the owners were not sure they wanted her at the time of her return'. Only a few months later – the time it took the director on leave to convince the owners of her professional and personal qualities – she was reinstated. The economic director's replacement remembers the way she was downgraded, after the previous director fought to regain her place:

> 'She did everything possible to get her old job back ... she told the CEO things to make it seem that I made mistakes with the banks. She really wanted that job. I really didn't care about it. But I returned from my holiday and they made the switch, without even telling me. That was really hurtful. Not even when I came back from the holiday did they tell me anything! ... It was only 2 weeks later that he [CEO] called for me and told me!' (F, 30, economic director's replacer)

The above extract shows the former director determined to prove herself worthy of her position, lost during her one and a half year period of maternity leave. The future possibility of children and a subsequent reconsideration of spare time for women in general, negatively affect management's plans towards them. Seen as probable betrayers who might favour family time or leisure activities, such as 'reading books' or 'grooming' and 'attending fitness classes' (as the CEO once remarked), women are treated as problematic individuals and they have to work more so as not to be discriminated against and gain promotion. Unlike men, they bring into the working relationship much more than is actually required from a managerial perspective: a potential for demanding flexible time or days off (caused by babies, sick relatives, their own illnesses which they tend to care for more than men), a potential for imbuing the workplace with emotional reactions, which men tend to camouflage better due to their putative masculine 'natural' coolness and detachment.

Nonetheless, the company has learnt that women's femininity and bodies are not liabilities in all cases, but in fact, they can be valuable assets, and it would be a smart choice to exploit beauty combined with intelligence and/or 'friendliness', especially when dealing with important multinational representatives. When dinner parties or inaugurations take place, top management invites to these events the women in the firm who best correspond to the above description. By so doing, the business can vary and increase the utility of its members of the female staff. Some women participate knowingly in these strategic games and commit to the expected image by dressing in revealing clothes and trying to be funny and witty to better entertain important clients. Some women employees are not suited for this role, while others participate less willingly, making a presence so as not to be considered insubordinate or lacking the capacity to have fun. Many of them, nevertheless, are skilled dancers and party lovers and fit perfectly into that environment. Moreover, the entire performance put on by the management is understood as a business move. Those women in important managerial positions fully understand the ascribed qualities of successful business women. They usually dress businesslike, while still feminine, and at corporate parties somehow more enticingly. Role playing is taken extremely seriously as they conform to a model of successful femininity that speculates on bodily attractiveness and keeping fit. Also, they are careful to maintain a clear distinction between their dress code and the male dress code, dressing in the customary medium length dress with matching high heels. More than once I found myself having gripping conversations about shoes or accessories stores with the financial and economic directors and the other women middle managers. This perpetuation of female dressing and interest in appearance, despite the formal business milieu which normally transforms clothes into a more masculine style, points to a certain consciousness about what constitutes a woman, transcending work type or attributed responsibilities. Men, as well as women, have clear gender distinctions that pressure for conformity. And a woman in both representations should remain feminine in spite of her success, workload, or managerial responsibilities. Still, femininity, while appreciated, does not ensure success and nomination to managerial roles. To conclude, valuable female employees, while feminine, are expected to display – and some successfully portray – characteristics perceived as typical of a manager; characteristics that actually help them to become one.

Conclusion

To sum up, I have discussed women's roles and role playing in the company to reach an understanding of their neoliberal utility and commodification. Women employees are expected to be veritable entrepreneurs of the selves regardless of their position and authority in the firm; whether they have 'traditionally' female occupations, or have surpassed the glass ceiling by climbing to managerial status, they should enhance skills and commit to continually improving their selves. Feminine traits and 'qualities' are welcomed in an adaptive post-Fordist company and exploited in a neoliberal fashion to suit business needs. The ostensibly egalitarian neoliberal discourse of self-improvement is internalized by female employees to the extent that they lose the ability to openly express dissatisfaction or participate in the few forms of resistance open to employees. Moreover, the case offers a novel interpretation of 'femininity' in managerial positions as not only conforming to previously-conceived 'masculine' authoritative methods, but also ruthlessly enhancing control and domination. Proving highly adaptive to perform jobs previously designed for men, successful women make excellent examples of neoliberal self-regulation, by tenaciously employing some of the feminine codes in combination with the perceived 'managerial' traits usually associated with men. In addition, the neoliberalization of women proves beneficial for corporate goals; the company constructing new standards of prowess with the aid of this novel, disciplined, female commodity.

References

Alexiou, A. 2010. A tale of the field: reading power and gender in the learning organization. *Studies in Continuing Education*, 27(1): 17–31.

Allen, J., Massey, D., and Cochrane, A. 1998. *Rethinking the Region*. London: Routledge.

Arulampalam, W., Booth, A.L., and Bryan, M.L. 2007. Is there a glass ceiling over Europe? Exploring the gender pay gap across the wages distribution. *Industrial and Labor Relations Review*, 60(2): 163–86.

Boltanski, L., and Chiapello, E. 2005. *The New Spirit of Capitalism*. London: Verso.

Boyce, L.A.H., and Herd, A.M. 2003. The Relationship Between Gender Role Stereotypes and Requisite Military Leadership Characteristics. *Sex Roles*, 49(7–8): 365–78.

Bruni, A., Gherardi, S., and Poggio, B. 2005. *Gender and Entrepreneurship. An Ethnographic Approach*. Abingdon and New York: Routledge.

Calàs, M., and Smircich, L. 1993. Dangerous Liaisons: The "Feminine-in-Management" Meets Globalization'. *Business Horizons*, 36(2): 73–83.

Geertz, C. 1973.*The Interpretation of Cultures. Selected Essays*. New York: Basic Books.

Handy, C. 1994. *The Empty Raincoat: Making Sense of the Future*. London: Hutchinson and Arrow.

Kalb, D. 1997. *Expanding Class: Power and Everyday Politics in Industrial Communities*. Durham, NC and London: Duke University Press.

Kalb, D. 2005. "Bare Legs Like Ice": Recasting Class for Local/Global Inquiry, in *Critical Junctions: Anthropology and History beyond the Cultural Turn,* edited by D. Kalb and H. Tak. London and New York: Berghahn Books, pp. 109–36.

Kelan, E.K. 2008. The Discursive Construction of Gender in Contemporary Management Literature. *Journal of Business Ethics*, 81(2): 427–45.

Lindgren, M., and Packendorff, J. 2006. What's New in New Forms of Organizing? On the Construction of Gender in Project-Based Work. *Journal of Management Studies*, 43(4), 841–66.

Massey, D. 1995. Masculinity, dualisms and high technology. *Transactions of the Institute of British Geographers*, NS(20), 487–99.

McDowell, J.M., Singell, L.D., and Ziliak, J.P. 1999. Cracks in the glass ceiling: Gender and promotion in the economics profession. *The American Economic Review*, 89(2), 392–96.

McDowell, L. 1997. *Capital Culture: Gender at Work in the City*. Malden: Wiley-Blackwell Publishers.

Messner, M.A. 2002. *Taking the Field: Women, Men and Sports*. Minneapolis: University of Minnesota Press.

Mojab, S., and Gorman, R. 2003. Women and consciousness in the 'learning organisation': emancipation or exploitation? *Adult Education Quarterly*, 53(4), 228–41.

Morgan, L.A. 1998. Glass-ceiling effect or cohort effect? A longitudinal study of the gender earnings gap for engineers, 1982 to 1989. *American Sociological Review*, 63(4), 479–93.

Pongratz, H.J., and Voß, G.G. 2003. From employee to 'entreployee': towards a 'self-entrepreneurial' workforce? *Concepts and Transformations*, 8: 239–54.

Puwar, N. 2004. *Space Invaders: Race, Gender and Bodies Out of Place*. Oxford: Berg.

Rudman, L.A., and Phelan, J.E. 2008. Backlash Effects for Disconfirming Gender Stereotypes in Organizations. *Research in Organizational Behavior*, 28, 61–79.

Stobbe, L. 2005. Doing Machismo: Legitimating Speech Acts as a Selection Discourse. *Gender, Work & Organization*, 12(2): 105–23.

Wajcman, J. 1998. *Managing Like a Man: Women and Men in Corporate Management*. Cambridge, UK: Polity Press in association with Blackwell Publishers Ltd.

Wiley, M.G.E., and Eskilson, A. 1985. Speech Styles, Gender Stereotypes, and Corporate Success: What if Women Talk More Like Men? *Sex Roles*, 12(9–10): 993–1007.

Williams, C. 1993. *Doing Women's Work: Men in Non-Traditional Occupations*. London: Sage.

Chapter 4

The Authorial Self and Acquiring the
Language of Neoliberalism in Slovakia

Jonathan L. Larson

Introduction

> According to experts many Slovaks lack the ability to express their thoughts
> clearly, or to argue. Slovak language and literature instructors complain that
> even students preparing for college do not master the basics of stylistic genres.
> Often they do not differentiate between the essay, analysis and narrative, and
> they even fail to write their own résumé correctly (Gáliková 2002).

In September 2002 the Vice Chair of the Slovak Government and Minister of
Finance Ivan Mikloš announced the third year of a student essay contest. The topic
was 'The World after September 11th 2001 – Is membership of NATO and the EU
still a guarantee of stability, safety and prosperity for you?' The newspaper article
that announced the competition paraphrased the need for it in the terms cited above:
national communicative deficiencies with implications for Slovaks' abilities to think
and debate with one another. While this article did not illustrate how the winners
for the secondary school and university categories demonstrated clear thought
and argument, it did make a point of describing what the winners had gained. The
contestants had 'plug[ged] themselves into public life'. The college winner spoke
of the pleasure of a three week trip to the UK, as well as the personal satisfaction
that apparently he had something to offer the field of defence and security. The
secondary school winner beamed over having achieved this 'small' success with her
own strength and purposefulness. Minister Mikloš himself weighed in. He claimed
to have accepted a request for a letter of reference for college from a previous winner.
The dean of the winner's eventual university in the Czech Republic wrote later to
confirm that the student was indeed one of the best in his class.

It might strike some readers as odd that a minister of finance would preside
over a contest in writing essays. After all, Slovakia, like most European states
for decades, has had a state minister responsible for education. However, this
competition's quirk reflected something about the timing and manner in which the
writing of essays was being promoted. Touted as an opportunity to 'plug themselves
into public life', or perhaps demonstrate their analytical skills, the winners had
earned the opportunity to travel to a 'Western' country (Britain) and practise
English, demonstrate their talents to future employers, prove to themselves their

'strength' and 'purposefulness', and secure the patronage of a young neoliberal economist renowned for his commitment to dismantling the socialist state. In sum, we could say that – over and above writing essays – the contestants (or at least the winners) in this competition had learned something about how to author the first chapter in the novel of a successful post-socialist life. For any minister of finance in the region seeking to cultivate enterprising individuals and reorient subjects toward the capitalist West, encouraging students to write a simple essay might indeed prove a solid investment.

This chapter explores notions of 'enterprise' in post-socialist Slovakia through one of its key emergent features: notions of the authorial self. The neoliberal philosophy of reformers such as Mikloš has sought to transition allegedly 'passive individuals coddled by the paternalism of socialism, and characterized by pessimism, dissimulation, an attraction to populist demagogy and a lack of civic virtues' (as the introduction to this volume paraphrased) to a 'new ethic of the active, choosing, responsible, autonomous individual obliged to be free, and to live life as if it were an outcome of free choice' (Miller and Rose 2008: 18). To the extent that notions of enterprise and entrepreneurship undergirding this project globally have taken on broader meanings of 'initiative, action and agency', they suggest that subjects should consider themselves more self-consciously the authors of their own lives. In this chapter, we will see how this idea of an authorial self articulates with other notions of authorship embedded in a practice that has received little attention by scholars of neoliberalism: secondary and tertiary instruction in writing academic essays. Drawing on one year of fieldwork in secondary lessons of Slovak language and literature – as well as in college lessons of English – I describe ways that students were introduced to ideas of crafting 'original' topics and assuming a voice of relative expertise in their acquisition of this genre. According to how Slovak students were learning it, the essay served as a particular technology of the self-governed by particular graphic ideologies (Hull 2003; Larson 2008, Schieffelin et al. 1998): a means by which students articulated and inscribed subjectivities within larger neoliberal projects.

This chapter traces three particular features of Slovak students' encounters with the notion of an authorial self through writing academic essays in English. First, in learning how to form and perform an authorial self, students showed substantial confusion over their rights to claim authorship. Students' confusion over the authorial self that they were expected to project in their essays had less to do with their 'socialist' conditioning and more to do with their puzzlement over the historically deep ideologies of language that one must acquire with this genre in English. Second, we discover more about why the genre of essays might matter to the neoliberal ministers and the reporters who cover them: the kind of covert semiotic inversion of foregrounding and back grounding traces of the self that typifies a Western C.V. (Larson 2008) is also a deeply rooted element of composing an Anglo-American style of academic essay. To the extent that this is the case, these technologies are less about broadcasting arguments as one's own than they are about the discursive management of the voice of a single author appearing in print to an audience in relation to the voices of others. Third, this expository quality of authorial personhood is an imperfect boon for a desired reawakening of the self-confident, engaged and enterprising spirit of capitalism in a post-socialist society. It may indeed embolden persons to broadcast their ideas to wider publics, but whether it truly engenders productive deliberative democracy is another matter. The foundation of neoliberalism in post-socialist Slovakia, observed through the introduction to students of a genre supposed to encapsulate many of its values, is a heteromorphic bricolage of Western beliefs and practices that yield a surprisingly homogeneous surface cohering in ideologies of written language.

In the rest of this chapter I will first describe motives and projects of educational reform in post-socialist Slovakia and East Central Europe. An underlying concern has been how to shift the educational foundations of society to socialize students to a post-socialist liberal capitalist order. Some reforms were pushed from a centre engaged with Western actors who readers might expect would promote neoliberal government. Other reforms, such as the introduction of Anglo-American ideas about essay-writing over the early years of the new millennium, emerged less uniformly from grassroots initiatives. Through interviews and observations of university instructors in Bratislava, I outline some of the work of these efforts to refashion the self and its public presentation through the genre of the academic essay. While some of these ideas regarding voice and authorship show a strong affinity with neoliberal ideologies, I suggest how they had just as much to do with the introduction of a different academic tradition and rhetorical culture, the lineages of which do not align very neatly with one commonly established for 'neoliberalism'. The technology of the self that is the essay forges a neoliberal subjectivity in ambiguous ways.

Educating for Liberal Democracy

Since the collapse of Communist rule, people in the former Czechoslovakia have engaged in extended debates over changes in educational practices needed for the order to follow. Given education's modern prominence as material for sculpting nations and subjects (see e.g. Kaplan 2006, Larson 2013, Mitchell 1988), it has probably come as no surprise that many of these debates, in one form or another, have entailed what kind of persons would emerge from the socialist experiment into a post-socialist modernity.

Neoliberal politicians, using the state, have assumed one role. By the turn of the millennium several governmental ministers in areas of finance, economics, labour, health care and other resorts had risen to power from earlier work for think-tanks engaged with the theories of Austrian liberal economist Friedrich von Hayek. Among their explicit aims was the devolution of risk and responsibility from the state to individuals in areas ranging from retirement, to health care, to higher education (Fisher et al. 2007). Among the most prominent figures have been the Czech Václav Klaus and Slovak Ivan Mikloš. These goals have been brought to bear on the educational system as well, frequently clashing with other agendas (see Larson 2013: 132–57 for a summary). Through not infrequent changes of government and public figures of reform, general patterns have emerged. In Slovakia they would correlate to a large degree with those with which Laura Perry characterized the region as of 2009: 'depoliticizing education', 'removing the state's monopoly on education by allowing private or nongovernmental schools to be established', 'increasing parents' and students' ability to choose a school', and 'decentralizing educational governance by giving more autonomy to local and regional authorities' (Perry 2009: 170).

These four patterns are bound by a common logic holding that reducing the role of the state and pluralizing options in education will necessarily depoliticize it while reproducing enterprise and autonomy in students, parents, schools and regions. To some degree this pattern has survived changes in government ministers because 'the state' has served as a popular discursive foil for Catholics, nationalists, liberals, localists and opportunists alike. Yet this attention to issues of governance has been in concert with initiatives addressing curricula and pedagogy only infrequently. Indeed, the state has actually *increased* its centralizing role in establishing curricular standards and guidelines as well as reforming school finishing exams (for one description, see Prendergast 2008). Outside of this shift from the socialist era governance of education, reform of curriculum and pedagogy has either not transpired because of the priority given governance, or it has emerged from individual or local initiative. On the one hand we have seen an inconsistent logic fostering autonomy, freedom of choice and local enterprise. On the other hand we have seen less thorough and consistent adjustment of post-socialist curricula and pedagogies than one might have expected.

Some 'post-socialist' curricular and pedagogical reforms – such as encouraging student voice while seeking to reduce the authority of individual teachers – have had a 'neoliberal' flavour, even if the two motives should not be collapsed. After all, theories of 'totalitarianism' cited citizen passivity as a feature of the Communist bloc long before 'neoliberal' attacks on an allegedly overly paternalistic state began to gather momentum in the West in the 1970s. Furthermore, we should remember that it was possible to have been against state socialist governance without being a neoliberal, just as any open-minded pedagogue in the West might question existing practices without a clear ideological agenda (see e.g. Perry 2009: 171). For instance, in Slovakia, the clamour for reforms resonant with today's went unanswered as early as the 1950s (see Larson 2013). Perhaps for these reasons, reforms of a 'neoliberal' character have not been solely top-down or bottom-up: they have cut from a variety of directions. New ideas on pedagogical practices and educational technologies have emerged from offices of foreign agencies such as the Open Society Institute and British Council; professional exchanges (such as Fulbright); informal opportunities to experience and exchange thoughts on teaching (such as chance encounters with foreign educators); and reading from newly accessible books and periodicals. These interactions have occurred at all levels of the educational system, from primary to tertiary, through informal workshops and formal classrooms alike. They have emerged from a plethora of sources, prominent among them workshops run by non-governmental organizations in ambiguous relation to the state (Berdahl 2005, Greenberg 2006, Junghans 2001, Larson 2008, also Prendergast 2008). 'Neoliberal' patterns to the teaching of particular technologies of the self, as we are about to see in more detail, have been assemblages of inspirations, ideas, habits and in situ solutions.

Finding a Topic, Finding an Authorial Voice?

After 1989 the population of educators that has most forcefully articulated a greater need for students to 'think for themselves' has been the same as those coming in most frequent contact with Anglo-American modes of self-expression: recent college graduates transitioning into roles of teaching new college students in Slovakia's metropole, Bratislava. These educators have encountered Brits and Americans in the metropole itself, and have tended to be more driven toward new opportunities for travel and professional development abroad than colleagues working in other regions. For some of these educators, encounters with Anglo-American academic communities piqued their curiosity without leading them to firm conclusions. For others, these exchanges had either unsettled their assumptions about 'normal' academic practices or alienated them enough from local traditions so they came to believe they had found a key to post-socialist pedagogy.

Of keen interest to numerous instructors was students' ability to 'find a topic' for their writing assignments. The problem of 'finding a topic' was in the air, coming up in college debate programs that the Soros Foundation sponsored throughout the region, and as a component of cultivating critical thinking at a 2004 national conference on primary education sponsored by a team of educators from the University of Northern Iowa, and by the Soros Foundation. Elsewhere in the region, 'finding a topic' appeared in the 2003 program of the European Association for the Teaching of Academic Writing's conference in Budapest, and in 2006 was serving as a focal concept for educational NGOs in Poland and Bosnia.

'Finding a topic' mattered to some because of its direct implications for post-Communist political dispositions and civic engagement. Consider, for instance, the following lament I heard at a 2004 conference in Bratislava of mostly Slovak ethnologists and historians marking the fifteenth anniversary of the Velvet Revolution. After the first presentation the discussion took on problems of helping current students understand the recent history of the socialist period, such as how the Velvet Revolution of 1989 or the Warsaw Pact invasion of 1968 really looked. One speaker decried her sense that not only did parents not discuss these events with their children, but that new textbooks that adequately addressed the subject had yet to appear. After some debate about whether historians, book distribution, economic conditions or the Ministry of Education were to blame, a young and fairly widely published lecturer in history stood up:

> In my opinion it's that students don't know how to explore any of these topics
> for themselves. When I ask them to go and write a seminar paper on a topic of
> their choice related to the Communist past, they give me these blank looks! Then
> they resolve the problem by talking amongst themselves and all settling on one
> topic that's in fashion, like 'the underground Church'. They go and read some
> secondary literature and paraphrase it. They don't apply what they're reading
> outside of class toward thinking up their own topic.

For this young historian, students' inability to come up with a topic on the Communist past individually triggered concern over levels of students' literacy ('what they're reading outside of class'); over their level of engagement with current events and recent history begging moral questions for the present; and over students' excessive trust in leaving research to professional experts. Underlying these concerns was a sense of Slovak students' deficiency or abnormality in these areas relative to other parts of the world.

For other instructors the problem of finding a topic implicated post-socialist subjects' abilities to script a new lifeworld. One young college instructor I knew directed his frustrations with students' expressive styles and academic skills into his attempts to teach them new forms of writing. Jozef was a state university instructor of English. About 30 years old, he was one of several peers from neighbouring post-socialist states to have studied as an undergraduate for a few years in the US through an exchange with Central European University in Budapest (yet another institution supported by investor-philanthropist George Soros). Jozef's class, 'English Composition', met once a week for about an hour and a half over ten weeks. He taught two sections of it: each with 15 to 20 students, mostly female (as were most students in the department) and in their second or third year out of five. Jozef's example is useful for breaking down the pedagogical problem of 'finding a topic' as acquiring a new technology of the self. In this process we see that Jozef's analysis of his students' work was not simply a matter of dissecting it to identify the topic or the thesis statement, but evaluating it according to criteria of how provocative, bold, or able to draw attention it was.

When I first met Jozef and told him about my interest in 'critical thinking' as a concept for explaining Slovakia's transition from Communist rule (Larson 2013), he launched very quickly into a contention that the heart of 'critical thinking' involves conceiving a thesis and defending it. To him, the ability to 'find a topic' reflected deeper issues of socialization to proper or improper civic discursive behaviour:

> The students I get, they arrive here trained like monkeys to repeat what their
> teachers have asked them to. Teachers give them the question, and they respond.
> But what if they aren't given a question, like if they're asked to write an essay

on any topic? They're lost. They can't think for themselves – coming up with a topic is probably the heart of critical thinking.

Students' main assignment was a final paper. Over the weeks Jozef alternated between points of style and building students up to the task of writing papers with their 'own topics'.

During a lesson that Jozef suggested I might find particularly interesting, he tried to orient students to appropriate topic sentences. At the start of the lesson he gave students a hand-out with several sample paragraphs and asked them to identify which sentence contained the topic. After some discussion about each example, he asked them to look at five sentences at the bottom of the page:

1. Life in a large city has many advantages.
2. Hollywood films have both good and bad features.
3. People must assume responsibility for their actions.
4. Computers may or may not be tomorrow's teachers.
5. Everyone believes that travel is educational.

'These five topic sentences at the bottom are all too broad to be used–why?' Students did not have much to suggest, so Jozef ended up guiding them through the sentences with his critiques of why the sentences were inappropriate for opening an essay. Regarding the first sentence, he said:

> Ok, you have to be more specific … in regard to the advantages, or to the city. You can say that the citizens of Bratislava think that the city has many advantages. For many people it is difficult to think of a specific topic sentence or a thesis statement for the whole essay because they think that they can just show what the advantages are and that would be it. Yes, but it would not be interesting because everybody knows that life in the city has many advantages – it also has many disadvantages. It's like saying 'sometimes I like to eat chicken for lunch, and other times I like carrots'.

Self-evidence seemed a significant concern. Jozef continued,

> [L]ast year … we spent about an hour discussing why, say, 'capital punishment is a controversial issue' is not a good topic or a thesis statement … because that's what it is – it is a controversial issue. Everybody knows that it is not an easy thing to decide about, to form an opinion about. … Same thing with 'life in the city has many advantages'. You know, it's banal. Yes it does, and so what? You don't want to read an essay that starts with something that you already know.

As above, Jozef targeted statements that in his view were not 'interesting' because 'everyone knows', for instance, that 'life in the city has many advantages'. Jozef seemed to be asking students to take on a role that they might use in debates or polemics: to spark exchange, rather than 'report' information to demonstrate a competency.

As the semester progressed, I observed how students applied these ideas, and to what degree they satisfied Jozef. In one session in his office, students discussed with him their planned paper topics and arguments. A few students actually brought prepared drafts, and two came with completed papers, seeming to treat the meeting as an oral presentation of them. Topics usually started broadly: 'abortion', 'homosexuality', 'loss of identity to globalization', and 'women in the Old Testament'. Jozef probed, 'What aspect?' "What theme is supposed to bind different examples of 'women in the Old Testament' together?" In response to the second question, that particular student searched a bit for an answer, and then responded, 'Beauty--the Old Testament talks about women's beauty'. The student elaborated on the topic, but still did not produce the kind of bold position that Jozef had encouraged in class.

All pedagogues (including I) struggle to size up and assess their students accurately to teach in helpful ways. These interpretations synthesize features of students' behaviour with beliefs about the meaning of it. Encounters such as Jozef's with his students were further taking place within a highly politicized post-socialist framework for evaluating the past and envisioning the future. A large anthropological literature on postsocialism has described these epistemological politics and ways that they might unfairly or inaccurately characterize the behaviour of postsocialist subjects (e.g. Dunn 2004, Lampland 2002, Lemon 2009). So rather than see the classroom exchanges that I have described as evidence that lingering socialist era conditioning had dulled students' cognitive and communicative skills fundamental to authorial personhood, what confusions might reveal Jozef's approach to be that of a particular socio-culturally and historically situated graphic ideology?

To begin, let us return to Jozef's discussion of a proposed topic sentence, 'Life in a large city has many advantages'. From my previous experience teaching English at a Slovak *gymnázium* (college-preparatory secondary school) from 1994 to 1996 and later conducting fieldwork there, the sentence reminded me of oral discussion topics that students might have received on their secondary school finishing exam (or *maturita*). Examining committees used such topic statements to evaluate students' active vocabulary for ability to perform in anticipated social interactions in the foreign language. Jozef was therefore critiquing a sentence – 'Life in a large city has many advantages' – and calling for its use within a genre (the essay) that students might not have fully understood yet, but had sought to grasp within their range of experiences in Slovak educational communities. Indeed, below we will see evidence of this application of a previously known genre or type of speech event to a situation for which Jozef held different expectations. When students brought whole drafts or whole completed texts to their consultation session and started to explain their papers to Jozef in a 'presentation' format, their actions suggested that they did not expect only a consultation about topic and argument.

Other nations' students show similar confusions over issues of authorship in writing academic papers. Part of this might arise from how they are taught to think of the figure of *the author*: a creative persona of public reputation that might seem to exclude them (see Foucault 1984, Larson 2009). This might illuminate their difficulty grasping the mechanics of a thesis statement, linear argument and rules of citation, as those mechanics represent the conventions of academic discursive communities for presenting and managing claims, evidence and the relationships of an authorial voice and the voices of other interlocutors to passages in a text (Blum 2009, Jones, et al. 1999). In the Slovak classrooms I observed, differing suppositions of genre and rights to assume participant roles governed how students evaluated the *esej* and *thesis* ('tay-zis'). Concepts of both the 'essay' and 'thesis' circulate in Slovak, but with divergent semantic domains and ideologies of writing. How do meanings and practices surrounding the *esej* and *thesis* differ in Slovak discursive communities from the Anglo-American?

'The essay' is not a new genre in East Central Europe, but the ways in which it has fit with East Central European (or Slovak) discursive communities look different from its practice in Anglo-American ones. This should not surprise us, as even though scholars of the genre frequently trace its origins through the conscious use of the label for 'attempt' beginning with de Montaigne, the spirit of the essay has been claimed for works from ancient Babylon and turn of the millennium (1000 A.C.E.) Japan (see e.g. D'Agata 2009). Its forms and meanings are in fact quite variable in English: for instance, there are personal essays, argumentative essays and academic essays written by students. Expectations for the form of each depend on whether an essay is published in *The New Yorker* magazine, appears as a monograph (such as John Locke's *An Essay Concerning Human Understanding*) or is taught in school.

Students in Slovak schools have been exposed to something called the *esej* for at least several decades (see e.g. Mistrík 1985: 29). However, that exposure has been quite different from Anglo-American schooling. Rather than build up the essay as a prominent site for the development of thought and self-expression,[1] Slovak schools have taught the essay as part of a larger framework for learning about language called *jazyková kultúra*, or 'language culture'. This framework descends significantly from the interwar Prague Linguistic Circle's structuralist and functionalist approach to language: breaking down linguistic systems into their component parts, studying their functionality and identifying ways to develop them out of moral obligation to self and society (Larson n.d.). Students learn about language and society as series of social events calling for variable discursive practices. The *esej* is but one practice in an atelier of communicative tools that includes other genres of argumentation, such as the polemic. The pedagogical discussions that I highlight here – ones into which even members of the Slovak government have inserted themselves – have clearly sought to raise the essay's import for post-socialist subjectivities.

---

1 See Blum, *My Word! Plagiarism and College Culture* and essays in Jones, Turner, and Street (eds), *Students Writing in the University: Cultural and Epistemological Issues* on writing as a distinctive feature of US academic culture.

Communicative practices are not utilized evenly across society; they vary, for instance, by profession. Slovak textbooks have noted this. In late socialist Slovakia the textbook for language and grammar used throughout secondary schools identified the *esej* with such highly regarded writers and elite masters of the national language as Alexander Matuška, Vladimír Mináč and Milan Rufus (Mistrík and Pauliny 1977). The name of the genre itself in Slovak suggests that it was borrowed from French, as have been related intellectual genres such as the feuilleton (Slovak: *fejeton*) (see e.g. Osvaldová and Kopáč 2007). In fact, the essay has been characterized in one Slovak secondary school textbook written by two late leading linguists in a fashion not unlike how Anglo-American readers might know the feuilleton: 'written personally, expressively and with the striking presence of the author in the text' (Mistrík and Pauliny 1977: 109). While this understanding of the essay might describe one of its manifestations (the personal essay) in Anglo-American discursive communities, this is a different orientation to the genre than Jozef was teaching his students and that Natália, another instructor we will encounter below, learned from British instructors: to *depersonalize* in style while simultaneously presenting a text's central ideas as *one's own*.

To elaborate on this point, consider Theresa Lillis's observation that in Anglo-American classroom essays

> [i]mportant relationships are not signaled between speakers or between sentence and speaker, but between sentence and sentence. The reader has to constantly monitor grammatical and lexical information and, as such, there is a need for the writer to be explicit about logical implications. ... The author is a fiction *since the process of writing and editing essayist texts leads to an effacement of individual and idiosyncratic identity* (Lillis 1999: 131, italics in original).

So Anglo-American classroom essays are not only built around a thesis statement (a detail that we will see confused Natália) and the 'logical implications' of each sentence; they also '[efface] individual and idiosyncratic identity'. Yet if Slovak students write essays, do they by contrast insert or broadcast their own identities in the text, as one textbook's definition states they should? In my months of observations of Slovak language and literature classes during the 2002–2003 school year, I not only did not see students practicing this genre (the *esej*) about which they were reading. I also sensed that there was a fundamental reason concerning ideologies of authorship. To write an essay as it is known in Slovakia – 'personally, expressively and with the striking presence of the author in the text' – is the work of professional writers such as Matuška, Mináč and Rufus. For students in Slovak secondary schools – even those preparing for college – an essay has been something to read and admire, not write. Moreover, if (as I noted above) the model of language that Slovak students acquire is one of linking types of texts to contexts, the 'denial of real participants' (which Lillis identifies in the Anglo-American form) might puzzle students as to how to locate essays socio-culturally.

Authoring and Owning

Let us now consider students' apparent confusions over genre by comparing them with someone slightly outside their peer group – a recent college graduate – who had joined the ranks of instructors. Around the same period as I was getting to know Jozef and observing his classes, I met Natália, an administrator and occasional lecturer at another institution. Natália was about the same age as Jozef and recalled how it had felt as a student to be confronted with the different demands that foreign lecturers had placed on her classmates both in Slovakia and during coursework in the UK. She attributed her confusion to suppositions about learning communicative acts that she had acquired while at a *gymnázium*. She recounted to me in an interview her experience of these foreign lecturers:

> [T]hey started to ask us for essays, which we didn't totally understand. ... They essentially wanted a specific structure from us. They wanted us to submit a thesis, but we had been taught ... that a thesis was a larger work for a degree. Well, at first quite a confusion broke out. Why? What kind of thesis? Why, a thesis is fifty pages long! ... Then I understood that I have to think up something new, which seemed impossible. Why, I'm not a historian, not even a fifty-year-old or thirty-year-old one! ... It took me quite a while to understand that in essence an essay is about ... a kind of brainstorming and knowing how to use multiple sources, and put them together. And form something somewhat new, even if it really isn't. ... It simply took me a while to understand that ... one just has to show there that he's mastered the material. That means that if in a lesson someone explains the process of expanding the European Union, why it's important, then I just need to write an essay that the process of expanding the Union is inevitable. ... And it's considered an original piece because I wrote it. ... I finally understood that it's not anything that marvellous.

Natália's account of her path to grasping what her foreign lecturers wanted in a 'thesis' invoked earlier suppositions of which genres were a normal part of classroom evaluation (her confusion over the term 'thesis'), but also *which stances or voices* her instructors expected her to assume toward the texts she produced. In the end, she claimed to have realized that 'an essay doesn't have to be something new' and 'it's not anything that marvellous'. All she recollected needing to do to satisfy them was to argue coherently one side of a debate, such as the inevitability of European expansion, and thereby demonstrate mastery of *existing* positions or voices (existing textual content) on the topic. Stance, attitude or conscious channelling of a particular 'authorial' voice toward the work seemed to matter just as much as anything else: 'it's considered an original piece because I wrote it'.

By the time I met her, Natália had accepted these premises for classroom writing, was teaching them herself, and found that her own Slovak university instructors had 'lacked a scientific approach'. Her criticism of those Slovaks who had taught her, however, did not mean that she was completely charmed by the

Anglo-American approach she had learned. Note her revelation at the end of her narrative that 'it doesn't have to be my own absolutely new idea'. Her relief even suggested that she understood these rules of thesis and voice could be applied to new, predictable 'opinions'. Students just needed to sort out the new 'correct' positions to voice: 'If in a lesson someone explains the process of expanding the European Union, why it's important, then I just need to write an essay that the process of expanding the Union is inevitable'.

Understandings of how to classify a text or event by genre trigger suppositions of participant roles. After all, when we size up an event as one that requires listening to a monologue (such as a speech) or allowing for dialogue (such as a debate) we assess our own rights to speak or listen. Beyond Slovak students' confusion over how to classify the literacy events in which they were being introduced to a new conceptualization of the essay (as opposed to the *esej*), fundamentally different understandings of structure and voice inhabit knowledge and practice of essays in each educational community. The teaching of Anglo-American understandings to Slovak students, as practised by young college instructors such as Jozef and Natália, introduces new thinking about the writing self that is embedded in a text. Clearly, some assumptions of expertise were being upended: East Central European academic communities tend to set accumulated and credentialed knowledge as a prerequisite for voicing opinions on certain matters (on this phenomenon, see e.g. contributions in Duszak 1997). Writing an analysis of recent Slovak history, therefore, would fall under the purview of a professional historian, as Natália suggested in her surprise over what she was asked to do.

Now, British and American discursive communities of course lend weight to the opinions of persons credentialed as professionals or experts. One difference I have just described is the distribution of the right to claim an authorial voice, something that seems less restricted for students in Anglo-American classrooms than in Slovak. But we have also seen hints of a semiotic basis to the crafting of this authorial voice: the back grounding of an authorial persona with the foregrounding of authoritative claims. The origins of this interesting inversion – a second feature of Slovak students' encounters with academic essays in English and one that I noted earlier appears in the self-claims that occur in a standard Western curriculum vitae – seem to have arisen within the modern history of the essay in Anglo-American print publics.

From Steven Shapin's *Social History of Truth* (1994) we have learned that seventeenth-century science began to trust more in signs of individual *dis*interest and less in intertextual cited authority. 'Disinterest' was part of a larger designation of 'virtue' used to evaluate the standing of gentlemen to make claims as early scientists. Being virtuous might have included the performance of agreement, rather than dissent in conversation; exhibition of self-control; and the avoidance of self-promotion through one's intellectual claims. Note, however, that the avoidance of self-promotion did not mean that these early scientists were not engaged in forms of self-claims: they might have bracketed off traces of an *interested* human author while their claims relied significantly on others' trust in their intentions and judgment.

Around this time in the West the figure of 'the author' was coalescing. Although origins of Western notions of 'the author' can be traced to multiple sources (see e.g. Foucault 1984), Shapin's and legal scholar Mark Rose's work suggests that the legitimacy of an individual's claims to an idea and the right to promote it in print, possibly through collaboration with publishers on its distribution, date at least partly from this point. Crucially, the possibility of laying claims to ideas as one's 'own' was facilitated by the increased moral legitimacy of accumulating private property. John Locke's *Two Treatises* contributed significantly to the intellectual work of shifting attitudes toward property (Bauman and Briggs 2003: 57). Locke's interest lay not only in forms of physical property such as land, but also in naturalizing 'private' property such as an individual's person. As Mark Rose puts it, 'With its concerns for origins and first proprietors, the liberal discourse of property blended reality with the eighteenth-century discourse of original genius'. If the right to profit from ownership of land was increasingly naturalized, so too was the notion of an individual's right to claim ideas as (predominantly) his own (Rose 1993: 5–7, Verdery 2003: 16). Possession and self-possession started to become a precondition of freedom (Macpherson 1962).

John Locke's arguments have of course become part of a canon of liberal political and economic theory. But to understand extensions of his and other late seventeenth-century thinking to authorship of ideas requires a summary of shifts in thinking about the role of language in intellectual knowledge. Up to that point in British thought, many of Locke's peers had seen language as an untrustworthy basis for inquiry because of its interaction with other objects in the world. Language was imbued with dangerous powers of persuasion and agency, eminently malleable according to context, and infused with traces of others' words in the construction of one's own authority as a discursive subject. But, Locke argued, one could also reimagine language as the transmission of more fixed, purified, semantic meaning stripped of social ties (and therefore of features subject to malevolent manipulation) to serve the individual minds that form the basis for a potentially more enlightened public sphere (Bauman and Briggs 2003: 45). One should see language, he argued, as part of the faculties and powers with which an individual is born, but which not all persons manage to cultivate in equal fashions (Bauman and Briggs 2003: 41–2). Within this apprehension of language, what replaced an interlocutor's ties to other trusted sources as the basis for trust? Locke insisted that sincerity, and therefore pure *disinterested* meaning, could be presumed when an interlocutor is a *gentleman*: a property-owning individual (usually male) whose independence from material stakes could be more plausible (see also Peters 2005, 1999).

This late seventeenth to early eighteenth-century transformation in scientific thought turned on shifts in thinking about language and how to interpret it. Arguments about the plausibility of Robert Boyle's or even John Locke's claims to objectivity legitimized more broadly the notion that an individual could not only claim disinterest, but that persons could claim ideas and arguments as theirs to publicize and circulate. But these new possibilities for performing the self arose from shifts in thinking about language and communication. Their reverberation today through countless genres and communicative contexts is central to current valorisations of neoliberal personhood in the public sphere.

Authorial Selves and their Audiences

Although students are taught often painstakingly to craft their essays to be accessible and logical for readers, contexts and motivations for reading are typically elided: the 'audience' is an undifferentiated mass. Recall Theresa Lillis's earlier observation that Anglo-American classroom essays tend to 'den[y] real participants'. Yet even though pedagogies of the essay might teach it in this intentionally sterile fashion, this does not mean that students and audiences apprehend it this way. Suppositions of audience underlie the use of this technology of the self: to whom are these student authors of essays (and selves) projecting their claims and to what effect?

An immediate answer is the pedagogical figure assigning the essay: Jozef, Natália, the young historian or even Minister Mikloš. But often in this era's imperative to 'broadcast yourself' (as YouTube would have it), the awareness of the relationship between an author and her audience is less explicit. At this juncture in the chapter, it would be fitting to complement the previous pages' digression in time to now situate ideas governing academic essays in space. One recent exploration of US students' struggles to conform to the expectations of their instructors for writing essays argues that US educational culture has undergone a longer shift away from demonstrating authenticity toward the discursive performance of a more mutable self that can acclimate to different interactive needs (Blum 2009). Yet from what we have seen of my brief exploration of the history of essays and authorship in Anglo-American discursive communities, an ideology of performance allowing for a more broadly distributed right to make authorial claims is not new, even if its origins were grounded in the implicit inequality of property ownership. We might therefore speak of a slow evolution toward 'performance' as a more conscious language ideology, while continuing to ask how such an ideology is not hegemonic. As Susan Blum herself notes in her study of plagiarism, one challenge for US students seeking to negotiate the performance of competent academic selves is the widespread practice of encouraging interdiscursive (although unattributed) quoting and sampling from sources in popular culture. Students must learn to bracket off the practices appropriate for certain genres of sociability (hanging out, joking with friends) to acquire different rules governing genres of argument, such as essays.

The heterogeneity of any speaker's repertoire and beliefs governing language use is a central tenet for many contemporary anthropologically informed approaches to language and communication. Yet so often North Atlantic thinking about language slides into more totalizing and homogenizing views, despite the exceptions that may be right before our eyes. So how might a consideration of audience pry open a sealed package view of language that posits the academic essay as key to performing a felicitous authorial self? In what ways do we see the liberal ideologies embedded in notions of writing essays as failing to note conditions and contexts for students or citizens to successfully generate and hold an audience's attention?

Recent political events around the globe have shown us that the use of genres quite different from academic essays *can* prove much more powerful for an authorial voice. Audiences have rallied in the name of occupying Wall Street or toppling the Egyptian government around the short, often anonymous suggestive bursts of Twitter (for example, Juris 2012) as well as the equally short, less anonymous verses of poets (Saad 2012). Neither genre follows the guidelines of argument and evidence for the essay, but both emerge from egalitarian notions of the right to authorship. Yet other recent scholarship on the introduction of new media forms into various contexts has shown how certain genres or practices for expositing the self are not in and of themselves authorial-felicitous even if they are authorial. Tomas Matza, building on earlier insights by Barbara Cruikshank (e.g. 1996), has pointed out that while recent talk shows in Russia have encouraged the sharing of the self's experiences and opinions, doing so does not necessarily advance liberal democracy. Rather than serve as democratic 'participation', sharing one's experience might simply serve as the exposing of an interior self or ownership over a self. In fact, the workings of talk shows in a context such as contemporary Russia suggest 'a ... disappearance of political possibility and the emergence of a feeling subject, left to negotiate a denuded landscape of pure affect' (Matza 2009: 512–13).

We should not conclude that a genre such as the talk show is an inherently limiting political technology. Ambiguous findings have been made regarding the use of social media such as Facebook, blogs and YouTube. As the contributions to one recent volume on digital media show (Thurlow and Mroczek 2011), new media might enable the expression of an authorial voice in new ways, but they do not do so in and of themselves: they can also script and channel interactions in ways that re-inscribe inequalities and reinforce worldviews of race, class and cultural difference. What might liberate one author of a text might generate others' social disadvantage. Slovak students' articulation of an 'original' opinion or argument in an essay would seem to beg similar questions over whether such a shift in discursively based personhood really engenders transcendent debate. The academic essay may simply foster a classroom of students epistemologically isolated from each other in their claims to personal distinction. In the context of global attacks on the welfare state, it may also (for instance) substantiate an author's bourgeois status through his racially charged critique of persons allegedly on the dole. The remedy, perhaps, lies with how these students go on to use their newly acquired knowledge.

Conclusion

This chapter has explored some of the implications of introducing post-socialist Slovak college students to Anglo-American forms of academic essays. I have argued that students' apparent confusions with these new forms had more to do with the ideologies of performance and writing governing the forms than with the forms themselves. A central difference between these ideologies is a notion of what I have characterized as the authorial self, a form of personhood closely related to neoliberal notions of enterprise. Through the ad-hoc post-socialist pedagogies of young cosmopolitan Slovak college lecturers such as Jozef and Natália, we have sketched some of the ideological and semiotic work through which essays might endow an authorial self with social force. This force, however, does not appear to have been equally accessible to all, as the social distribution of the right to make claims as an author was in question. The standing of the authorial self is achieved, ironically, through a surface back grounding of a writer's distinctive personal features which puzzles some interlocutors. An essay's performativity, I suggest, is often locatable in elites' beliefs in its powers, rather than in a measurable reality of how a democratic public sphere emerges dialogically or interactively through the genres which its constituents extend and employ. After all, among the notable advocates of essay-writing that we encountered in this chapter were an anti-Communist economic reformer (Ivan Mikloš) and a global capitalist and patron of liberal governance par excellence, George Soros. As with their seventeenth-century counterparts such as John Locke, we see a collapse of authorship and ownership, whereby those who are properly economically engaged have also earned the right to share their views with others publicly.

I would hesitate to lament the introduction of these new ideas governing the genres in Slovak students' communicative repertoire. After all, these ideas currently provide students with access to performances of the self widely expected across the globe; indeed, they seemed to open a door to university study for one winner of the essay contest. Moreover, Slovaks (as with other peoples) have long encountered new discursive habits and appropriated them (a case in point being the essay itself). A fascinating question to follow is how Slovaks are proceeding to negotiate these new ways of thinking about language and communication in a capitalist world, and how they are integrating them into existing models.

Acknowledgements

I would like to thank a Fulbright-Hays Dissertation Abroad Fellowship for funding this research, and the permission of several instructors I leave unnamed for allowing me to observe their classes and talk with them over several weeks. I would also like to thank Susan Frekko, Ivan Lacko, the Department of Anthropology at Grinnell College, and the Department of Communication Studies at the University of Iowa for very helpful feedback.

References

Bauman, R., and Briggs, C.L. 2003. *Voices of Modernity: Language Ideologies and the Politics of Inequality*. New York: Cambridge University Press.

Berdahl, D. 2005. The Spirit of Capitalism and the Boundaries of Citizenship in Post-Wall Germany. *Comparative Studies in Society and History*, 47(2): 235–51.

Blum, S.D. 2009. *My Word! Plagiarism and College Culture*. Ithaca, NY: Cornell University Press.

Cruikshank, B. 1996. Revolutions within: self-government and self-esteem, in *Foucault and Political Reason: Liberalism, Neo-liberalism and Rationalities of Government*, edited by A. Barry, T. Osborne and N. Rose. Chicago: University of Chicago Press, pp. 231–52.

D'Agata, J. 2009. *The Lost Origins of the Essay*. St. Paul, MN: Graywolf Press.

Dunn, E.C. 2004. *Privatizing Poland: Baby Food, Big Business, and the Remaking of Labor*. Ithaca: Cornell University Press.

Duszak, A. 1997. *Culture and Styles of Academic Discourse*. New York: Mouton de Gruyter.

Fisher, S., Gould J. and Haughton, T. 2007. Slovakia's Neoliberal Turn. *Europe-Asia Studies*, 59(6): 977–98.

Foucault, M. 1984. What Is an Author?, in *The Foucault Reader*, edited by P. Rabinow. New York: Pantheon Books, pp. 101–20.

Gáliková, M. 2002. Aj súťaž v písaní esejí môže dať nový impulz. *Sme*, 3 September, 1.

Greenberg, J. 2006. Noć Reklamoždera: Democracy, Consumption, and the Contradictions of Representation in Post-Socialist Serbia. *PoLAR: Political and Legal Anthropology Review*, 29(2): 181–207.

Hull, M.S. 2003. The File: Agency, Authority, and Autography in an Islamabad Bureaucracy. *Language & Communication*, 23: 287–314.

Jones, C., Turner, J. and Street, B. 1999. *Students Writing in the University: Cultural and Epistemological Issues*. Philadelphia: John Benjamins.

Junghans, T. 2001. Marketing Selves: Constructing Civil Society and Selfhood in Post-Socialist Hungary. *Critique of Anthropology*, 21(4): 383–400.

Juris, J.S. 2012. Reflections on #Occupy Everywhere: Social media, public space, and emerging logics of aggregation. *American Ethnologist*, 39(2): 259–79.

Kaplan, S. 2006. *The Pedagogical State: Education and the Politics of National Culture in post-1980 Turkey*. Palo Alto, CA: Stanford University Press.

Lampland, M. 2002. The Advantages of Being Collectivized: Cooperative Farm Managers in the Postsocialist Economy, in *Postsocialism: Ideals, Ideologies, and Practices in Eurasia*, edited by C.M. Hann. New York: Routledge, pp. 31–55.

Larson, J.L. *The Bold and the Beautiful: 'Cultures' of Opinions and Encounters with English in Slovak Classrooms*. n.d.

Larson, J.L. 2008. Ambiguous Transparency: Resumé Fetishism in a Slovak Workshop. *Ethnos*, 73(2): 189–216.

Larson, J.L. 2009. Cosmologies of Criticism: Taste, (Dis)trust, and Uses of Literature in Slovak Secondary Schools. *Critique of Anthropology*, 29(4): 447–69.

Larson, J.L. 2013. *Critical Thinking in Slovakia after Socialism*. Rochester, NY: University of Rochester Press.

Lemon, A. 2009. Sympathy for the Weary State? Cold War Chronotopes and Moscow Others. *Comparative Studies in Society and History* 51(4): 832–64.

Lillis, T. 1999. Whose 'Common Sense'? Essayist literacy and the institutional practice of mystery, in *Students Writing in the University: Cultural and Epistemological Issues*, edited by C. Jones, J. Turner and B. Street. Philadelphia: John Benjamins, pp. 125–47.

Macpherson, C.B. 1962. *The Political Theory of Possessive Individualism: Hobbes to Locke*. Oxford: Clarendon.

Matza, T. 2009. Moscow's Echo: Technologies of the Self, Publics, and Politics of the Russian Talk Show. *Cultural Anthropology* 24(3): 489–522.

Miller, P. and Rose, N. 2008. *Governing the Present: Administering Economic, Social, and Personal Life*. Cambridge: Polity Press.

Mistrík, J. 1985. *Štylistika*. Bratislava: Slovenské pedagogické nakladateľstvo.

Mistrík, J. and Pauliny, E. 1977. *Slovenský jazyk pre gymnáziá a pre stredné odborné školy*. Bratislava: Slovenské pedagogické nakladateľstvo.

Mitchell, T. 1988. *Colonising Egypt*. Berkeley: University of California Press.

Osvaldová, B. and Kopáč, R. 2007. *O fejetonu, s fejetonem*. Praha: Karolinum.

Perry, L.B. 2009. American Academics and Education for Democracy in Post-Communist Europe, in *American Post-conflict Educational Reform: From the Spanish-American War to Iraq*, edited by N.W. Sobe. New York: Palgrave Macmillan, pp. 169–88.

Peters, J.D. 1999. *Speaking into the Air: A History of the Idea of Communication*. Chicago: The University of Chicago Press.

Peters, J.D. 2005. *Courting the Abyss: Free Speech and the Liberal Tradition*. Chicago: The University of Chicago Press.

Prendergast, C. 2008. *Buying into English: Language and Investment in the New Capitalist World*. Pittsburgh: University of Pittsburgh Press.

Rose, M. 1993. *Authors and Owners: The Invention of Copyright*. Cambridge, MA: Harvard University Press.

Saad, R. 2012. The Egyptian revolution: A triumph of poetry. *American Ethnologist*, 39(1), 63–6.

Schieffelin, B.B., Woolard, K.A. and Kroskrity, P.V. 1998. *Language Ideologies: Practice and Theory*. New York: Oxford University Press.

Shapin, S. 1994. *A Social History of Truth: Civility and Science in Seventeenth-Century England*. Chicago: University of Chicago Press.

Thurlow, C. and Mroczek, K. 2011. *Digital Discourse: Language in the New Media*. New York: Oxford University Press.

Verdery, K. 2003. *The Vanishing Hectare: Property and Value in Postsocialist Transylvania*. Ithaca: Cornell University Press.

Chapter 5

Losing the Enterprising Self in Post-Soviet Estonian Villages

Aet Annist

Introduction: Another World Record!

Late in the evening of 29 January 2012, the Estonian Ministry of Finance issued a press statement in which the Minister of Finance, Jürgen Ligi, urged Estonian inhabitants to accomplish a collective world record by completing the e-population census (Laev 2012). Following the catchy slogan of the Estonian Statistics Board 'Everyone counts!' (*Igaüks loeb!*)[1] and the final appeal 'Let's count ourselves!' (*Loeme ennast üle!*), Estonians beat the Canadians' world record of participation in self-e-census by 8 per cent. Sixty-two per cent of the estimated population demonstrated an astonishing choice to voluntarily self-report to the state, with minimal cost to the government: savings would have been substantial in the cost of printing of questionnaires and their delivery, otherwise done by interviewers at the doorstep. Despite the concern some expressed in the social and public media regarding the complexity and the highly personal nature of some questions, the majority chose to plough through the maze of inquiries out of their free will, establishing a collective 'world best' that the country could write on its wall of honours for e-practices. The population acted like an excellent example of self-governed, actively compliant citizens and handed the state free tools to govern and regulate them effectively. People gave up their time and offered voluntary commitment which was turned into state resources both for administrative purposes, but also for symbolic purposes as the political elite quickly settled onto its global laurels for successful e-governing.

Although e-governmentality is obviously a new phenomenon brought about by new technologies, voluntary compliance with the requirements of the state is an interesting feature that Estonians have for long mocked and prided themselves for. Having promised to eat 'potato-skins' in the name of an independent state, the Estonian population has indeed showed extreme patience, or has for some reason been unable to protest, during the shock therapy of the 1990s and beyond. IMF structural adjustments in the 1990s, negotiations with various global bodies, most prominently WTO and European Union, have triggered various changes in

---

1   The dual meaning is there also in Estonian. This advert was placed all over the urban regions of the country for a month before the actual e-census opened.

local laws, regulations and tax levels, and have rolled the state way back from the Scandinavian model, the source of early visions of capitalism in Estonia. More recently, further fiscal stringencies in order to join the euro-zone in 2011 in the midst of budget cuts and rising unemployment tested Estonians' tolerance and willingness to enable the neoliberal state, and found it to still be going strong. The trust in the ruling neoliberal politics can be gauged from the nearly 20-year rule of such parties. The elite touting Estonia as a glowing example of fiscal balance and budget cuts to their Baltic neighbours, to other East and West Europeans, and even to the world, has only recently started to lose credit.

Such lasting credence of (post)modern capitalism has been greatly helped by the legacies of socialism. The temporal and spatial proximity of the 'failed model' of a socialist state has played a considerable part in generating the evidence for trust in its political opponent, the liberal state. Moving away from the socialist model and anything resembling it in words or deeds (social democracy, unions, even communal organisation of society) was in Estonia a highly nationalist project. This role makes it very significant for understanding the processes there that, since 1992, the country has been ruled by the neoliberal variety of liberalism. That is, one that represents in itself, according to Nikolas Rose, a 'new game of power', ethico-politics which:

> concerns itself with the self-techniques necessary for responsible self-government and the relations between one's obligation to oneself and one's obligations to others. Ethicopolitics has a particular salience at the close of the twentieth century. For it appears that somehow 'we' – the subjects of advanced liberal democracies – in the absence of any objective guarantees for politics or our values, have become obliged to think ethically. (1999: 188, emphasis in the original)

Think ethically, that is, towards the state – the extension of one's self, in the 1990s and 2000s Estonia is still very highly nationally defined. The link between personal freedom and market freedom, so strong in neoliberal discourse (e.g. Harvey 2007: 7) has been particularly strongly linked to national independence in Estonia and has become a compelling association to make. In the case of those nation states where the majority of adult citizens still remember struggling for freedom from an oppressive rule, there has been an overwhelming need to assume these links truly exists and depend on the rigorous following of various self-techniques for self-governing.

Studies on neoliberalism suggest that the politico-economic reality structuring people's lives has profoundly changed (e.g. Harvey 2007, Ong 2006, Rose 1999), redeploying or re-engineering the state (e.g. Wacquant 2012, Hilgers 2012). However, the coming of this new regime has not meant the materialisation of the features that appeared to characterise the capitalist regime to those gazing from behind the Iron Curtain: welfare, accountability of power, equal opportunities etc. Yet, the obligation of succumbing to neoliberal ethicopolitics has not been rejected even if the associated expectations have not been met. What is more – in the process, the neoliberal state has been freed from the obligation to act ethically towards the citizen. The state, as Nikolas Rose (1999: 144) suggests, sees itself no longer as 'providing' but as 'enabling', creating both organisational and subjective conditions for a particular kind of citizen: an enterprising self. Such enabling, according to Rose, requires very particular features oriented to market freedom and an apparent freedom of entrepreneurial opportunities. On the organisational level,

> de-nationalization of publicly owned enterprises, minimization of rigidities in the labour market; ensuring ample availability of skilled labour; acting against all that which seeks to inhibit the freedom of the market. The subjective conditions: restructure the provision of security to remove as many as possible incitements to passivity and dependency; make the residual support conditional, wherever possible, upon demonstration of the attitudes and aspirations necessary to become an entrepreneur of oneself; incite the will to self-actualize through labour through exhortation on the one hand and sanctions on the other.

The changes on the organisational level have been meticulously applied in Estonia, purporting to be one of the greatest success stories in converting from socialism to capitalism.[2] In fact, whilst the usefulness of the term 'neoliberalism' has recently been questioned in various anthropological outlets (e.g *Focaal* 2008, *Social Anthropology* 2012), Estonia may well present one real example of the 'actually existing neoliberalism' (Collier 2005). In this success story of neoliberalism, Estonia emerged from a Soviet planned economy in the 1990s to become an advanced liberal economy, providing the conditions for the *Homo Economicus* to evolve into a self-sufficient, active individual. As this entrepreneurial self uses the freedom and enabling environment offered by the state for their own advantage, they also advance the state (cf. Rose 1999: 145, 174–5). When some sectors – such as the agricultural population – have fallen hard, they are assumed to have failed the new quest for self-governed, thus free individuals. To explain this failure the finger is habitually pointed at the Soviet mentality that has suffocated people's capacity for freedom and enterprise.

The following chapter intends to tackle three interlinked topics. Based on the data from my 18 months of fieldwork in two ex-state farm villages during the 2000s, I will discuss, firstly, the type and form of enterprising that characterised the Soviet rural inhabitants and propose that the definition of entrepreneurship in common and academic use contrasts the Soviet and neoliberal, post-Soviet circumstances and as a result hides rather than reveals something very significant about neoliberal societies.

---

2   Such measurements are regularly presented in Estonian media, referring to various global hierarchies such as the 'Index of Economic Freedom' by the Heritage Foundation which ranked Estonia in 2013 as the 13th country in the world, ahead of most West and all East European countries (Heritage Foundation 2013).

Secondly, I wish to demonstrate that the rural regions of post-socialist Estonia do not offer a classic example of the process of dispossession where people lose their means of production, subjugating them to pressures from the capitalists acquiring those means. Some of the "dispossessed" may very well have acquired and still own forest, land, property, vehicles and other means of production. However, means of production do not necessarily empower people. Ownership does not convert directly into subsistence, and even less, into stability, but generates inequalities in access and value.

This discussion links with the third topic – unravelling the circumstances after the Soviet collapse in Estonia helps us understand what propels the neoliberal process of dispossession in this stage. Inequalities coupled with a rolled-back yet nationalistically supported state, the ideal of entrepreneurial self-sufficiency, and the distrust of social solidarity, have triggered a remarkable fragmentation of the social fabric. In fact, I propose social dispossession – not in the sense of marginalisation but rather disintegration and separation from one's fellows – is at the very centre of the neoliberal demise in Estonia. This aspect of dispossession has seldom been discussed in anthropological (but see O'Brien 2006, Goode and O'Brien 2006, de la Rocha 2001) and post-soviet literature, leaving people's inability to adequately respond to post-soviet changes a somewhat mystified process.

Soviet and Enterprising

Whilst certainly not a social paradise, accounts of contended Soviet social life both at work and during leisure were common amongst the age-group who were adults during the Soviet period. Rural life was in relatively high public regard in many respects both then and before 1940. In fact, there was bitter pride in all circles, including amongst the dissenting urban intellectuals, for Estonia's position as economically the most successful Soviet republic. Reportedly, between 1987 and 1990, Estonian GNP per capita was USD4,646, far ahead of all other Soviet republics except for Latvia (USD4,582) (Lerman et al. 2002: 4). Agriculture had played an important part in achieving this. Estonia had the highest labour productivity in agriculture in the Soviet Union (Johnson and Brooks 1983: 142); in 1983 Estonian agricultural output in roubles was 12.5 thousand per worker, again more than other Baltic republics and way above the rest of the Soviet Union (Lerman et al. 2002: 6). Soviet milk yields were the highest in Estonia (Johnson and Brooks 1983: 144) and hay yields were one of the highest despite climatic disadvantages (Johnson and Brooks 1983: 104).

People's memories of Soviet Estonian agriculture presented it as the one helping disastrous Soviet agriculture to survive. Stories and anecdotes about both Estonian worker-heroes, as well as those referring to Estonian pork being transported to Moscow whilst 'only screams, tails and ears stayed in Estonia', were common. The pork industry is also pictured in the following joke: 'Q: What is the largest animal in the world? A: Estonian white pig: head and feet are under the counter in Estonia, bottom on the counter in Moscow'. Such jokes contain both criticism of the failed Soviet economy as well as sour pride over the achievements of Estonians, seen to be much better-educated than other Soviet citizens, leading to greater capacity for contributing to modern agriculture. Those stories, strongly implanted in my own memories and revived by my informants in the villages, also contain a description of the centrality of agriculture in this pride.

By the 1970s, the period from which most positive Soviet memories were derived (see also Jõesalu and Kõresaar 2013), life in the countryside had become wealthier than in the urban areas (cf. Creed 1998). This was on the one hand a result of the activities of the 'providing state': wages were higher, farming staff's opportunities to meet their everyday needs (apartments, cars, etc.) and some cultural needs (rural clubs, health resorts, etc.) were greater. On the other hand, some of the opportunities in rural areas had little to do with state provisions: rather, the condition of shortages triggered an enterprising response which was then not curbed, for whatever reason – possibly out of the recognition that such private activities were providing produce that the planned economy was itself unable to deliver. For instance, Lane (1985) estimates that by 1980 in the whole Soviet Union, the private plots represented about 0.05 per cent of the total cultivated area but contributed 49 per cent of potatoes, 15 per cent of vegetables, 14 per cent of meat, 6 per cent of milk, and 6 per cent of eggs.

In conversations about such activities, people, however grateful for the collapse of the Soviet rule, tended to draw contrasts with the present:

> The sellers were all taken together to Leningrad[3] and everything was bought up there ... well but now it is so bad, people have nowhere to put their produce, like those people by the lake, in Mustvee and – they have nowhere to take their onions and all this, we do have produce and that butter and they cannot, they cannot [sell these] ... . This saddens my soul ... (Koidu, 84, Kureste village)

Astrid, now a pensioner, lives with her husband and sister-in-law in Kureste village. In charge of the Soviet time piggery, she used to grow pigs and bulls for selling on the market. She was certainly better positioned to be enterprising in such a way than many; yet, most farmstead dwellers kept a considerable variety of farm animals and used this produce far beyond family sustenance. Those living in apartments had access to small allotments, the only type of land under the private control of the people. Strictly speaking, they were not owned by the people but rented from the *sovkhoz/kolkhoz*, but in reality the ability to make decisions about produce gave this land a special status, which was very similar to viewing it as a private plot. People cultivated these plots with considerably greater dedication than the communal farm land. Crucially, these plots provided a basis not only for strong interdependent relations amongst the locals but also for various urban

---

3   St Petersburg.

relations, which the 'land allotment farmers' would maintain with the help of their harvest. Such activities, commonplace amongst the working-age villagers, were never their only income but they were vital for both social and economic benefits. Indeed, the possibilities for increasing personal wealth were greater in agriculture than in any other branch of the economy during the Soviet period and the villagers were certainly not characterised by unwillingness or inability to be enterprising or to take charge of their own prosperity. The importance of these activities for the social functioning of the villages is only becoming clear decades after the collapse of this system.

The presence of this enterprising spirit is not an isolated example characterising only Soviet Estonia. Several classical sociological studies have demonstrated the capitalist seeds in non-capitalist societies. Secondary economies that existed in most socialist countries offers similar examples: Hann's (2003) overview of Polish, Hungarian and Bulgarian changes suggests an existence of entrepreneurial capacities before the beginning of 'capitalism' in those regions. Some authors redefine what 'capitalists' means in discussing how Eastern Europe made capitalism without capitalists. Eyal et al. (1998) point out that instead of capitalists, bourgeoisie from an earlier era is at the centre of the new processes. Szelényi et al.'s (1988) embourgeoisment thesis suggests a continuation of pre-socialist mentality observable in socialist entrepreneurs' career history. Hann (1980) offers a detailed ethnography of the 'market socialism' in Hungary and Creed (1998) describes the process of 'domesticating' the socialist revolution in Bulgaria with entrepreneurial skills and mind-sets. Even the term 'entrepreneurial selves' has been considered within non-neoliberal environments (e.g. Kipnis 2008, Ong 2006).

Despite such examples of personal entrepreneurial capacities outside neoliberalism, the idea of an entrepreneurial or enterprising self tends to derive its centre from a sense of novelty and connection to a particular economic order. Yet, what is it that is specific to the socialist enterprising individuals, differentiating them from their neoliberal counterparts?

I suggest some of this is purely a matter of ideological definitions that are then given formal status. Whilst registering as an entrepreneur was impossible during the Soviet period and nobody would officially be labelled an entrepreneur, being enterprising, as I have demonstrated, was widespread. Stable work guaranteed social safety and subsistence and enterprising activities offered access to deficit goods, personal prosperity within certain limits, and social networks. In the new era, a particular new form of enterprising is defined and carved out to signal the presence of considerable change: formal entrepreneurial activities become possible and only people who are registered formally as self-employed or who establish an enterprise are defined as entrepreneurs. It is those individuals only who are now seen as enterprising, which now equals entrepreneurial. As a result, those who engaged in profitable activities in the rural regions prior to the Soviet collapse now fall out of such a category – although, admittedly, there are various gradations of this, and the terms '*spekulant*' and '*ärikas*' (both referring to profitable activities that were considered dubious and somewhat exploitative by nature) are still under-researched. However, in the media, statistics or even academic discussions, comparisons between Soviet enterprising activities and neoliberalist 'entrepreneurial selves' do not take into account such shades of grey.

Post-Soviet, Non-Entrepreneurial

Due to this ideological lack of 'entrepreneurs' in the Soviet statistics, and a similarly ideological lack of the category of enterprising individuals beyond self-employed entrepreneurs[4] very little comparative statistical data would allow us to contrast the Soviet enterprising activities with the official entrepreneurship of the post-collapse years. However, interviews I carried out during my fieldwork with middle-aged and older inhabitants, i.e. those who were active in the market in the late 1980s and early 1990s, describe a sharp sense of loss: of opportunities to produce, sell, and be self-reliant.

Before relating to the real experiences of people in the villages, some of the macro-processes need to be explained. Certainly, rural regions were affected differently by the new possibilities for enterprise than towns. In the latter, changes did indeed increase opportunities for trade which were missing before. The discourse of entrepreneurial freedom was high on the agenda of all the parties that were active before the first free elections in 1989 (see Maandi 1995), and rural farms envisaged a return to the golden era of a successful European economy that the media pictured the First Estonian Republic to have been between 1920 and 1940. Yet many declined the possibility of becoming a private farmer (see Alanen et al. 2001), which led to the public conclusion that rural people, mentally debilitated during the Soviet years, were incapable of taking up the challenge of 'being their own masters' (*iseenda peremees olema*), an expression and a capability that has its historic roots in the discussion of the first farmers buying their own farmsteads in the 1860s.

However, this challenge was anything but mental. To start with, becoming a farmer since the late 1980s demanded a different setting than starting to sell filled waffles or burnt caramel cockerels in market stalls, emerging in train stations and high streets in the late 1980s Estonian towns. Those who did start farming, even if they often had just acquired means of production rather than lost them in the process of change now had to face severe structural transformations. Firstly, the loss of the Russian market played an important part: there were no Western consumers hungrily waiting for post-Soviet Estonian produce. Secondly, the disappearance of large-scale buyers, e.g. state and collective farms buying milk from the locals, eventually led to a monopsonistic situation with low procurement prices. Thirdly, the quick dissolution of state farms resulted in different forms of 'grabbing' (of machinery and other movables), especially practised by those in

---

4   Officially, *füüsilisest isikust ettevõtja* or FIE.

more privileged positions due to their access to information and relationships (see Alanen et al. 2001 for a thorough analysis of this process in Estonia). Fourthly, the restitutional land reform of the 1990s tried to generate land ownership not by offering land to the people who had been working it during the Soviet years, but to the original pre-1940 owners, undoing the injustice of the violent 1940s land nationalisation and deportations but creating new injustices which were widely discussed in the Estonian media in the early- and mid-1990s. New landholdings were often small and landowners were not necessarily interested in or skilled at working the land (cf. Szelenyi et al. 1988). Fifthly, there was a deliberate effort to undermine (both in public and in state structures) such disfavoured sectors as agriculture (and even certain industries). Such strategies as dumping the market (e.g. Salum 2001) and stripping away any protective measures were established for agricultural produce,[5] whilst the service and, in particular, financial sectors were privileged. Sixthly, cooperatives, including cooperative banking and machinery exchange arrangements, could have created an 'enabling environment' of mutual support, but without any support to set up and run such schemes they were short-lived (see Leetsar 2003). Finally, in the regional structure where European Union requirements increasingly affected the national and local processes, large-scale farms were much better able to meet EU requirements demanding considerable investments, and to make use of various, often EU-derived funds.

As a result, during my fieldwork in the early 2000s, farming was unusual as a sole means of subsistence in both of the studied villages, Kureste and Saadoja. In Kureste where the reformed *sovkhoz*, now the only large-scale enterprise in the village, dominated access to the buildings and rented most of the private lands, farming seemed particularly scarce as a main activity. Whilst selling the milk produce on to the *kolkhoz* or *sovkhoz* was commonplace during the Soviet years, cow ownership has steadily declined. In the 1990s the villagers had been forced to sell their livestock to abattoirs, and this process has been continuing through most of the post-Soviet years. This was one of the most heart-breaking accounts of the changes that I heard from my informants. When I visited Miili (82) in the local old people's home in Kureste, she matter-of-factly described her life full of loss to me. Her story ran over losing her brother during the Second World War, and her mother shortly after, losing her first born child in the 1950s, her husband in the 1960s, and her grown up son in the 1980s. She finally broke down in tears when describing how, in the 1990s, she had to help her cow onto the abattoir's truck when keeping the animal had become impossible in the new economic climate.

Before the 2000s, milk trucks used to come regularly to villages' 'milk stands' (*piimapukid*) from where the milk of villagers' private cows was collected. These humble stands have become iconic symbols of the bygone era

---

5   Although any support was then discussed as against capitalist development *per se*, in comparison, today, the same political powers support large scale EU assistance to – mostly large scale – agricultural industry.

Figure 5.1   A monument to abandoned milk stands in Luiste village, Estonia

Note: The monument carries the following text: 'There were five milk stands in Luiste village. This one here was the largest, where cow keepers brought more than 1000 litres of milk every day. In 2001, the milk purchasing from the milk stands was discontinued. The milk stand was [also] a source of quick information for the villagers'. Beneath a picture of black and white cows, the text continues: 'The milk truck will come no more'. (Courtesy of Heiko Kruusi)

of a thriving trade: several villages have recently built monuments to the 'milk stands' (Figure 5.1). At the end of the 1990s, abattoir trucks replaced the milk trucks. Whilst in 2001, 31 per cent of households were still keeping a dairy cow, by 2010 this had declined to 17 per cent (Eesti Statistika 2010).

In 2003 only one family in Kureste and another nearby were keeping cows. A few more were growing vegetables and sold their produce to locals. In Saadoja, no cows were in sight. Three families were predominantly engaged in vegetable production and one considered this their main employment, although the wife had many other sources of income. One family was growing grain and rapeseed and a couple of families were active in smaller villages nearby, primarily in meat and dairy farming. Most of the villagers did not buy milk or vegetables from the farmers.

Parallel to the structural changes, however, something even more vital was happening in the villages, affecting the potential of self-sustaining and enterprising. At the age of 70 Astrid, who still came across as dynamic and active, in full possession of knowledge of the market and opportunities then as well as today, and now in possession of her own means of production, was relaying her reasons for giving up enterprise, raising and selling livestock, as related to more than her age:

> I remember how we at first had a very close-knit collective [at the *sovkhoz*], all of us kept together, like really a close-knit family but then when [society] started to stratify and those new directors came [during the reforms], then we were no longer [close-knit]. Some became richer and some became poorer and this was stratifying (*kihistus*) … as soon as they became richer and now, well, yes … .[long pause]
>
> I have been working in piggeries all my life and – I wanted to mill some grain [in the ex-*sovkhoz* mill] – and [the director] does not let me! Does not let me and that's that. […] I told him: Ivo, we have both lived here nearly 50 years and you do not let me mill! And he gave some silly reasons. I was sitting in his car, when we were talking about this – so I told him I won't leave this car [knocks on the table between each word to show how decisive she had been], I will drive with you the whole day if you do not let me mill. Well then he asked how much do you have and I said one tonne. And well he let me mill it. Gave me some piece of paper to take to the miller but I heard that others could not, they had to go [to the neighbouring village]. He did not let [them mill]. (Astrid, 70, Kureste village)

Another story from the same village describes how the director switched off electricity in the barn that had been used by *sovkhoz* workers during the Soviet era to raise calves, goats and chickens. Unable to confront or negotiate with the director who most only saw zooming through the village in his car, limiting his socialising to other entrepreneurs and managers, the locals struggled to continue keeping their animals – but 'still go there using torches' (Laine, 54, Kureste village).

In a much smaller village some distance away, the locals used a drying house a few miles from the village centre to dry their grain in the autumn. The house was communal and people paid into the municipality to use the mill without any restrictions. In the early 2000s Tõnu, a new, rather successful private farmer and politician who did not live in the area bought the drying house, usefully near to the municipal centre and the railway station. Tõnu was asked to continue allowing the villagers to use it – their production had diminished considerably and accommodating the needs of the villagers as well as his own should have been possible. However, soon after acquiring the drying house, Tõnu restricted the villagers' access. Their protests were ignored. They had no means of communal control to influence Tõnu as he was beyond their reach (cf. Hivon 1998).

Those vignettes emphasise the changes in ownership and power even when the possession of means of production and property has increased for many. But it demonstrates also that, under the new conditions, personal relations became rearranged on a different level. In both of those cases, the new entrepreneurs – in one case, with a high position already in the Soviet era – were actively dissociating from the villagers who might interfere with the total control they expected to establish over their newly acquired means of production. But significantly, the successful villagers also preferred and were able to exclude themselves from the rest in daily interactions. They no longer participated in the mutual relations and lacked interest in such reciprocity.

Such circumstances might appear as if they could trigger the need and thus capacity to be self-reliant, and as a result boost the numbers of those self-employed. The reality demonstrates constraints to self-reliance. On the one hand, the percentage of self-employment has steadily been greater in the rural regions than in urban areas. On the other hand, it has never reached over 10 per cent of the rural population in employment (Eesti Statistika n.d). Replacing the lost job with entrepreneurial activities has clearly not become more likely in the new, supposedly favourable, atmosphere. This is well characterised by the story of a widow in her mid-40s, with two children. She had lost her job at the limited company and was hopelessly looking for work both in the village and a nearby town. She had registered as unemployed and had enrolled in courses oriented to the unemployed to increase their entrepreneurial capacity. Yet after having attended a course oriented to teaching her to become self-employed she told me, baffled by the experience:

> What is it that they think I could sell? I am no artist. After learning to do silk painting, I have nothing more in me I can sell – nothing but my readiness to work. But there isn't any [work].

Such struggles cast a different light over the position of freedom to become self-reliant in neoliberal conditions. For the majority of the villagers freedom, including the freedom to be enterprising, has often lessened rather than increased (see also Hann 2006). Previously, they could choose to engage in entrepreneurial activities, but could also carry on working as simple *sovkhozniks* without losing their social guarantees and other opportunities for sustenance. Now, they often lack the option of working as an employee as well as the choice to become self-employed or to sustain their livelihood by being enterprising. Although registering as an entrepreneur was encouraged, being self-employed or a small-scale entrepreneur rarely offered sufficient sustenance to live on. At the same time, registering as self-employed brought considerable personal risk, remarkable administrative duties and an obligation to self-report to various state bodies – all this in return for limited access to certain social services (e.g. healthcare) and for a rarely realised potential for an income above the bare minimum.

Ethnographic examples above appear to depict how 'the actually existing neoliberalism' is 'uplifting and liberating' to those who have managed to climb to take their positions on the 'right hand' of the state, yet 'castigatory and restrictive' to those who have fallen to the bottom, offering work instability, inequality and blame (Wacquant 2012: 73, 74).

Indeed, from these examples, what transpires is one of the key differences between the two socio-political systems under which the villagers have lived. During the Soviet era, enterprise was enveloped within state structures within which risk was minimal and support structures both institutional as well as social. Blame for any failures were, within this system, taken by the carriers of the ideology: the state and the collectives. In contrast, the individual is placed in the centre of the neoliberal order, the internal logic of the enterprising selves is directly linked with the support the neoliberal order requires:

> The notion of enterprise thus entails a distinct conception of the human actor – no longer the nineteenth-century economic subject of interests but an entrepreneur of his or her self. The human beings who were to be governed – men and women, rich and poor – were now conceived as individuals who were *active* in making choices in order to further their own interests and those of their family: they were thus potentially active in their own government. The powers of the state thus had to be directed to empowering the entrepreneurial subjects of choice in their quest for self-realization. (Rose 1999: 142)

However, whilst this process of empowering signals certain freedoms and opportunities, it entails an imbalance that these do not settle. As Nikolas Rose puts it, the individuals in neoliberalism are both 'autonomised' (Rose 1999: 174) and 'responsibilised' (p. 178). As responsibility is laid on the individual, it is removed from the state and the collective bodies, even if those are the sources for both the massive structural changes gripping the individuals and the resulting social grievances affecting the actual availability of freedoms and livelihoods. In a diffuse and decentralised manner the state that places responsibility on the individual creates conditions which are the opposite to empowering.

Crucially, risks and blame, piled on the individuals struggling in response to processes that they cannot control, affect more than people's link with the state structures and trigger a loss of entrepreneurial capacity, rather than increase it. Understanding this process in Estonia requires explaining the interrelated nature of lack of stability, access to social networks and the disappearance of widespread capacity for being that very enterprising self which the neoliberal discourse purports to encourage.

Post-Soviet, Post-Social

Stephen Collier's recent book *Post-Soviet Social* (2011) on Russia is one of the latest ethnographies providing minute details of the profound changes after the collapse of the Soviet Union. Its task is twofold: on the one hand Collier notes the massive changes following the Soviet collapse. On the other hand, he tracks how neoliberal reforms have provided a justification for redistribution and social welfare, and how they have worked to preserve the norms and forms of social modernity characteristic to the region. Resistance to the market was 'not a rapid adjustment to new circumstances but a sustained and painful struggle to preserve existing mechanisms of need fulfilment' (Collier 2011: 133). Collier pits the small cities that he is looking at against the markets and suggests that those 'seemed to embody the battle of markets versus the existing organisation of collective life'. His message is that this has been the battle which the markets have not won, challenging 'the great transformation' story of the post-Cold War world.

This 'iron law of market resistance' (Burawoy and Verdery 1999: 7) has been described by many researchers of the region. They have demonstrated that as the old regime crumbled, various strategies were utilised to retain the old links and relations by those sectors of the society for whom much was to be lost along with the old. And with those old relations, the 'mentalities' survived. Thus, contrary to the descriptions of market reforms as dramatic rupture, detailed ethnographies describe surprising continuities between socialism and post- or market-socialism (Humphrey 1999, Verdery 1996, Ledeneva 1998, Nonini 2008, West and Raman 2009). In many if not most of those depictions of the post-socialist reality, community plays a vital role as the provider of continuity as well as relief from the painful changes that people have had to face. The communal solutions studied include, amongst others, a greater dependence on earlier structures and networks (Humphrey 1999, Verdery 1996), the strength of the community in resisting the new forms of moral economy (e.g. Hivon 1998, Pine 1998, Seabright 2000) and a capacity to reorganise old structures into new 'suzerainties' or communities as strategies of survival in stringent times (Humphrey 1991, Pine 1998). González de la Rocha's (1994) description from Latin America summarises the approach well. As she studies the social networks providing cooperation, mutual help, exchange of services and goods for those hit by the changes, she labels these the 'resources of poverty' which enable a certain level of welfare even during the difficult times. Poverty consolidates and appears to activate the social. Thus, the collapse of the Soviet system would not trigger a total social rupture. Instead, whilst the overarching structures vanish or crash, people would manage to retain their connections, rearrange their systems of mutual help and sources of subsistence. Despite newly appearing inequalities and rapid stratification, people consolidate the relations that had formed during the Soviet time, in some cases tightening their ranks against the outside (Pine 1998).

As my fieldwork suggests, however, the rupture is not always bridged by lasting or renewed social relations, perhaps particularly clearly in the case of neoliberal rule established with greater efficiency (cf. Peck and Theodore 2012: 183). Thus, the centralised villages experienced a more-or-less total collapse of both their economic systems and their social networks. On the one hand, work at the *sovkhoz* was the basis of people's daily social connections, creating in large part relatively equal relations, mutual knowledge and support. On the other hand, the need for acquaintance networks for acquiring goods in the midst of shortages was the second main connecting factor, yet, by nature, somewhat forced, sometimes semi-illicit, often slightly unequal. This nature created the basis of the rejection of some of those relations as soon as the necessity disappeared. Yet it certainly did not atomise people during the Soviet era (cf. Chris Hann 1985). On the contrary, as the accounts above demonstrate, the memories of those years communicate integration, either in response to hardship or simply too tightly-knit lives in the same work collective.

The neoliberal reforms of the 1990s transformed the state farms, and the villages that had been built around these in 1950–1980 to accommodate the agricultural work-force needed.[6] Now, the two villages became the centres of small rural municipalities of about a thousand inhabitants with very few agricultural jobs available. As work vanished, people's capacity to invest in and utilise their social relations, or what Bourdieu (1986) would call their symbolic and social capital, changed beyond recognition. Since the Soviet collapse the most reliable jobs have been linked to the state structure: municipal governments, schools, kindergartens, libraries and rest homes, although even those jobs were in danger: schools were closing all around due to lack of children, municipal structures were in constant fear of profound reforms and amalgamations etc.

In Kureste the reformed *sovkhoz,* now a private enterprise with about 50 workers, offered fairly reliable jobs, although many of those are unskilled, low paid, and often seasonal. In Saadoja, enterprises were even fewer and hired mostly low-paid seasonal agricultural workers. The pay was considerably higher than the rural average only in the government offices and schools, where work was available all year. A few more posts came from the post offices and medical aid stations. As change had been abrupt, many if not most people appeared to have fallen hard and were to some degree sharing the 'fellowship of the flawed' (Herzfeld 1997: 28). In Kureste more people had work, yet within very different salary structures with different guarantees and levels of stability. There, stratification was far more obvious and judging people according to their success more common.

However, a certain negative egalitarianism characterised both villages. The new positions and livelihoods people acquired and the survival strategies they adopted were not simply accepted – people questioned them. Even such a generally respected occupation as teaching was problematised as a manifestation of unfair differences. Most often, people's success was put down to their comfortable positions during the Soviet period, or to kin relations which were seen to have sometimes smoothed people's entry into certain jobs. Both reasons were considered unacceptable.

Work places that previously formed an interrelated system were now separated from one-another and became much more competitive within; schools and nurseries no longer brought together the children of relative equals but had become the rare windows through which people could peek into the increasingly differentiated social conditions of their fellow villagers, with whom they had no work and other social connections. Lack of trust between colleagues as well as between employees and employers was obvious from most conversations I had in the villages.

---

6   Both villages had about 300–400 inhabitants most of whom lived in 2–4 storey apartment blocks built for the *sovkhoz* workers between the 1950s and 1980s.

Withdrawal and unwillingness to engage with others was striking, even if understandable. With their social 'armoury' in tatters, people removed themselves from situations of close contact, created 'fences' and managed inaccessibility (Gullestad 1986) to lessen proximity and the discomfort of displaying their current condition. Although they would have benefited from mutual relations, dependency between villagers with and without means of production had become unidirectional and could easily be rejected by those with resources. People avoided dependency relations even at moments of need and expanded social distance by unfriendliness, exclusion and migration. Stories of asking for as well as offering help were filled with extreme discomfort and feelings of loss of connectedness with fellow inhabitants. The recently developed unequal relations were considered undignified and people often withdrew from such relations rather than establishing them anew (cf. Creed 1998: 265).

At the same time the social services were crumbling and the need for others had become more vital for some. Yet there was no willingness to cooperate or to tackle difficulties together. In solving any common (e.g. sanding the streets or cleaning the village) or personal problems (e.g. transport to hospital, financial needs) people with diminished, crumbling or painful relations preferred to appeal to state resources and structures.

The following offers a telling description of the effects of such changes to entrepreneurial abilities. Selling handicrafts was an activity that supported the small pensions that many elderly people received during the Soviet era. Perhaps even more importantly, this helped maintain social networks and contributing to those as an equal. Today, this is no longer a viable resource for either economic or social benefit. Seventy-five-year-old Maali and her sister knit beautiful socks and mittens as well as various other handiworks. These have lost, however, almost all of their social and trade value. Social value, as disconnected people no longer participate in mutual exchanges of small, sometimes insignificant items: trade – as in a saturated market such local crafts had no competitive value. Reaching the market outside the village where authenticity value could have increased had become a problem in the 'post-social' reality where help between neighbours had become so disagreeable. With no transport to take their crafts to the market, the old ladies presented them to occasional visitors in their home in a desperate display of their unrecognised diligence, skill and effort.

Gerald Creed (2011: 143) describes how in Bulgaria, self-reliance is achieved by subsistence production for which the family unit is reinforced over individual and personal connections. Relations with those better resourced (e.g. tractor drivers) are established through reciprocal assistance and gifts, exchanges and cooperation (2011: 144). In Estonian ex-Soviet centralised villages help was rarely sought, and the response to the lack of likelihood of cooperation was withdrawal, rather than struggle or conflict, as in Creed's Bulgarian account. And although, following Creed's interesting analysis of Bulgarian communities, we could potentially suggest that a withdrawn community is the ideal community in Estonian terms (a conclusion which would not be entirely untrue) it is also obvious that this withdrawal has had very real consequences for people's ability to be self-sufficient and economically autonomous. Being enterprising in such circumstances was simply no longer an option.

The success of being an entrepreneur 'hinges on the extent to which [the entrepreneur] can parlay their social relations into hard currency' (Dolan 2012: 6). If the social relations are fragmented and social interaction divides more than unites, if social capital has been devalued, enterprise becomes a display of the willingness to aspire only (cf. Appadurai 2004), rather than a device of self-realisation, survival or connection.

Through various structural transformations, people were facing immediate changes in their social relations in the villages. Their capacity for enterprise was dissolved in the midst of the loss of mutually beneficial social support networks. These new, 'post-social' relations between villagers had a very important role in destroying the enterprising capacities and the entrepreneurial spirit. The direct loss of means of production has been less significant in this than the less obvious but nevertheless debilitating change in social relations. And further, without the base from which to share and exchange, people could no longer be self-sufficient, nor stand against the pressures of dispossession and exploitation.

Conclusion

This chapter has described how the post-Soviet era has provided few new avenues for self-sufficiency, whilst enabling successful disengagements of the new capitalists from the rest of the population and triggering a massive loss of social linkages which, in turn, has undermined the wide base of relative economic autonomy that characterised Soviet-period rural inhabitants. Although neoliberal condition has been thoroughly discussed, this social effect of neoliberal reality has remained rather understudied. Characteristically, Dunn (2004: 6) has suggested that 'the successful creation of a market economy requires changing the very foundations of what it means to be a person'. Concentrating on the person or, alternatively, on the macro-level changes has left the relational changes in the shade. Yet, a change much more likely to occur within a short time frame is a profound transformation of relations between people, and relations of power and possession. Rather than contrasting the 'dependency' of the socialist-era individuals on state provisions with the liberating and enabling conditions of neoliberalism, this chapter has contrasted the reciprocal ties and needs of an oppressive, economically deficient regime with the fragmented conditions of today's rural regions, where entrepreneurial opportunities have become primarily objects of desire (Comaroff and Comaroff 2000) and disappointment, triggering rapid withdrawal from the social networks, and has considered the role that the neoliberal regime plays in this.

Scholars' efforts to discriminate between Soviet enterprising activities and capitalist "entrepreneurial selves" play into an ideological argument which establishes neoliberal capitalism as the enabling condition for the enterprising spirit and for human potential. This ideological argument contributes to disguising the real daily constraints to self-sufficiency in neoliberalism. It also hides from the view that not delivering the promise of prosperity and equality was the failure of socialism as much as not delivering the promise of prosperity and equal opportunities is the failure of capitalism. Yet, as individuals are at the centre of the latter ideology, the blame for the latter failure, when admitted, is shifted from the state to the individual, allowing the system to continue without serious criticism or alternatives.

The story of success of neoliberalism in Estonia is present in its continuing discourse of the hands-off state that does not even collect its own statistics but can hand this over to competent and willing citizens. This story conceals the reality of a strong state legislating for the benefit of the top layers and against the rest whose main connection with the state is increasingly one where the state is 'omnipresent and strangely absent' (Hilgers 2012: 85): absent from managing any structural constraints that people are facing in the new economic climate, and present to capitalise on any appearance of collective proof of successful and self-reliant citizenry. As the state capitalises on the statistically-proven success to 'govern at a distance', it can also easily dismiss the criticism that is present in the distant past, as missing data on ideologically defined variables of population censuses from two opposing regimes hide the changes that have truly affected the rural population.

References

Alanen, I., Nikula, J., Põder, H., Ruutsoo, R. 2001. *Decollectivisation, Destruction and Disillusionment: A Community Study in Southern Estonia*. Aldershot: Ashgate.

Appadurai, A. 2004. The capacity to aspire: culture and the terms of recognition, in *Culture and Public Action*, edited by V. Rao and M. Walton. Washington, DC: The World Bank, pp. 59–84.

Bockman, J. 2012. The political projects of neoliberalism. *Social Anthropology*, 20(3): 310–17

Bourdieu, P. 1986. The forms of capital, in *Handbook of Theory and Research of Education*, edited by J.G. Richardson. New York: Greenwood Press, pp. 241–58.

Burawoy, M. and Verdery, K. 1999. *Uncertain Transition: Ethnographies of Change in the Postsocialist World*. Lanham: Rowman and Littlefield Publishers.

Collier, S.J. 2005. The spatial forms and social norms of 'actually existing neoliberalism': toward a substantive analysis. [Online]. Available at: http://www.gpia.info/files/u1/wp/2005-04.pdf [accessed: 17 March 2013].

Collier, S.J. 2011. *Post-Soviet Social: Neoliberalism, Social Modernity, Biopolitics*. Princeton: Princeton University Press.

Comaroff, J. 2000. Millennial Capitalism: First Thoughts on a Second Coming. *Public Culture*, 12(2): 291–343.

Creed, G.W. 1998. *Domesticating Revolution. From Socialist Reform to Ambivalent Transition in a Bulgarian Village*. University Park, Pennsylvania: The Pennsylvania State University Press.

Creed, G.W. 2011. *Masquerade and Postsocialism. Ritual and Cultural Dispossession in Bulgaria*. Bloomington: Indiana University Press.

Debate. 2012. *Social Anthropology*, 20(1)–(3).

de la Rocha, G.M. 1994. *The Resources of Poverty: Women and Survival in a Mexican City*. Oxford: Blackwell Press.

de la Rocha, G.M. 2001. From the resources of poverty to the poverty of resources? *Latin American Perspectives*, 28(4): 72–100.

Dolan, C. 2012. The new face of development: The 'bottom of the pyramid' entrepreneurs. *Anthropology Today*, 28(4): 3–7.

Dunn, E. 2004. *Privatising Poland: Baby Food, Big Business and the Remaking of Labour*. Ithaca: Cornell University Press.

Eesti Statistika n.d. Piirkondlik Statistika. [Online]. Available at: http://pub.stat. ee/px-web.2001/Dialog/varval.asp?ma=TT218&ti=H%D5IVATUD+ELUKO HA+JA+H%D5IVESTAATUSE+J%C4RGI&path=./Database/Sotsiaalelu/15 Tooturg/02Heivatud/02Aastastatistika/&lang=2 [accessed 15 February 2013].

Eesti Statistika 2010. Põllumajandusloendus. [Online]. Available at: http://pub. stat.ee/px-web.2001/Dialog/varval.asp?ma=PMS001&ti=LOOMAKASVA TUS+MAJAPIDAMISTES+MAAKONNA+JA+MAJAPIDAMISE+LIIG I+J%C4RGI&path=./Database/Majandus/13Pellumajandus/04Pellumajand uslike_majapidamiste_struktuur/02Loomakasvatus/&lang=2 [accessed 21 January 2013].

Eyal, G., Szelényi, I. and Townsley, E.R. 1998. *Making Capitalism Without Capitalists: Class Formation and Elite Struggles in Post-Communist Central Europe*. London, New York: Verso.

Focaal. 2008. *Forum: Putting neoliberalism in its place(s)*. 51(Summer): 135–60.

Goode, J. and O'Brien, R.T. 2006. Whose social capital? How economic development projects disrupt local social relations, in *Social Capital in the City: Community and Civic Life in Philadelphia*, edited by R. Dilworth. Philadelphia: Temple University Press, 159–76.

Gullestad, M. 1986. Symbolic fences in urban Norwegian neighbourhoods. *Ethnos*, 51(3): 52–70.

Hann, C. 1980. *Tázlár: A Village in Hungary*. Cambridge: Cambridge University Press.

Hann, C. 1985. *Village without Solidarity: Polish Peasants in Years of Crisis*. New Haven: Yale University Press.

Hann, C. 2003. Introduction: Decollectivisation and the moral economy, in *The Postsocialist Agrarian Question: Property Relations and the Rural Question*, edited by C. Hann. Münster: LIT Verlag, 1–46.

Hann, C. 2006. *Not the Horse We Wanted! Postsocialism, Neoliberalism and Eurasia.* Münster: LIT Verlag.

Harvey, D. 2007. *A Brief History of Neoliberalism.* Oxford: Oxford University Press.

Heritage Foundation 2013. *2013 Index of Economic Freedom. Country Rankings.* [Online]. Available at: http://www.heritage.org/index/ranking [accessed: 14 February 2012].

Herzfeld, M. 1997. *Cultural Intimacy: Social Politics in the Nation State.* London and New York: Routledge.

Hilgers, M. 2012. The historicity of the neoliberal state. *Social Anthropology*, 20(1): 80–94.

Hivon, M. 1998. The bullied farmer: social pressure as a survival strategy? in *Surviving Post-socialism: Local Strategies and Regional Responses on Eastern Europe and the Former Soviet Union*, edited by S. Bridger and F. Pine. London and New York: Routledge, pp. 33–51.

Humphrey, C. 1991. 'Icebergs', barter and the mafia in provincial Russia. *Anthropology Today*, 7(2): 8–13.

Humphrey, C. 1999. Traders, 'disorder', and citizenship regimes in provincial Russia, in *Uncertain Transition: Ethnographies of Change in the Postsocialist World*, edited by M. Burawoy and K. Verdery. Lanham: Rowman and Littlefield Publishers, pp. 19–52.

Johnson, D.G. and Brooks K.M. 1983. *Prospects for Soviet Agriculture in the 1980s.* Washington, DC: First Midland Book.

Kipnis, A.B. 2008. Audit cultures: Neoliberal governmentality, socialist legacy, or technologies of governing? *American Ethnologist*, 35(2): 275–89.

Laev, S. 2012. *Jürgen Ligi: e-loendus pakub Eesti elanikele ajaloolise rekordi võimalust.* [Online, 29 January]. Available at: www.fin.ee/rss_uudise. [accessed: 12 February 2012].

Lane, D. 1985. *Soviet Economy and Society.* Oxford: Basil Blackwell.

Ledeneva, A.V. 1998. *Russia's Economy of Favours: Blat, Networking and Informal Exchange.* Cambridge: Cambridge University Press.

Leetsar, J. 2003. *Ühistegevus globaliseeruvas ühiskonnas.* Tartu: Vanemuise Seltsi Kirjastus.

Lerman, Z., Kislev, Y., Kriss, A. and Biton, D. 2001. *Agricultural output and productivity in the former Soviet republics.* [Online]. Available at: http://ideas.repec.org/p/ags/aaea01/20471.html [accessed: 17 March 2013].

Maandi, K. 1995. *Elections and Referendums in Estonia 1989–1995: A Brief Overview.* Tallinn: National Electoral Committee.

Nonini, D.M. 2008 Is China Becoming Neoliberal? *Critique of Anthropology*, 28(2): 145–76.

O'Brien, R.T. 2006. Unemployment and disposable workers in Philadelphia: Just how far have the bastards gone? *Ethnos: Journal of Anthropology*, 71(2): 165–90.

Ong, A. 2006. *Neoliberalism as Exception: Mutations in Citizenship and Sovereignty.* Duke University Press.

Peck, J. and Theodore, N. 2012. Reanimating neoliberalism: process geographies of neoliberalisation. *Social Anthropology*, 20(2): 177–85.

Pine, F. 1998. Dealing with fragmentation: the consequences of privatisation for rural women in central and southern Poland, in *Surviving Post-Socialism: Local Strategies and Regional Responses on Eastern Europe and the Former Soviet Union*, edited by S. Bridger and F. Pine. London and New York: Routledge, pp. 106–23.

Rose, N. 1999. *Powers of Freedom. Reframing Political Thought.* Cambridge: Cambridge University Press.

Salum, M. 2001. Eesti talumees ja tema kanake. *Õhtuleht*, 28/04.

Seabright, P. 2000. *The Vanishing Rouble: Barter Networks and Non-monetary Transactions in Post-Soviet Societies.* Cambridge: Cambridge University Press.

Szelényi, I., Manchin, R., Juhasz, P., Magyar, B. and Martin, B. 1988. *Socialist Entrepreneurs: Embourgeoisement in Rural Hungary.* Madison, WI: University of Wisconsin Press.

Verdery, K. 1996. *What was Socialism and What Comes Next?* Princeton, NJ: Princeton University Press.

Wacquant, L. 2012. Three steps to a historical anthropology of actually existing neoliberalism. *Social Anthropology*, 20(1): 66–79.

West, H.G. and Raman, P. 2009. *Enduring Socialism: Explorations of Revolution and Transformation, Restoration and Continuation.* New York: Berghahn.

Chapter 6

Good Work: State Employees and the Informal Economy in Cuba

Maria Padrón Hernández

Introduction

When people in contemporary Cuba make a living they do so in a market, for labour as well as for consumer goods, which is more diverse than it has been since the socialist revolution of 1959. In late 2010, the Cuban Worker's Union announced that 500,000 state employees were to be laid off in the first months of 2011. These employees, the Union assured, would find new means to make a living in the expanding private economy. New possibilities of formalizing private entrepreneurship were created and, for the first time, these entrepreneurs were allowed to employ workers.[1]

This chapter builds on anthropological fieldwork carried out among state-employees in Havana during eight months in 2006 – the same year Fidel Castro announced that he was in too poor health to continue as the leader of the country. In retrospect, then, this text emerges as an image of the last months of an important phase of the Cuban revolution: the time between the reforms implemented to deal with the economic crisis of the 1990s[2] and the ones being implemented at the time this is written by the new leader, Raúl Castro, in order to 'rationalize' the state economy. In 2006, I would say that *the* fundamental problem faced by people in Havana was that state salaries were insufficient to cover household needs. At the same time, the Cuban economy was structured around salaried work for the state, since laws and regulations created a situation where few other options were legally viable. In other words, the alternatives to income-generation through salaried work were more often than not situated within the informal economy (see Espina Prieto 2004: 224).

---

1   Some employees (who had to be relatives of the license-holder) had previously been allowed in businesses such as private restaurants.

2   Since Cuba was economically dependent on the Soviet Union its fall provoked a deep economic crisis in Cuba called 'the special period in times of peace', or 'special period' for short. The first half of the 1990s is vividly remembered by Cubans as a time of scarcities: frequent power-cuts, empty stores and virtually no public transport, made life very hard for everybody in Havana. In contrast, the 1980s are remembered as a golden age when it was possible to live a 'normal' life and buy what you needed with a state salary.

In this chapter, I will focus on personhood and work by looking at the informal income-generating activities used by state-employees to make a living in Havana in 2006, as well as the moral negotiations surrounding these activities. Being a socialist country situated in the global south in a post-Soviet world, Cuba occupies a strange geography. Relevant questions concern, for example, the context in which research on Cuba should be put as well as the theories that should be used.

Since Cuba is a poor country in the Caribbean, one way to understand income-generating activities is to use theories of development. I will look closer at the so-called livelihoods approach (see, for example, Meikle 2002, Moser 1998, Rakodi 2002) and my main point in this chapter is that the use of such an approach in the Cuban context shows it to be problematic in at least two senses. Firstly, the livelihoods approach fails to give sufficient attention to the limits of resourcefulness and the moral anxieties that surround income-generating activities. Secondly, this approach operates within a very specific view of the self that can have negative theoretical (and political) implications. While it might seem paradoxical at first glance – Cuba is, after all, a socialist country – I will use theories on neoliberal governmentality and personhood to develop this critique. I propose that such theories are 'good to think with' in relation to contemporary Cuba. Not only do they help us understand important complexities and contradictions in everyday economic life; they also help us see ourselves, as scholars, and the sometimes unexpected effects our explanatory models might have.

The chapter will be structured as follows. First, I will develop my critique of the livelihoods approach uncovering the neoliberal self which hides behind it. Secondly, I will explore state-employees' informal income-generating activities in Havana in 2006 through the emic notion of *inventar*, to invent. Of great importance in this analysis will be the abilities needed to *inventar* – creativity, flexibility, risk-taking. This part of my argument will show how the livelihoods-approach may seem like an attractive, intuitive and neat explanatory model. Thirdly, I turn to the moral anxieties that surrounded income-generating activities and which the livelihoods approach is likely to miss. Fourthly, I argue that far from being typical of socialist societies, these moral anxieties are understood as an integral part of the making of personhood in both socialism and capitalism. The difference lies in the way the ethical plurality is solved and the consequences this solution has for personhood. Finally, I return to my main point arguing that models such as the livelihoods approach not only contain an implicit assumption of the enterprising self but fail to acknowledge important moral obligations.

The Livelihoods Approach and the Enterprising Self

The impossibility of relying solely on salaried work and the need to diversify income–generating activities and venture into the informal market is obviously far from unique to Cuba. The so-called 'livelihoods approach' has been devised within development studies as a way to deal with situations where people's incomes cannot be measured by their pay-checks.

Conventional poverty analyses using a 'poverty line' – that is, a minimum income which separates poor from non-poor people – focus on income-levels which are both difficult to measure (informal incomes are often excluded) and insufficient in order to evaluate the material lives of the people in question (non-monetary incomes might be important). Proponents of the livelihoods approach try to address these problems by taking a broader view of economic life. Rakodi (2002: 3) cites Chambers and Conway: 'a livelihood is defined as comprising "... the capabilities, assets (including both material and social resources) and activities required for a means of living"'. The unit of analysis is the household and instead of a negative view focusing on what households lack, the focus lies on what they *have* and what they actually *do* in order to secure their livelihood. Scholars using this approach thus talk about households' *assets* and *strategies*.

Within the livelihoods approach, assets are commonly classified as financial, natural, physical, human or social (Meikle, 2002: 46–7, Rakodi 2002: 11). Assets are part of households' 'asset portfolio' (Moser 1998, Rakodi 2002) and people are described as 'managers' of these portfolios (Moser 1998: 1). Overall the language used is highly economistic, and Moser (1998: 5), for example, quotes Corbett to tell us that: '... households select from a range of nutritional, economic and social responses available to them with sequencing "the product of a number of complex (through largely intuitive) calculations concerning the feasibility, relative costs and expected return of each option, both immediately and for the future"'.

Elsewhere (Padrón Hernández 2012) I have argued that, with some adjustments, the livelihoods approach is a useful model through which we may understand the diversification of income-generating activities in Cuba. As we shall see in the discussion of the emic notion of *inventar*, a focus on assets is in accordance with how people in Havana express what is needed to generate an informal income. However, in this chapter I will shift focus. Instead of searching for explanatory models through which we may understand how people in Havana make a living, I will look at how the application of explanatory models such as the livelihoods approach may (i) obscure the moral anxieties around the abilities needed to *inventar* and (ii) implicate scholars in the making of personhood by promoting the enterprising self.[3]

Nikolas Rose and Peter Miller highlight work as an important site through which to study governmentality and personhood. They argue that: 'For the last century, ways of thinking about and acting on work have been fully engaged with the philosophical question of what kinds of persons human beings are. Work has been a key site for the formation of persons' (Miller and Rose 2008: 174). Miller and Rose have looked at contemporary capitalist societies in Western Europe and

---

3   My critique of the livelihoods approach is not the only one. Wolf (1990) has pointed out that the concept of household strategies obscures intra-household conflict, treats households as rational beings and fails to give attention to people's own voices.

the US finding the 'enterprising self' to be the prime image of what kind of beings we are, at work as well as elsewhere. 'Energy, initiative, ambition, calculation and personal responsibility' (Rose 1998: 154) are the rules by which subjects in late capitalism conduct their everyday lives.

In Emily Martin's writings, neoliberal personhood serves as a powerful image shaping not only how we see ourselves in our working lives, but also how we describe the immunological system (Martin 1994) and how we understand manic depression (Martin 2007). Martin argues that personhood in late capitalism is fundamentally flexible where persons are imagined as mini-corporations, 'collections of assets that must continually be invested in, nurtured, managed, and developed' (Martin 2000: 582). Martin's mini-corporations and Rose's enterprising selves are similar in their representation of persons as rational actors continuously changing themselves, many times with the help of experts, in order to become the autonomous, free, entrepreneurial, competitive beings they imagine themselves to be.

The view of the person hidden in the livelihoods approach is a carbon copy of this 'enterprising' self. Martin and Moser echo each other when they talk about portfolios or collections of assets that are continuously managed by rational calculating individuals. This is nothing more than a *homo economicus*, rationally using and combining material and non–material assets in order to yield a profit and make a living. It is also a neoliberal (or late capitalist) version of the *homo economicus*, endlessly adaptable and flexible, always doing things to get by, always finding new ways to make a living and always creative in her use of what resources she has access to.

At least in its substantivist vein, economic anthropology has counteracted such views of the self by emphasizing persons as social moral beings and, since Polanyi, pointed at the embeddedness of economy in other areas of life. The study of 'other' pre/non-capitalist societies has been a way for economic anthropology to formulate a powerful critique of conventional economic theory and modern capitalism (Wilk and Cliggett 2007: 171–2). The problem of this critical ambition is that is has led scholars to be as unfair to the complexities of the world as the conventional economic theories it sought to correct. I am not the first to point out that emphasizing morality to the point of forgetting calculation is just as problematic as doing the opposite.[4] My ambition here is, therefore, to combine critical ambition with attention to both calculation and morality. Thinking in terms of assets and calculation only show us part of the picture and has to be complemented with, but not replaced by, descriptions of the moral negotiations which infuse economic everyday life.

This aim of counteracting a dichotomous view of morality and economy might, however, be especially hard when studying Cuba. Both emic notions and politico-

---

4 For a detailed critique see Bloch and Parry (1989), Browne (2009), Gudeman (2001), Humphrey and Hugh-Jones (1992), Medick and Warren Sabean (1984), Miller (2001), Zelizer (2005).

economic traditions in Cuba reproduce the dichotomy I want to question. Issues of maximization and solidarity have, in fact, a long history in Cuba. The so-called Great Debate took place in Cuba in the 1960s and to a large extent it revolved around whether incentives to work should be material or moral.[5] Advocates for material incentives tended to lean more towards the Soviet model and argued that Cuba had to retain capitalist elements in its organization of the socialist economy. This was necessary, they argued, in order to create the right material conditions for communism – especially considering Cuba's state as an underdeveloped country. The other side argued that a socialist consciousness was paramount for creating the conditions for communism. Retaining capitalist elements would be fostering a capitalist mentality that could only be negative in the long run and Latin American dependency theory was used to argue that Soviet 'help' would threaten national independence. Intimately linked to the position favouring moral incentives was Guevara's vision of the 'new man', largely defined by his or her willingness to work for the good of society rather than for individual gain (see Guevara 1965). The different changes in Cuban economic policy since the 1960s, where market mechanisms have been introduced or excluded (such as the private agricultural markets introduced 1980, closed down in 1986 and re-opened in 1994), have all made reference to this debate. Thus, the dichotomy expressed in the Great Debate is still present both in official discourse, in emic notions about work-ethic and, as we will see below, it echoes in the moral negotiations surrounding income-generating activities. In Cuba, as in Europe and the US, work has been a key site for the formation of persons.

But the dichotomies of morality/economy and solidarity/calculation are not the only ones that have to be questioned and transcended in the case of Cuba. Being a socialist country Cuba is an example *par excellence* of an economic and political 'other' which, as argued by Yurchak (2005), is often understood in binary terms. Several authors (see for example Brotherton 2008, Smith and Stenning 2006, Yurchak 2005) have argued against clear-cut divisions between capitalism and socialism, pointing instead at the contradictions in *all* societies and economic systems. In fact, tensions, anxieties and fears seem to surround the entrepreneurial spirit in both capitalism and socialism.

Zelizer's (2005) work on modern USA shows how there is a persistent scepticism towards economy *in certain areas of life*. Intimacy and economy, Zelizer (2005: 32–5) argues, are considered 'separate spheres and hostile worlds' so that calculation is only celebrated as long as it does not invade intimate spheres and relationships. Rose, with reference to Weber and his different 'spheres of existence', also points out an ethical plurality in contemporary western society. At the same time, Rose argues, the solution to the tensions created by this plurality

---

5   See Mesa-Lago (1972), Kapica (2000: 132–9) and Gordy (2006: 390–91) for more about the Great Debate. Kapica is particularly interesting since he shows how the two positions represent two different visions of *cubanía* (Cuban national self-image) that have surfaced in Cuban history since colonial times.

is situated in the individual with the help of experts such as psychologists, life coaches, self-help services and HR-departments. Rather than becoming a threat to the entrepreneurial self, these tensions are solved by using this self in *all* spheres of life. In the words of Rose (1998: 157): '[T]he new experts of the psyche promise that modes of life that appear philosophically opposed – business success and personal growth, image management and authenticity – can be brought into alignment and achieve translatability through the ethics of the autonomous, choosing psychological self'.

I will now turn to a description of informal income-generating activities through the notion of *inventar* to see how the livelihoods approach is, at first glance, an attractive one in the case of Cuba. Then I will return to the question of ethical plurality by looking at the moral negotiations which infuse everyday economic life in Havana.

Inventar

The emic notion of *inventar* (to invent) and the related terms *resolver* and *luchar* (resolve and struggle respectively) have received attention by various scholars studying Cuba (see Gordy 2006, Powell 2008, Rosendahl 1997: 175, 2001: 93, Weinreb Rosenberg 2009: 65–82). According to anthropologist Mona Rosendahl (2001: 93), *inventar* 'refers to all activities and transactions in which people used their imagination to find solutions to the lack of food, clothing and other necessities'. This definition is in accordance with how it was used by the people I spoke to: *inventar* was about finding solutions to specific problems, identifying opportunities to make a living and having the skills necessary to take hold of them.

Informal possibilities of material gain could be found unexpectedly and suddenly, and being able to see them and carry them through was a much valued trait. During my fieldwork – in which I hoped to learn more about the mystery of how people managed to get by – I could sometimes walk away after a two-hour interview without actually being able to describe how the household made a living. It seemed like some people survived by pure coincidence and I could only repeat the words of one of them: 'Something always comes up'. While this total reliance on unexpected opportunities was not that common – most had employments or businesses that had at least a couple of months' duration and on which they relied at the time of the interview – it was true for most unskilled workers, at least in a long-term perspective. Many people, especially those without a higher education, had no stable and reliable solution to their livelihood which lasted from one year to the other. To get by under these circumstances required a lot of the person's creativity, flexibility and street-smarts.

Historically, *inventar* has been a very useful ability described in numerous studies of the poor in Havana before and immediately after the revolution (see Butterworth 1980, Calderón González and Loy Hierro 1970, García Alonso 1968, Lewis, Lewis and Rigdon 1977a, 1977b, 1978). In other words, it is not something new but has been important to Cubans at various points in modern history when faced with difficult economic situations. As the saying in both Spanish and English goes: necessity is the mother of invention (*La necesidad es la madre de la invención*). Rosendahl (2001: 100–101) makes the following statement about the special period when the ability to *inventar* was absolutely crucial for the livelihoods of people in Havana:

> In Cuba, external circumstances have been important factors in triggering the economic activities of the special period, but these activities often *reactivated or strengthened already existing relationships, norms and networks*. The informal activities became less important during a time when the standard of living was high and the state could provide; the second economy was a way of supplementing what was received from the planned economy. During the special period, however, when scarcity became 'normal', people turned to the cultural values of reciprocity, patronage, inventing (*inventar*), resolving (*resolviendo*) and trust (*confianza*). ... Flexibility and the skill of seizing the moment, which has always been important in times of scarcity, became a necessity for many Cubans. (Rosendahl, 2001: 100–101, first emphasis mine)

Many visitors to Cuba are amazed by and celebrate the population's creativity when it comes to finding solutions to everyday problems. Examples of such creative solutions are making a satellite dish (for receiving US TV-stations) with an aluminium tray, repairing cars without spare parts and, ultimately, getting by without a sufficient stable income. Mexican anthropologist Mercedes González de la Rocha (2001) has criticized too enthusiastic celebrations of the informal market and the 'resilience' of people living in difficult economic circumstances. More specifically, she has emphasized the importance of salaries and employments as a prerequisite for other income-generating activities. With her fieldwork in urban Mexico in mind, González de la Rocha points to employments as crucial since the stable and fairly high salaries associated with them make other income-generating activities possible. In the Cuban context of low salaries, her critique is still important, but we must be attentive to *other* ways of benefitting from employments. I would argue that, in Havana, employments were seen as opening up important possibilities to informal income–generation.

When my interlocutors spoke about an employment and evaluated it, the salary was often much less important than the other opportunities for material gain this could lead to. In Havana in 2006 employments could be used in several ways. First, there were the formal non-monetary rewards for salaried work. Roberto worked as a custodian and received a monthly shopping bag with attractive hard-currency[6] goods such as cooking oil, chicken and soap. Other employments included a snack

---

6   Cuba has a dual-currency economy with important goods sold in hard currency while state salaries are almost exclusively paid in soft currency. This is one of the reasons why state salaries are unable to cover household needs.

– a baguette with ham and cheese and a can of soda – which had generated a whole informal economy of middle-hands passing by workplaces to buy snacks and then re-selling them in the street. Informal taxis in Havana often had plates indicating that the car belonged to the state, which meant that the person moonlighting as a taxi-driver was using a car he had access to as part of his employment. All these privileges could thus either be enjoyed directly by the employee or sold and converted to money. Rather than seeing this money as part of the salary, it was the result of informal income-generating activities conducted in parallel with, and thanks to, the employment.

Second, if the employment meant a position of power over or control of important information, knowledge or skills, it could also generate material benefits such as gifts. Employees of state bureaucracy or public health exemplify people who received gifts from clients and patients at a more or less regular basis (see also Andaya 2009, Rosendahl 2001: 95). In both cases these employees cater the needs of people in desperate situations of bureaucratic pressure or ill health, and in both cases the clients are willing to give gifts in order to show their gratitude, establish strategic relations, skip long waiting hours or be taken care of with extra considerations. The following was related to me by a nurse at a waiting room in a polyclinic attending Cubans. She had worked at a gynaecological division and one day a young pregnant woman arrived desperate to skip the queue. The nurse described the woman as a *jinetera* (a word often used to talk about sex-workers) with an Italian boyfriend:

> She offered me money. Lots of it. But I refused: 'Take that away. Are you crazy! I can lose my job and I can't afford that. If I help it's because I want to. Because you are in a difficult situation and deserve help. Not because you give me things'. I helped her and the following day she came back with a shopping bag full of food and things: 'I know you don't want anything but you were good to me and I want to help you in the same way. Because I just feel like it and don't give a damn (*porque me sale de la papaya*). Not in order to pay anything'.
>
> I helped her during the whole pregnancy and was at her side during the delivery. The whole time she bought me and my children things: clothes, shoes, food. Finally she migrated to Italy and when she came back to visit she invited me to dinner and brought all kinds of things to my children: toys, clothes, shoes … everything! To me she brought, amongst other things, a bikini that I use to this day. It's very nice, Italian. She said she had chosen to do it because of what I had said that first day: 'I noticed that you wouldn't take advantage of me, that you weren't a shameless jerk (*una descarada*). You helped me and I helped you'. Then she returned to Italy and I've never heard from her since.

In this narrative the nurse – carefully portraying herself as helping others without material interests – follows her patient through pregnancy and delivery almost like a private nurse. This is not uncommon for doctors and nurses, who regularly follow patients informally through their convalescence, with home visits and personalized care. At times, the rewards are ample and I have even heard stories about doctors inheriting old people's houses for helping them during their last years in life.

Since bribing is strictly forbidden and heavily punished if brought to light and since there are emic notions about interpersonal relations as ideally free from economic interests, gifts are given in subtle ways. For example, it is common for people to hand over the gift after the service has been completed – as in the narrative above – and maybe also at the person's house. The exchange of gifts for services is also more likely to occur between people who know each other or who at least have an acquaintance in common.[7]

In other words, social relations are highly important and this is the third way in which formal employments are important for informal income-generation. Employments give access to valuable social networks opening up for opportunities to exchange all kinds of material and non-material wealth. The workplace itself could, for example, mean a good market for informal petty trade with stable clients and relative security. Selling coffee or snacks at a daily basis at one's workplace was fairly common but sales of a more irregular nature could also be conducted at work.

Last but certainly not least the employment could give access to valuable goods that could be 'gotten hold of' by the employee (see Rosendahl 2001: 96). For example, working as a chef was considered a very good job since it meant the possibility of taking home foodstuffs, mainly for the household to consume but also for selling – food being *the* most sought after product in the informal market. While the state actors certainly conceptualized this as stealing of state property, the word *robar* (to steal) was only used by the people I spoke to when criticizing state salaries. In that case *robar* was used rhetorically: 'when paying low salaries the state forces people to actually steal' – something that, of course, was seen as both hypocritical and immoral on part of the state.

Looking only at the income-generating activities used by people in Havana, it is easy to see how the livelihoods approach could provide a good explanatory model. This is especially so since the approach fits so well with emic narratives of *inventar* as seizing the moment and making something of the things that 'always come up'. Also, it is easy for Euro-American scholars to think in terms of assets precisely because, as pointed out by Miller, Rose and Martin, this is the way people in Europe and the US are encouraged to think about themselves. Another feature that makes it attractive is that it provides us with a neat list of types of assets with which to classify the chaotic wheeling and dealing in the

---

7 Similarities with practices in Eastern Europe during and after socialism abound. See Ledeneva (1998, pp. 39–42) for a discussion of the similarities and differences between gifts and bribes in Soviet Russia. See Pawlik (1992) for a description of gift-giving in socialist Poland and Makovicky (2008) for a discussion of gift-giving to doctors, teachers etc. in contemporary Slovakia.

informal economy. However, while it certainly contains more than a grain of truth – people in Havana often act as mini-corporations in the informal market – the question is what this deceptively simple and intuitive model hides and, ultimately, what it does. I argue that it hides the contradictions, strains and moral anxieties that people in Havana experience and which present a different view of the self. I will turn to these moral aspects of economic life now.

Morality in Economic Life

Being able to *inventar* is an art surrounded with mixed feelings. On the one hand it was celebrated and seen as typical of people in Havana (see also Weinreb Rosenberg 2009: 65 and Powell 2008: 187); on the other hand the need to *inventar* was born out of a deeply stressful situation of material scarcity and insecurity where solutions always depended on the possibilities of the moment and where planning was almost impossible (see for example Solberg, 1996: 50). Inventing in order to make a living could also easily become cheating others in the informal market which created an undercurrent of moral anxieties. In the words of Powell, ' ... the ability to *inventar, resolver, luchar* as part of the daily work of social reproduction – as well as offering opportunities for individual advancement – has become a capacity which is both essential and permeated with anxieties' (Powell, 2008: 182). This is reflected in the many uses of the word. Besides the above connotation, it was used to describe adulterated products. Coffee-powder diluted with *too much* toasted and ground yellow peas was, for example, *un invento* (an invention). In this case the person selling the coffee certainly had invented a way to make more money by diluting the powder, but it had been done at the expense of the buyer. The flexibility, intelligence and creativity had been abused. To quote Powell again, 'celebrations of the capacity to *inventar, resolver, luchar* overlook the immense strain on the very social relations which underpin this economy of practices' (Powell, 2008: 187).

When speaking about taking things from work, *llevar* (take away) or *conseguir*[8] (to get hold of) were the preferred terms. These words lacked the strong moral force of *robar* (to steal) and instead expressed a necessity and something 'everybody' did. When pressing the issue, it was argued that the moral breach had already been done by the state. The people I spoke to reasoned that by paying insufficient salaries, the state failed to fulfil its obligation to provide for its citizens. In other words, getting hold of things from one's workplace was

---

8   Other authors, for example Weinreb Rosenberg (2009: 72–5) and Rosendahl (1997: 43) have analyzed several different meanings given to the word *conseguir*. Here only one of those will be dealt with: the way it is used in relation to 'getting hold of' things from workplaces. See also Ledeneva (1998: 13) on the Russian word *dostal* used similarly in Soviet Russia and Firlit and Chłopecki (1992) on 'lifting' in socialist Poland, including a thorough discussion of the differences between 'lifting' and theft.

just a way to make up for the low salary. In the following excerpt from my field-diary, Sara tells me about a disturbing phone call from her godmother:

Sara: She was crying, poor thing ...

Maria: Why?

Sara: Well you see, she is not working now and neither is her husband and it seems like her knee has been swollen for a couple of days.

Maria: Oh ... How come she lost her job? Did they fire her?

Sara: No. The thing is she had been working at a laundry for many years. It was a good job because she could take (*llevarse*) detergent ... You know how it is ... But then they had to make cut-downs and she was sent to another laundry too far away from her home. It didn't include transportation[9] and she couldn't leave her little daughter for more than a few hours with her grandmother. So she said no and now she's filling in all the paperwork asking them to give her work closer to where she lives. Her husband also had a good job. He worked in a hotel kitchen but they too had to do reductions and since he was just substituting for a regular employee he was one of the first to go. And that job was good because he worked in a buffet and at the end of the day they got the leftovers and distributed amongst them. All of them, even the chef. And you know that the most difficult thing here is the food.

When Sara talks about these people's employments she classifies them as 'good' and in both cases she does so with reference to the possibilities they offer to get hold of valuable goods, namely food and detergent. The salaries are not even mentioned. With small comments like 'you know how it is' and 'even the chef' the moral dubiousness of the behaviour of the people in the story is countered with reference to the economic situation and how generalized this practice is. Sociologist Alena Ledeneva has studied informal exchange in the Soviet Union and lists 'people's excuses' (1998: 70–71) for engaging in this practice. Common sense and references to necessity, shortage, scarcity, and social conventions are the ones that echo Sara's above.

Note, however, that things got more complicated when the goods employees got hold of were taken more directly from customers rather than from the state. Susana told me happily that her boyfriend had offered to get her a job at a nearby school-canteen: 'I asked him if there was any chance of taking home

---

9   Cheap organized bus-rides between the house/neighbourhood and the work-place is a common privilege connected to employments. Given the crowded, irregular and unreliable nature of Havana's public transport it is highly valued.

some chicken or anything and he said yes!' The next time we spoke her daughter Yanelis was visiting and Susana had broken up with her boyfriend:

> Susana: Let me tell you something to see what you think about it. Yesterday I quarrelled with my boyfriend because of something Yanelis said. Remember I told you he offered to get me a job at a school?

> Maria: Yes?

> Susana: Well, I told Yanelis about it and she said something that really made me think. 'Mommy', she told me, 'please don't steal in places where there are children and old people. I think about my daughter [Susana's granddaughter] and imagine somebody taking away what little chicken or the few eggs they give at school'. I thought a lot about that and I believe she's right. I think that's wrong and so I went to his house and told him that. He got mad and told me he cannot be thinking about these things, he lives with his old parents and has to get hold of what he needs and I left him like that, in mid-sentence. I asked him to think about it and tell me [what he planned to do about it] the next day.

> Yanelis: I wouldn't be thinking the way I do if it wasn't for my daughter but just imagining that they take away what little food they give her ... If she [Susana] steals at a hotel I don't care because there is lots of food there. And if it's grown-ups it's not the same thing, but children and the old ... There are so little resources there and they barely give rice, beans and eggs, a little bit of chicken once a week and that's that. And not all kids can eat at home either. They need what little food they get at school.

In this narrative, taking things from the workplace is not the problem *per se*. It is stealing food from needy children that is questioned as immoral and contrasted rhetorically with stealing food from rich adult tourists in a context where state resources seem to be channelled to the latter. Taking things from the state was, again, just compensating for the unjust salaries but taking things from other people was more complicated in a moral sense.

Within the livelihoods approach we are encouraged to view interpersonal relations explicitly as 'social assets' when it comes to income-generation. This is contrary to emic notions about morality. According to these notions, the pursuit of material gain threatens the obligations inherent in social relations since intimacy and solidarity should be strictly separated from material interests and money. In the nurse's narrative above she repeatedly stressed the fact that she helped her patient *without interest* and it seemed like it was precisely this disinterestedness that was amply rewarded materially.

As mentioned above, Rose and Miller identify work as a key site in which questions of personhood are articulated. In Havana, I argue, the moral anxieties associated with informal income-generating activities reveal scepticism towards commercial activities, calculation and the making of profit. These might be necessary in order to diversify incomes by venturing into the informal economy but could become too much and spiral out of control[10] thus threatening the social fabric of solidarity. The everyday moral negotiations described above are attempts to check the entrepreneurial spirit by appealing to social obligations and moral values. Through these negotiations a different view of the person is put forward, namely a social and moral being motivated not only by the maximization of profit but also by a will to do good (or at least not to do harm).

There is a trend in accounts of post-Soviet Cuba where moral anxieties such as these are described as typical of socialism. These are the ruptures, it is argued, that occur when socialist utopia clashes with capitalist reality or when 'old' socialist values have outlived their time. For example, Cubans are described as 'experiencing a dissonance between their personal values and the strategies they employed in order to earn a living informally or illegally' (Weinreb Rosenberg, 2009: 6, see also Eckstein 2003: 25–6).

I break with this trend in two ways. Firstly, by arguing that far from being ineffective rationalizations, the moral negotiations described above were effective in the sense that most employees did find ways to use their employments that did not come into conflict with their conscience. In this way the moral standard of the person, created precisely through these on-going negotiations in everyday encounters, shaped the income-generating activities which she or he engaged in. My interlocutors often complained about people doing anything for material gain but they never described themselves in that way. The reason they engaged in moral negotiations was not in order to justify their behaviour or bitterly point at the ways in which they were forced to hypocrisy, but precisely in order to find good strategies. While complaining about the hardships and scarcities of everyday life and lamenting the need to break laws, people spoke about their specific income-generating activities without shame or bad conscience. Breaking the law was not the same thing as being immoral and while their strategies could often be illegal they were 'good' strategies both in an economic and moral sense.

Secondly, I want to question the simple dichotomization of socialism versus capitalism in labelling these anxieties as typical of socialist societies. As argued above, the entrepreneurial self is surrounded with tensions and anxieties in capitalist societies as well. But while Rose (1998: 157) shows how these tensions are solved by expanding the enterprising self to all spheres of life in the societies studied by him, this does not seem to be the case in Cuba. In Cuba the tensions surrounding the entrepreneurial self are solved by negotiating morality so as to strike a balance between calculation and moral values – both of them

---

10   Besides these moral anxieties there are other aspects at play here, for example status and the construction of distinction and class. For a university graduate, street peddling is seen as shameful, even though it might be more lucrative than an employment. For more about this see Padrón Hernández (2012).

needed to do good work. While the neoliberal solution to ethical plurality never becomes a threat to the ethics of the enterprising self the Cuban solution could become such a threat.

In other words, the moral negotiations dealt with in this chapter can be seen as a continuous problematization of the entrepreneurial self by putting forward the moral self. By applying a livelihoods approach we not only fail to acknowledge these local processes of the making of personhood but risk intervening in these processes by promoting a very particular view of the self as a mini-corporation.

Conclusion

Paradoxically perhaps, theories on neoliberal personhood and governmentality have proven useful in understanding contemporary Cuba. The reasons for this are twofold. First, rather than starting from an assumption about what human beings are like, these theories explore the making of the self, especially in the area of work. Second, attention is given to the contradictions, ethical pluralities and anxieties which characterize human life in both socialism and capitalism. Because of this, they help us break apart the dichotomization of morality/ economy as well as socialism/capitalism and open up for a reflexive critique of the ways in which scholars, particularly scholars from western Europe and the US, participate in the making of personhood.

Instead of choosing between portraying people in Havana as either enterprising selves or moral selves, the ethnography in this chapter presents a complex picture. On the one hand the enterprising self is increasingly needed in order to make a living in the informal market as wages lose their ability to fulfil household needs; on the other hand this self is effectively questioned and moderated through intense moral negotiations in relation to income-generating activities. Far from being typical of socialist societies, as is sometimes argued in the literature about Cuba, strains, contradictions and fears surround the enterprising self in capitalism too. Rose shows how these contradictions are solved in capitalist societies by applying the enterprising self to *all* spheres of life. This serves not only to solve the ethical strains experienced by particular individuals but also effectively hinders these strains from turning into a questioning of neoliberal personhood. I argue that the solution to the ethical plurality in Cuba is, instead, sought in the on-going moral negotiations I have highlighted here through which people find ways to be good human beings doing good work. In contrast to the situation described by Rose these negotiations offer a critique of the entrepreneurial self and a counter-image: the self as a social and moral human being balancing calculation with solidarity.

Returning to my main point I argue that models such as the livelihoods approach not only fail to acknowledge these important moral negotiations but contains an implicit assumption of the self as a mini-corporation managing a portfolio of assets. The simplified picture of reality which these types of explanatory models generate emerges as the lesser problem compared to the ways in which these models implicate scholars in the 'changing of souls', to quote the introduction to this volume. Rather than describe and analyse the on-going moral negotiations through which personhood is shaped in Cuba models such as the livelihoods approach participate in this negotiation by promoting the enterprising self and muting the moral self.

References

Andaya, E. 2009. The gift of health: socialist medical practice and shifting material and moral economies in post-Soviet Cuba. *Medical Anthropology Quarterly*, 23(4): 357–74.

Brotherton, S.P. 2008. "We have to think like capitalists but continue being socialist": Medicalized subjectivities, emergent capital, and socialist entrepreneurs in post-Soviet Cuba. *American Ethnologist*, 35(2): 259–74.

Butterworth, D. 1980. *The People of Buena Ventura: Relocation of Slum Dwellers in Post-revolutionary Cuba*. Urbana and London: University of Illinois Press.

Calderón González, J. and Loy Hierro, A. 1970. *Amparo: millo y azucenas*. Havana: Casa de las Américas.

Eckstein, S. 2003. Diasporas and dollars: transnational ties and the transformation of Cuba. *The Rosemarie Rogers Working Paper Series 16*. The Inter-University Committee on International Migration.

Espina Prieto, M. 2004. Social effects of economic adjustment: equality, inequality and trends toward greater complexity in Cuban society, in J. Domínguez, O.E. Pérez Villanueva and L. Barberia (eds), *The Cuban Economy at the Start of the Twenty-first Century*. Cambridge, MA: Harvard University Press, pp. 209–43.

Firlit, E. and Chłopecki, J. 1992. When Theft is Not Theft, in J.R. Wedel (ed.), *The Unplanned Society: Poland During and After Communism*. New York: Columbia University Press, pp. 95–109.

García Alonso, A. 1968. *Manuela la Mexicana*. Havana: Casa de las Américas.

González de la Rocha, M. 2001. From the resources of poverty to the poverty of resources? The erosion of a survival model. *Latin American Perspectives*, 28(4): 72–100.

Gordy, K. 2006. "Sales + economy + efficiency = revolution"? Dollarization, consumer capitalism, and popular responses in special period Cuba. *Public Culture*, 18(2): 383–412.

Ledeneva, A.V. 1998. *Russia's Economy of Favours: Blat, Networking and Informal Exchange*. Cambridge: Cambridge University Press.

Lewis, O., Lewis, R.M. and Rigdon, S.M. 1977a. *Four Men: Living the Revolution – An Oral History of Contemporary Cuba*. Urbana and London: University of Illinois Press.

Lewis, O., Lewis, R.M. and Rigdon, S.M. 1977b. *Four Women: Living the Revolution – An Oral History of Contemporary Cuba.* Urbana and London: University of Illinois Press.

Lewis, O., Lewis, R.M. and Rigdon, S.M. 1978. *Neighbors: Living the Revolution – An Oral History of Contemporary Cuba.* Urbana and London: University of Illinois Press.

Makovicky, N. 2008. The Object of Morality: Rethinking Informal Networks in Central Europe, in H.G. West and P. Raman (eds), *Enduring Socialism: Explorations of Revolution and Transformation, Restoration and Continuation.* New York: Berghahn Books, pp. 103–24.

Martin, E. 1994. *Flexible Bodies: Tracking Immunity in American Culture from the Days of Polio to the Age of AIDS.* Ipswich: Beacon Press.

Martin, E. 1999. Flexible survivors. *Anthropology Newsletter*, 40(6): 5–7.

Martin, E. 2000. Mind-body problems. *American Ethnologist*, 27(3): 569–90.

Martin, E. 2007. *Bipolar Expeditions: Mania and Depression in American Culture.* Princeton: Princeton University Press.

Meikle, S. 2002. The Urban Context and Poor People, in C. Rakodi and T. Lloyd-Jones (eds), *Urban Livelihoods: A People-centered Approach to Reducing Poverty.* London: Earthscan, pp. 37–51.

Miller, P. and Rose, N. 2008. *Governing the Present.* Cambridge: Polity Press.

Moser, C.O.N. 1998. The Asset Vulnerability Framework: Reassessing Urban Poverty Reduction Strategies. *World Development*, 26(1): 1–19.

Padrón Hernández, M. 2012. *Beans and Roses: Everyday Economies and Morality in Contemporary Havana, Cuba.* Dissertation, University of Gothenburg, Gothenburg.

Pawlik, W. 1992. Intimate Commerce, in J.R. Wedel (ed.) *The Unplanned Society: Poland During and After Communism.* New York: Columbia University Press, pp. 78–94.

Pérez Izquierdo, V. 2007. Cuba: Alcance y Desafíos de la Política Social, in R. Domingo and R. Tansini (eds), *Cuba y Vietnam: Un nuevo análisis de las reformas económicas.* Montevideo: Departamento de economía, Facultad de Ciencias Sociales, UDELAR, pp. 91–140.

Powell, K. 2008. Neoliberalism, the special period and solidarity in Cuba. *Critique of Anthropology*, 28(2): 177–97.

Rakodi, C. 2002. A Livelihoods Approach – Conceptual Issues and Definitions, in C. Rakodi and T. Lloyd-Jones (eds), *Urban Livelihoods: A People-centered Approach to Reducing Poverty.* London: Earthscan, pp. 3–21.

Rose, N. 1998. *Inventing Our Selves: Psychology, Power and Personhood.* Cambridge: Cambridge University Press.

Rosendahl, M. 1997. *Inside the Revolution: Everyday Life in Socialist Cuba.* Ithaca: Cornell University Press.

Rosendahl, M. 2001. Household Economy and Morality during the Special Period, in C. Brundenius and J. Weeks (eds), *Globalization and Third World Socialism: Cuba and Vietnam.* Basingstoke: Palgrave, pp. 86–101.

Smith, A. and Rochovská, A. 2007. Domesticating neo-liberalism: Everyday lives and the geographies of post-socialist transformations. *Geoforum*, 38: 1163–78.

Smith, A. and Stenning, A. 2006. Beyond household economics: articulations and spaces of economic practice in postsocialism. *Progress in Human Geography*, 30(2): 190–213.

Smith, A., Stenning, A., Rochovská, A. and Swiątek, D. 2008. The Emergence of a Working Poor: Labour Markets, Neoliberalisation and Diverse Economies in Post-Socialist Cities. *Antipode*, 40(2): 283–311.

Solberg, M. 1996. Liten by, stort helvete: magfoldige overlevelsestrategier i 90-årenes Cuba. Hovedoppgave, Universitetet i Oslo.

Wedel, J.R. 1992. *The Unplanned Society: Poland During and After Communism.* New York: Columbia University Press.

Weinreb Rosenberg, A. 2009. *Cuba in the Shadow of Change: Daily Life in the Twilight of the Revolution.* Gainesville, FL: University Press of Florida.

Wolf, D.L. 1990. Daughters, decisions and domination: An empirical and conceptual critique of household strategies. *Development and Change*, 21(1): 43–74.

Yurchak, A. 2005. *Everything Was Forever, Until It Was No More: The Last Soviet Generation.* Princeton: Princeton University Press.

Zabala Argüelles, M. 2010. Poverty and Vulnerability in Cuba Today. *Socialism and Democracy*, 24(1): 109–26.

Zelizer, V.A. 2005. *The Purchase of Intimacy.* Princeton: Princeton University Press.

Chapter 7

Building on Trust: Open-Ended Contracts and the Duality of Self-interest in Romanian House Construction

Radu Gabriel Umbres

Introduction

Self-interest has two paradoxical features. On the one hand, classical economic thinking has proposed that markets are created by self-interested individuals who enter into economic exchanges following their private interests. Bernard Mandeville and Adam Smith have argued that, perhaps against our first intuitions, actions based exclusively upon selfish motivations, articulated with the division of labour and with market relationships, lead to an increase of the common good. These early contributions to classical economics have been immensely influential in economics and political thinking, and the loose set of ideas grouped under the banner of 'neo-liberalism' owes no small debt to the classical liberal image of private vices turning into public benefit under the guidance of the invisible hand of the market. But self-interest has another property which threatens to annul its brighter side. If self-interest is unbridled, if nothing else but self-interest reigns supreme, can we even hope for markets to do their hidden work? Can self-interest exclusively by itself guarantee that people will become market actors, that individuals can successfully follow their private good in the anonymous, atomised market of textbook economics?

These questions are particularly apposite in the context of post-socialist societies where economic and political reform was informed more by the optimistic first image of self-interest than by the more pessimistic view which puts unlimited self-interest as the problem rather than the solution to economic development and human freedom (Hayek 2011 is a classic text; a more recent scholar and policy-maker is Jeffrey Sachs 1989). As other contributions to this book prove, the discourse of post-socialist transformations was often built upon the image of the individual as a mini-corporation, a 'Me Inc'. as Makovicky puts it, cultivating its assets for market performance, speculating on opportunities for personal enrichment; a transformation of the self from a tainted, 'collectivistic' past to the bright future of individualism. As I will purport to demonstrate, this image of change is inaccurate, and even misleading as a solution for human welfare and economic development.[1]

The problem lies inside the ontological contradictions of 'individualism' itself. MacPherson's famous discussion on classical liberal theory misleadingly included Thomas Hobbes alongside the likes of Adam Smith or John Locke (Gauthier 1969: 108). Hobbes' main insight was into the self-defeating nature of self-interest in the absence of a higher authority or moral order (Hobbes 1998). Individualism alone is a problem rather than the solution for human freedom and social harmony. This chapter will discuss precisely the tense relationship between unfettered individualism and market relationships, arguing that successful economic exchanges entail a curbing of self-interest in the form of mutuality just as much as they rely upon each actor's attempt to maximise returns. Taking my cue from Gudeman and Rivera (1990),[2] I will analyse the folk representations of economy and morality found in the predicament of a Romanian rural entrepreneur trying to establish a business in the post-socialist village society. The case study reflects the problem of tackling the dark side of self-interest and the culturally-adapted way of taming and harnessing its economic power.

I will analyse the story of Mihai, who left Sateni to work as a builder in Greece, and subsequently returned to his home village to start a local business. His genuine entrepreneurial intentions faced severe obstacles in Sateni, from uncertainty about his skill and business strategy to the widespread mistrust of exchange partners in Sateni economy. Mihai tackled these problems in two related ways. First, he started working for relatives rather than unrelated villagers, building upon the inherent trust attached to social relationships between kin. The second practice was to defer payment and price negotiation indeterminately in the future. Both builder and client delayed the moment of financial reckoning by ostensibly relying upon each other's trustworthiness and fairness through the means of an informal open-ended contract rooted in culturally-elaborated ways of creating moral social relations. I will explain the role of kinship and the apparent financial coyness by focusing on the uncertainty of technological processes and the overcoming of mutual distrust. Finally, I will reflect upon Mihai's accomplishments and failures as a case-study for understanding how private interest is a self-contradictory phenomenon whose destructive expressions must be circumscribed for the benefit of mutually-rewarding economic relationships.

---

1   I would like to thank Nicolette Makovicky and Dimitrios Dalakoglou for organising a panel at EASA 2010 in Maynooth, Ireland, especially the former for the subsequent meeting in Oxford and her critical reading of drafts. The EU-funded INCORE project bursary fund has graciously supported the conference expenses. I thank Mihaiela and Radu Calin for their exceptional generosity in funding my fieldwork.

2   Like them, I became fascinated by the parallels between ethnography and classical scholarship, especially the commonalities of moral dilemmas discussed in this chapter.

Setting the Scene

Building upon two years of fieldwork in a Romanian village, I proposed that the shared world-view of villagers in Sateni comes impressively close to the ideal of a society in which everyone is ultimately responsible for their own life (Umbres 2012). There is little, if any, concern for something coming close to a 'common good', or a worldwide-oriented sentiment of mutuality and responsibility for others, an echo of the 'amoral familism' described by Banfield (1967) in rural Italy. Not to put too fine a point on it, Sateni villagers defy several stereotypes of post-socialist actors: they are neither relying on state or society for support with their livelihood, nor are they hoping for any external agency to help them in their life struggle. Just like a well-behaved neo-liberal subject, they see life as a competition against the wider world where just deserts come from one's own agency. There are no free lunches or social safety nets in the world-view of Sateni villagers, where every man has to make his own way in the intricacy of social life and be responsible for the results, or as Romanians would say '*sa se descurce*' – to get ahead by skill, resources, and cunning.

There is no need to teach self-interest or fashion a new capitalist personhood for the Sateni villager, as no-one expects altruism or self-denying practices from themselves or from others. Money, the epitome of capitalism and market integration, is never construed as morally dangerous or subversive (Parry and Bloch 1989), quite the opposite. Villagers assert vigorously that money is key to social fulfilment, that being rich is a worthy objective and any means to obtain it are legitimate. The economy of Sateni is thus an interesting testing ground for the success of self-interest in creating markets, developing the division of labour and reaping the fruits of specialisation and exchange.

Sateni is a village in North-East Romania, poor by national standards but rather well-off in comparison with its neighbours. After receiving land from the socialist collective farm, most villagers work in agriculture, especially at subsistence level. A few people managed to set up relatively successful farms, with stocks of cattle and sheep bring cash revenues from governmental subsidies and market sales. Productivity is rather low, as land strips are small and scattered across the village, with villagers fighting prolonged battles to guarantee land ownership and protection, the low levels of interpersonal trust rendered cooperation impossible in post-socialist Sateni (see Verdery 2003, Cartwright 2001 for parallels). The collective farm was literally dismantled, with people taking home bricks and wood from farm buildings, machinery was either taken apart for spare parts or privatised in shady deals. Attempts to consolidate land plots or create a pasture cooperative were also curtailed by the lack of trust in managers, leaders or anybody who tried to move on from the autarchic mode of production. Being an independent all-round producer, even though at a lower level of productivity than a professional, narrowly-specialised one, is seen as more as an accomplishment than a weakness, and people would look down upon someone who would leave her gardens fallow to spend time in more lucrative enterprises. There is a market for several products, either villager-to-villager or more formal ones in a nearby town, but the bulk of items and services are exchanged in low risk and low value spot transactions.

From the late 1990s, many villagers migrated to Western Europe looking for jobs and cash income on the background of continuous un-/under-employment in Romania (Sandu 2005). Transnational migration brought a wave of relative prosperity for some villagers, with remittances fuelling an increased demand for domestic goods and more significant investments. A spectacular impact was the drive to build new houses with conspicuous modern characteristics: panel steel roofing, elaborate woodwork, double glazing, central heating, etc. The tastes of clients were largely informed by their contact with Western architecture and were also an attempt to break with the past style of hay-and-clay bricks and asbestos roofing in terms of comfort and lifestyle. In fact, the immediate sign of successful migration was the erection of a two or more story house with expensive amenities. As economic theory has it, demand creates its own offer, and migration served as a two-pronged impetus for both processes, giving entrepreneurs a rare window of opportunity.

The Entrance of an Entrepreneur in the Economy of Sateni

Mihai left Sateni for Greece in his early thirties, after spending his youth as a small-scale trader in cereals and timber between Sateni and mountain villages. He made good money in the 1990s, but his commercial niche was soon exhausted. To support his family, he went to Serbia and ended up in Greece as a migrant builder. He climbed the professional ladder fast and became a master builder for a subcontractor working at the Olympic Games residence near Athens, the apex of economic and prestige gains in his migrant history. His portfolio included industrial, residential, private housing, especially in the early stages of construction, but often stretching to finishing work. However, the economic crisis hit the construction industry hard and Mihai decided to return home and start a construction business in Sateni. He invested around one year's worth of income in a set of equipment never seen in Sateni, specialist tools for carving wood, measuring, and fine tuning.

His approach was truly entrepreneurial in technology and skill innovation, fitting well with one of two established definitions of entrepreneurship found in literature. He returned home to become the best builder in the area, backed by specialist work equipment and ten years of experience at competitive standards. He was convinced that the way houses were built in his home village was obsolete and could be improved in terms of design, skill, and team management, doing away with inefficient practices in a sweep of 'creative destruction' characterising entrepreneurship (Schumpeter 1976). Moreover, like the entrepreneur of classical liberal economics, he was aiming to make a profit from a perceived opportunity to transform and link capital from different sectors of the economy, the accumulation of skill and capital on the offer side and the increased financial possibilities of clients (Kirzner 1978, Barth 1967)

Nevertheless, his aim to change the economic process of house building and gain from the economic arbitrage between social spheres had to overcome a difficult institutional barrier: the widespread mistrust characterising economic practices in Sateni in particular and rural Romania in general. Mihai was remembered from trader days as a shrewd negotiator, bargaining hard to get a good price and somewhat fussy in his choice of clients. Things were not looking much better in his reputation as builder. He was known for his history of work and migration and he already had one project running: his own house. This used to be by far the largest house built in the village and arguably his largest investment of time, effort, and money in recent years. But now the site remained an unfinished project, as Mihai's remittances stopped and he had to start anew in Sateni. No-one knew with certainty if he could complete a project successfully, the actual cost of materials used by Mihai, or the price he would ask for his services. Unlike most builders, he was known as a teetotaller but even this made him look stingy and too calculated. Mihai tried to find clients, but several months passed without any serious engagement. Despite ambitious plans and qualifications, Mihai's prospects were bleak as transaction costs (Williamson 1996) in terms of uncertainty and mistrust, seemed too high to engage in the local construction market.

After a few months of settling unfinished business and accommodating to the new realities of the village, Mihai got his first break. Ana, one of his many cousins, asked him to take down the roof of an old stable, build a new first floor the house and erect a new roof allowing the attic to be extended. The money for the repairs and extensions came from the cousin's son, Ilie, who regularly sent large amounts of his wage working as a roofer in Germany. Mihai was put in charge of the project, planning and designing the new housing arrangement. In a short time, he assembled a group of workers (the ethnographer included), designed the architectural setting appropriate for Ana's needs and resources, and started taking down the old wooden structure.

It is highly significant that Mihai's first client came from the sphere of kinship. Unlike most of the 1,000-odd villagers in Sateni, Ana and her family knew Mihai intimately, having first-hand knowledge of Mihai's proficiency as builder and both knew each other's quirkiness and preferences. They also shared a long history of reciprocity in agricultural and domestic work. Mihai's father was part of the work gang which helped Ana and her husband erect their first house without receiving payment as it is usually the case in close kin relations. While Mihai was in Greece, Ana helped his wife with garden work, and Mihai helped her son find work in Athens. Nonetheless, this new project was much more than the previous exchanges – Mihai's contribution was essential to the house building (unlike his father's) and he expected proper payment as a master builder. Conversely, Ana expected professional workmanship and was prepared to meet the costs. Whatever else their social relationship was about, this project was ultimately a business arrangement.

Given their specific economic interest in the project and the aforementioned ubiquitous talk about money, I was surprised by the absence of payment negotiations. Discussions between Mihai and Ana revolved around the price and quality of materials, construction techniques and design, yet at no point was Mihai's fee brought up. I initially considered that they had settled the matter in private, with their kin relation smoothing the monetary issue. Only later did it become clear that Mihai actually started work without asking for a fee. When around half of the work was done, Ana asked him to name an estimate fee. Mihai tried to avoid the answer as much as possible, then had to say something when Ana insisted to know how much money she should ask from her son. A sum of 4,000 RON (1,000 EUR) was forwarded with a provision for change in the future. After two weeks when the project was finished, Ana inquired Mihai about the final price. Mihai increased the sum to 6,000 RON and Ana accepted saying that she knows that even this fee was too moderate yet she would compensate with future aid for Mihai's family. The upgraded house became one of the novel designs in the village and jobs began pouring in the following months for the emerging Sateni entrepreneur.

A possible interpretation of this puzzling practice is that trust and reciprocity between relatives makes the problem of money superfluous. If we choose to see the deal between Mihai and Ana as enmeshed in larger social relations transcending mere business, this embeddedness could serve as an explanation for the absence of an explicit guarantee of a fair price. After all, he was not risking anything, as he trusted his cousin and he was certain that she would understand and agree to the fee that he would name at the end of the job. While this line of interpretation is not necessarily false, it is too limited to grasp the entire complexity of Mihai's economic agency. Several facts suggest a more detailed explanation of the relationship between kinship, trust and money. First, Mihai observed the practice of financially open-ended contracts in his future deals with clients from outside the sphere of kinship. Moreover, the estimation of a fair price for construction work was highly problematic for a novice entrepreneur fumbling through the darkness of economic and social uncertainties characterising home building in Sateni. Finally, the connection between kinship, trust and fairness proved highly tenuous when expectations of axiomatic amity or even promises were falsified by reality. The following sections explore the way Mihai developed his business by exploiting and creating fields of mutuality in the surrounding society using the power of imagining a different future than the endless cycle of distrust, even when promises and expectations turned sour.

Building with Trust

In his first two years, Mihai's business flourished in terms of number of jobs and complexity of building. He and his ever-changing team of labourers erected fences, stables, houses, reconstructed roofs and foundations, fitted windows and doors, insulated walls and roofs, etc. After one year, Mihai was known as the best master builder in Sateni and his reputation extended across village boundaries. He still had clients among relatives and friends, but most work was done for non-kin and even people he had never met before. Approximately half of his 'contracts' were still begun ahead of an advance fee.

The scare quotes of 'contract' remind that, although he had thought about formally registering his activity, Mihai's business remained entirely in the informal sector. He paid no taxes on his income, nor did he charge VAT, without contributing to or benefiting from health insurance, pension or welfare. Since his clients register the building site with the local authorities as using exclusively family work and day labourers, there is little chance of Mihai being accused of tax evasion or illegal construction as the proofs against him are weak. Pretty much everyone is interested in keeping their mouths shut and overlooking this minor illegality.[3] A very important consequence of informal arrangements is the lack of legal enforcement of verbal contracts between parties. Neither builder nor client can bring a matter in front of a court of law, and, without a third party to officially mediate a conflict, actors need to rely on other social mechanisms for solving disputes.

Given this insecurity and the prominence of money-talk in everyday life, I was further puzzled by Mihai's apparent lack of concern for settling an initial fee. His reasons for postponing money issues aimed to make the project possible in the first place in order to follow his entrepreneurial ambitions which included, paradoxically, making as much profit as possible. A crucial aspect is the uncertainty faced by Mihai in his start-up plans.

The first problem was reputation. Amateurish self-proclaimed 'master builders' who landed jobs by sweet-talking clients into disastrous projects baffled Mihai. While he was convinced of his superior cost-benefit offers, he considered marketing talk empty and unconvincing. He was fond of saying that work should do the talking. His unfinished house was a potential advertisement, yet Mihai was well aware that most villagers were primarily interested in shallow appearances and knew little about the intricacy of professional construction. He took prospective clients to see his incomplete project as proof of craftsmanship but, although he was adamant that structural work and durability were essential, had little ways to be convincing.

Technical aspects of building work raised a second uncertainty. Mihai had never worked as a construction entrepreneur in Sateni and faced difficulties in estimating inputs and outputs. He needed empirical evidence of workers' productivity to compute labour costs. He was unaccustomed to Romanian materials, which he later found cheaper, but of uncertain quality to the ones in Greece. The quirky requirements of his new clients added to the jobs' complexity. His techniques and architectural solutions were outstanding for local requirements, yet every client

---

3 Mihai is hardly unique. All builders in Sateni and surrounding villagers work informally, even though some projects are worth tens of thousands of euros. Officials turn a blind eye, since they are sometimes relatives and other times clients of workers and masters. Only when builders work for the state or corporate businesses (that is almost never) do they bring their practice into full legality.

had idiosyncratic ideas about their home (though Mihai often found them silly). He had to adapt to Sateni cultural representations of a 'proper' house.[4] Several strange demands proved that the minds of clients were a continuous source of uncertainty for his economic approach. In some projects, additional work was required over what was initially agreed, in others clients worked as labourers, and most investment estimations bore little resemblance to outcomes.

Since Mihai was still finding his way within a new social and technological environment, he became wary of venturing an initial fee. Lack of local experience in everything from labour relations to production bottlenecks hindered an accurate estimation. Afraid of asking too much and losing customers, he was also afraid of asking too little and reducing profits. He considered that his innovative building style made it difficult for non-specialists to understand the actual process. He was afraid to scare off potential clients with an initial estimation but was certain that, once he would get the project running, his intricate mastery would become evident, thus justifying his fee.

These difficulties were largely alleviated by working for kith and kin. Consociates had more information about his skill and accomplishments, both in Sateni and abroad, and identified his qualities and flaws to make for a harmonious economic interaction. They knew ways around his quirks (such as spending days on end to finding the perfect roof slope). The atmosphere in these projects was relaxed, with licentious banter, jokes and stories passing to-and-fro workers and hosts. After each sundown (the practical end of a workday), we spent several hours in intimate discussions characterising the sphere of kinship, interspersed with concerns for the construction project. Strong interpersonal trust inherent in this intense sociality helped Mihai find his first work opportunities and ultimately increase his reputation as skilled master builder. Under expectations of axiomatic amity (Fortes 1970), Mihai relied upon his relatives to trust him with a fair estimation of work effort and profitability, while he offered in exchange his trust that they would agree to his estimation and keep their side of the deal. Mihai could thus delay the moment of reckoning until enough information about costs and complexity became available to assess a 'fair' price for each party. Mihai's fee could be settled by subtle negotiation and piecemeal advancement to a level where everyone was satisfied with the transaction and no one felt short-changed. The deals were even an inter-family affair, underscoring the ramification of trust among kin. In a few cases, Mihai's wife was communicating with the wives of clients, passing information about costs and prices alongside other discussions found among kin. The management of risk using the ascriptive morality of kin

---

4   An interesting example was the preoccupation of older clients with the size and angles of interior walls: they wanted to make sure that coffins could be moved easily from the ritual room to the burial ground, unlike the cases run by the gossip mill where the dead person had to be extracted through the window – a shameful event for a 'proper' family. Mortuary rituals are essential moments in Sateni sociality and houses play a crucial role, as I discuss in my doctoral thesis (Umbres 2012).

reflects the importance of social networks and trust for entrepreneurial activities (Hart 1988). The kith and the kin offered Mihai an 'entrepreneurial breeding ground', a space of relative safety and trust to pursue his plans by controlling uncertainty and further advertise his skill and honesty to the wider village.

This being said, it is important to note that Mihai's open-ended contracts were also extended to non-kin, yet something of the atmosphere surrounding kin relations persisted. Most clients came personally to Mihai, either approaching him at home during a Sunday or on other holidays that involve work-interdictions, or during week-day evenings in one of the two central village pubs. Even when he did not know, or had just a faint acquaintance with his clients before these meetings, the conversation was cordial and informal, as the two men[5] got to some general discussions about the business, in private preferably, if they could get rid of the pesky anthropologist. Almost always the client approached Mihai by asking him about his work schedule in a certain period of the year. If Mihai was available during that time, the client would lay out his plans for the project. The rest of the conversation was spent with Mihai asking particular questions about the construction and offering advice for the future. At the end of a successful conversation, they would set up a meeting at the future building site to get real contact with the situation on the ground.

There was one particularity of conversation which always drew my attention. If he was interested and available for the job, Mihai started asking a lot of practical questions, as if the job was already secured. He inquired about available materials, gave advice on premium deals from suppliers, started laying out plans for the project's finishing, colours, aesthetic details, he asked many questions about the client's needs and resources, offered his solutions to technical problems, etc. The same process of communication happened during the first visit to the future building site, with Mihai surveying the area with an expert eye and mentally designing the steps ahead. I always felt that a crucial step was missing, the one of negotiating the fee for the construction, the intersection of offer and demand, the possibility of rejection, the question of cold hard money. It was as if the deal was already sealed and parties fully engaged in the process. If considerations of price were raised by either part, they were met with an optimistic 'we shall see about that, in the end we are all people (human), we will find a way'.

The image of actors engaged in this joint project without thinking hard about money is largely an illusion based on public communication. In reality, the issue was rarely far from their minds. From his first visit to a site and prior to agreeing to undertake the job, Mihai would keep a pocketbook where he scribbled surface and section outlays and jotted down facts and figures about days and wages. As time went by, the pocketbook amounted to a basic accounting system that helped Mihai compute costs and revenues. When Mihai had many concomitant jobs, his

5 It is mostly men who begin the talk although women play an important subsequent role.

wife took over the ledger and kept track of wages and investments, employing a simple accounting system to compute Mihai's profits and losses.

Interestingly, even when Mihai did offer a fee estimation, this was usually accepted with almost no haggling. The superficial disinterest in discussing money hides a more complex reality. In house-construction, monetary sums are less important than what they actually pay for. The initial price was just a starting point for an economic process fraught with uncertainty and unpredictable developments. Unlike spot markets, information about the object of transaction in construction work is hardly conveyed by prices, and must be built upon trust and intimate social knowledge. No-one can predict exactly what will happen during the actual construction. It is just that the moment of reckoning depends on more than the purely monetary ground and more on the moral inclination of partners. In particular, the issue of self-interest shows its perilous side for the success of mutually rewarding exchanges.

Mutuality and Self-interest

I have argued that the local configuration of interpersonal trust and axiomatic fairness between kith and kin lowered the monitoring and enforcement transaction costs. This resource, however, is not easily available in the wider Sateni economy, as folk representations of society portray villagers as driven by competitive individualism and mutual suspicion. This worldview is closely related to the pervasive presence of money in everyday conversations: everyone agrees that money is important, that all men try to accumulate as much as possible and, when interests diverge as it is usually the case, conflicting desire for money will end up in disagreement and hostility. The Hobbesian undertone of everyday representations is a powerful barrier to an entrepreneur such as Mihai who needs clients and successful deals to get ahead in life.

He was far from oblivious to the problem, and was painfully aware that conflict loomed large over each and every business deal. But, as an echo of Adam Smith, he also envisaged the business deal as a mutually rewarding process which left business partners better off than the alternative of no exchange. His decision was to turn the tables on the problem and step away from the vicious cycle of mistrust by a symbolic inversion. Where other builders started by asking primarily about prices and payment deadlines, he chose to put the project ahead of any other concerns. 'If I start by asking for money, for *arvuna* [advance payments], what would they think? That I am only interested in my money; that I do not care about the house, about how much they are spending. I could just as well hung an axe on my shoulder and go around the village collecting *arvune* never to return again if that's all' he once said to me. Even more puzzling was his reluctance to approach clients directly. I once found out that someone was looking for a team to building a house. I told Mihai about the opportunity but he refused to approach the potential client. 'If he wants me to build his house, he can come any time and ask. I would look greedy if I go first, he would feel threatened if I just show up saying that I know about his business and I want it. He knows that what I am doing and how I am doing it, so he can make up his own mind. I would only scare him'.

Delaying the moment of financial reckoning was just one form of communicating his honest intentions. From the moment he agreed to take on a job, Mihai and his family became involved in meaningful social relationships with his clients and their network of kith and kin. I have mentioned the insertion of preliminary business inquiries into practices belonging to the private sphere. Home visits are frequent after the start of the project, with Mihai and his clients drinking coffee and telling stories of their past exploits in Sateni and abroad. Mutuality and amity are also performed in the ritual domain, from funeral attendance to rites of passage. Mihai and Dorina, his wife, attended the wedding of a client who used to be just one of many unrelated Sateni villagers a few months before. They could have avoided the event and the substantive mandatory cash gift, by either claiming ritual mourning (Dorina's paternal grandfather had just died) or a previous engagement to a related family's baptism taking place the same day. However, they honoured the invitation and graciously reinforced the strength of social relationships. Even before the wedding, Mihai and Dorina, Andrei and Sorina (the client and his future wife) and the ethnographer had an evening out in a nearby town just like good old friends. Earlier in the day, Andrei visited some relatives in another village and Mihai acted as his driver and companion. In a matter of days, the two men got from being distant acquaintances to apparently close friends in a process mingling kinship, business, and shared migrant life histories. Months later, Andrei sent as gifts from Italy second-hand photo cameras and mobile phones and Mihai's son added the client to his Yahoo Messenger list to keep in touch across international borders.

Business-related sociality also permeates tavern interaction. Mihai often drinks with clients and his work-team, and introduces them to his friends and relative. Consistent with his general attitude, Mihai does not offer rounds to cajole potential clients. In fact, clients are the ones buying drinks for him and his companions. Villagers come with the business proposition and the round of drinks is part of their display of generosity and goodwill. There is no mention of any obligation on the part of the builder to consider the proposition and go ahead with the project, yet the first contact is made and expressed materially, in a small, yet visible token. On his part, Mihai does not want to appear manipulative by courting clients with drinks. If anything, I would describe this way of seeing economic communication as 'inverse car salesmanship'. This is entirely consistent with the peril of house building becoming a 'lemon' market like used-cars market (Akerlof 1970) given the uncertainty about construction quality, skill, and post-deal insurance in Sateni.

It is important to note that the intensity of social relationships correlated with construction stages. Mihai neither forgot nor ignored his ex-clients, yet the frequency of interaction and communication decreased once the project was over. Nonetheless, it is unduly superficial to consider the process of befriending as purely strategic. The social relationship is, above all, about following the interest of both parties to complete the project in mutually-beneficial terms. In significant ways, the wellbeing of Mihai and his clients was dependent upon the wellbeing of the other party. The intense social relationship between parties helped fine-tune the construction process, as practices of amity and reciprocity turned an apparent business arrangement into a flow of social exchanges with material and symbolic content which echoed the interaction between kith and kin.

This section concludes my exposition of how the self-interest of economic agents can coexist harmoniously when uncertainty and suspicion are alleviated by actions expressive of mutuality and fairness defining or echoing the axiomatic amity of kinship. In the last section, I tackle self-interest's conflictual side. The antagonism appears, somewhat paradoxically, in the entrepreneurial cradle of kinship yet becomes fully destructive when trust and reciprocity are unilaterally reneged.

The Limits of Kinship and Trust

I have showed that kinship and trust were central to Mihai's entrepreneurial project. However, neither of them conveys an easy solution to the problem of unbridled self-interest. The limits of kinship appear in an ethnographic vignette. Mihai was approached by Relu, cousin-once-removed, to start work on a new storehouse. A few weeks into the construction, after the largest part of work was completed, Relu's wife Mihaiela called Mihai's fixed line phone and talked with his wife Dorina. She inquired about the progress of the building and somewhere in the middle of the conversation brought up the issue of cost. Dorina did not know the sum but that she promised to ask Mihai. The second day, Dorina transmitted Mihai's answer that an approximate cost would revolve around 6,000 to 7,000 RON. Mihaiela was somewhat relieved and added that, since she expected an even higher price, she feels indebted for the future when she will reward the generous offer of Mihai. After a few weeks, Relu paid Mihai with money sent by Mihaiela from Italy.

On the face of it, the story appears as a mutually gratifying meeting of demand and offer as Mihai got his price and Relu paid an affordable amount. However, the situation has multiple ramifications that point to the tension in conducting business with relatives. One evening over coffee, Dorina hushed Mihai's attempts to intervene and urged me to use my newly-developed expertise in construction to estimate the 'fair' price for Relu's project. Mihai gave me a wink 'à la Geertz' to stop me from recalling that we already had this discussion a few days before. Taking into account the number of work days, the area of the building, and the fee that I knew Mihai had demanded, I came up with a sum of roughly 8,000 RON. Dorina was quite content with my higher estimate and started complaining that her 'generous' husband does not care enough for his household's needs. She thought Mihai had other people's benefit too much in mind, while no-one would, in turn, think of his household when need arises. Mihai agreed that his price was low, but came up with a detailed justification. Relu was one of his most trustworthy relatives, he was always there when needed, his son ran a lot of errands for Mihai's household without asking for payment, even if most of the times he got some pocket money. Relu's wife was also aware that the price was low and consequently promised to even the balance in the future. His final word on the matter, and the end of the discussion, was a firm 'and after all, Relu is Relu'. Condensed in this assertion is the belief in another person as a responsible and considerate individual who will show in the future that he was worthy of such trust and generosity.

This apparently minor friction was the tip of a quite problematic iceberg: Mihai's deals with relatives were far less profitable than business with unrelated villagers, and even sometimes he ended up with net losses. When several jobs came up at once, Mihai realised that, were he to work for kin rather than non-kin, opportunity costs increased severely. Undercharging friends and relatives, he was losing handsome projects from people prepared to pay market prices. Mihai wanted to ask the full price from relatives, and sometimes did, but dreaded their response if they expected preferential prices or treatment (such as more time and attention than given to regular clients), or priority for small projects when larger ones came from non-kin.

This imbalance became unsustainable in the long term, owing to the position of Mihai in the local division of labour.[6] It was not that Mihai wanted to extract himself from his sphere of kinship and its practices. He continued to maintain solid relationships with relatives and friends, embedded in extensive cycles of delayed reciprocity and mutuality, from rituals to everyday life. But he could no longer run his construction business exclusively according to the logic of generalised reciprocity when such practices threatened his future as entrepreneur and social person. This latter aspect is particularly important. Mihai was the sole breadwinner of his family and bore the responsibility for bringing money in the household. Dorina's discontent derived from her perception that Mihai shirked on his familial duties in gaining less money than possible. Moreover, Mihai and his family live in a social world where moral participation is inextricably linked to money. They need money in a great number of actions imbued with moral worth such as wedding gifts, loaning or donating money to relatives in distress, caring for their ancestors' graves, building a house to show their social worth, and offering their child education, inheritance and social prestige. It might be that it does not buy happiness, but when so much of Mihai's sociality is tied to using money, any detriment to the finances of his business were damaging his entire personhood.

Mihai's solution was to either treat his relatives as full-paying customers or to avoid working for them when their interests diverged so much as to threaten their deeper social relationships. This was one way of controlling the destructive side

---

6   I pursue this theme in the final chapter of my thesis; my argument, in a nutshell, is that Durkheim's (1992) insight that division of labour is associated with radical transformations in the forms of social solidarity should consider the causal direction going from morality to division of labour rather than the other way around, an argument which can be found in a reinterpretation of Marcel Mauss' work (1954).

of self-interest when moral commitments were found in conflict between different spheres of Mihai's social life. Nonetheless, the pernicious side of self-interest surfaced in far more harmful events: outright deception and cheating.

I have already mentioned Mihai's apprehensiveness in approaching monetary issues with clients. Amongst other peculiarities, he was often delaying the receipt of intermediary payments during construction. He only requested a weekly amount to cover his worker's wages and something for his everyday expenses, leaving a considerable amount to be handed over at the final delivery. Again I was puzzled, and I was offered the following rationale: grabbing money would have sent the wrong message of narrow self-interest, while a delay indicated Mihai's trustworthiness and, respectively, his trust in his clients' honesty. Performing significant services on a mere promise, often tacit, is a credible, hard-to-fake signal of one's cooperative intentions in the universe of Sateni cultural representation, an essential stage in the social construction of trust (Gambetta 1988).

By working with a provisional estimation of fees (or no agreement at all) and by leaving a large amount of payment due after the end of a project, Mihai overtly communicated his trustworthiness, but also exposed himself to the threat of opportunism or unilateral defection. Rare as these events were, moments when the self-interest of his clients overwhelmed the mutuality of the business are instructive regarding the limits of trust and amity in economic endeavours.

A mutual friend told Mihai that a publican in a nearby town wanted to hire the builder to refurbish a house. Mihai went ahead with the project and, as usual, proposed an initial fee, which was later amended upwards due to the usual vagaries of construction work. He vaguely knew his client, but they became socially intimate during the construction job, as usually happened with clients. He received his weekly fees, yet the client did not make the final payment of around 5,000 RON. The publican presented excuses about financial problems, but he soon stopped answering calls and gave Mihai the cold shoulder each time the master builder asked for his rightful fee.

Mihai was caught off-guard by this turn of events. He knew about the publican's reputation as a ruthless businessman, but there were no credible signs of potential malfeasance. Social intercourse on site and beyond had been smooth, although his client was tediously arrogant. Mihai attended the funeral of his client's mother-in-law, paid multiple visits to his town pub, and both displayed the amity found between reciprocally respecting persons. Mihai repeatedly said that he could understand and tolerate snags in transactions, as long as clients would discuss matters with him and mutually re-arrange a deadline for payment. He even believed that financial problems rather than malevolence had caused the delay, but changed his mind after months had passed without any sign of friendly intentions.

There was little left for Mihai as means of coercion. With no legal proof of contract and aware that informal work was illegal in terms of tax and safety regulation, he pondered upon threatening or even roughing up the bad payer. But the client was a heavy man in many respects, as brother of the town mayor, who enjoyed connections with local underworld figures and tough men. Overall,

Mihai was left with no alternatives with which to enforce the monetary contractual provisions once the moral contract disappeared. Two years since, Mihai has largely renounced any hope for receiving that important fee.

In this case, Mihai's self-interest was the victim of another person's self-interest. However, the unilateral pursuit of self-interest can also lead to mutual losses. In another project, Mihai deliberately erected a house structure requiring a roof which only he could have designed and executed. He charged a very large amount for the roof,[7] to the chagrin of his clients, captive in a technological trap. Although Mihai's stratagem worked against the short-term interests of his clients, it also damaged his own long-term economic opportunities, as other builders were brought to do the finishing work by the clients who thus punished his costly trick. This episode shows one more time that economic success is less dependent upon individual inclinations. The temptation of opportunistic gains may lead even generally-honest entrepreneurs to take advantage of their clients. In the long term, the economy based on division of labour may only thrive through mutualistic relationships informed by the local cultural repertoire.

These examples prove that self-interest's destructive side has real consequences which jeopardise the economic self-realisation of an entrepreneur such as Mihai. If clients can renege on their promises with impunity, if deception undermines the power of promises, then short-term opportunism can eliminate long-term mutuality. In retrospect, it seems amazing that Mihai managed to conduct such a successful business in a world where self-interest reigns supreme. The answer suggested by this paper is that Mihai, his clients, as well as all Sateni villagers, try to conduct their affairs within the cultural representations and social institutions of Sateni, from kinship to the symbolic elaboration of trustworthiness. Even failures and renegotiations of social position serve to prove that their economic agency is built upon harnessing the power of self-interest to create markets and exchanges, but only when the destructive force of self-interest is mutually-neutralised.

Conclusion

This chapter argued that, even before considering multiple forms of personhood enmeshed in the post-socialist reality (Dunn 2004), the model of possessive individualism itself is riddled with ontological contradictions when self-interest stands against itself, in an only apparent paradox. I have shown how Mihai's economic relationships continuously balanced the two facets of self-interest, the entrepreneurial self-reliance and the harbinger of conflict.

I have argued that sociality is more than mere 'fluff', epiphenomenal to the 'real' business of house construction. Several transactional costs make a moral covenant

---

7   His post-rationalisation was that he asked too little for the previous stages and was trying to recoup some of the losses. Be it as it may, he was consciously ensnaring his clients in a position which was against their interests.

between builder and client, the institutional backbone of economic prestations. The design is open-ended, initial price estimations are constantly revised and the amount of effort cannot be easily monitored or gauged by inexperienced clients. An important payment remains until the end of the project, and there is no recourse to official enforcing agencies.

Despite these problems, mutual satisfaction in terms of money and results is possible if each party fulfils its promise. Employing the terminology of game theory, both actors can maximise their gains if they respect their pledges, yet both could lose if mutually cheating. However, only one party could cheat and stand to gain at the expense of the other. Mihai could save work effort by fudging certain aspects, unnoticeable to non-professionals, while his clients could default on their promises. The irony (and logical consequence) is that mutual cheating leads to mutual loss. Everyone is worse off when all default on their promises in the Hobbesian 'warre'. A cooperative solution must be found for a potentially non-cooperative situation. In the absence of external enforcement, parties have to police themselves and each other from opportunism. The tension lies in the two-pronged feature of self-interest, simultaneously stimulant for, and latent subversion of exchange, while the solution is found in the cultural representations of trust and reciprocity and their social enactment.

If the neo-liberal project is about creating a personhood centrally defined by self-interest, it should look no further than a village in Romania. This chapter has showed that individuals in Sateni have no problem in defining and expressing self-interest, but they need to move further forward. To create an economy which rewards its participants, their agency aims to channel self-interest into the mutually-beneficial force of division of labour and exchange, rather than let it develop its destructive potential.

References

Akerlof, G.A. 1970. The market for 'lemons': Quality uncertainty and the market mechanism. *The Quarterly Journal of Economics*, 84(3): 488–50.
Banfield, E.C. 1967. *Moral Basis of a Backward Society*. New York: Free Press.
Barth, F. 1967. On the study of social change. *American Anthropologist*, 69(6): 661–9.
Cartwright, A. 2001. *The Return of the Peasant: Land Reform in Post-Communist Romania*. Aldershot: Ashgate Publishing.
Dunn, E.C. 2004. *Privatizing Poland: Baby Food, Big Business, and the Remaking of Labor*. Ithaca, NY: Cornell University Press.
Durkheim, É. 1992. *The Division of Labour in Society*. Basingstoke: Macmillan.
Fortes, M. 1970. *Kinship and the Social Order: The Legacy of Lewis Henry Morgan*. London: Routledge & Kegan Paul.
Gambetta, D. 1988. *Trust: Making and Breaking Cooperative Relations*. New York: Basil Blackwell.

Gauthier, D.P. 1969. *The Logic of Leviathan: The Moral and Political Theory of Thomas Hobbes*. Oxford: Oxford University Press.

Gudeman, S. and Rivera, A. 1990. *Conversations in Colombia: The Domestic Economy in Life and Text*. Cambridge: Cambridge University Press.

Hart, K. 1988. Kinship, Contract, and Trust: The Economic Organization of Migrants in an African City Slum, in D. Gambetta (ed.) *Trust: Making and Breaking Cooperative Relations*. New York: Basil Blackwell, pp. 176–93.

Hayek, F.A. 2011. *The Constitution of Liberty: The Definitive Edition*. Chicago: University of Chicago Press.

Hobbes, T. 1998. *Leviathan*. Oxford: Oxford University Press.

Kirzner, I.M. 1978. *Competition and Entrepreneurship*. Chicago: University of Chicago Press.

Mauss, M. 1954. *The Gift: Forms and Functions of Exchange in Archaic Societies*. London: Cohen & West.

Parry, J. and Bloch M. 1989. *Money and the Morality of Exchange*. Cambridge: Cambridge University Press.

Sachs, J. and Lipton, D. 1989. Poland's economic reform. *Foreign Affairs*, 69: 47–66.

Sandu, D. 2005. Emerging transnational migration from Romanian villages. *Current Sociology*, 53(4): 555–82.

Schumpeter, J.A. 1976. *Capitalism, Socialism and Democracy*. New York: Harper and Row.

Umbres, R. 2012. *Folk models of the social in a Romanian village*. PhD thesis. London: University College London.

Verdery, K. 2003. *The Vanishing Hectare: Property and Value in Postsocialist Transylvania*. Ithaca, NY: Cornell University Press.

Williamson, O.E. 1996. *The Mechanisms of Governance*. Oxford: Oxford University Press.

Chapter 8

Earning Money, Learning the Language: Slovak Au Pairs and their Passage to Adulthood

Zuzana Sekeráková Búriková

Introduction

Au pairing combines elements of paid domestic work undertaken by temporary migrants, cultural exchange defined by national and international law, and basic living arrangements. By law (European Agreement on Au Pair Placement 1969, Immigration Directorates' Instructions 2003[1]), au pairs are young foreigners, who stay for up to two years with families in order to learn English and acquire a better knowledge of the country. Au pairs must live 'as part of family'. They receive food, accommodation, and 'pocket money' (i.e. not a wage) in return for childcare and/or housework. Au pairs are supposed to spend a maximum of five hours per day helping their host families plus two weekly sessions of babysitting. They should have two rest days a week. In the United Kingdom they must be between 17 and 27 years old, unmarried, without dependants, and originate from a specified group of largely European countries. Until 1993, only females were approved. Families are bound to treat au pairs as equal (European Agreement on Au Pair Placement 1969); Immigration Directorate Instructions (Immigration Directorates' Instructions 2003, chap. 4 section 1 paragraph 1) and agencies usually suggest treating them as family members.

Au pairs were originally understood to be West European and middle-class girls coming for a gap year in order to learn the language or for cultural tourism. In the early 1990s, however, the dynamics of au pair exchange changed significantly, with a new generation of au pairs coming from the post-socialist countries of Central and Eastern Europe (Cox 1999, Hess 2001–2002, 2003, Williams and Balzac 2004); many of them from Slovakia, which is among the countries with the world's highest number of au pairs per capita (Behan 2005).

---

1   In November 2008 a points-based application system (PBS) was introduced as a revision to the UK immigration process. As a result, the au pair scheme has been closed and au pairs (together with other temporary workers, students on gap years and voluntary workers) fall under the more general Youth Mobility Scheme (YMS) of Tier 5 of the PBS.

Though being both a frequent route for migration for (not only East European) women and a popular source of childcare, researchers have until recently paid little attention to au pairs. The location of au pairs' work in private homes and their status as non-workers does not make them an obvious object of research on labour migration. Only in a last decade have researchers focused on au pairs as migrants and part of the domestic work industry (Anderson 2006, 2007, 2009, Bahna 2005, 2006, Búriková 2006a, Búriková 2006b, Búriková and Miller 2010, Cox 1999, Cox 2006, 2007, Cox and Narula 2004, Hess 2001, 2003, Hess and Puckhaber 2004, Macdonald 2011, Rohde 2011, Williams and Baláž 2004).

I spent a year[2] with Slovak au pairs, who worked in London just after Slovakia entered the EU. They were all reasonably young; mostly female, and many of them had left their parental homes for the first time. Trying to reconstruct their histories of migration, and talking to them on numerous informal occasions over the course of my fieldwork, I found that the reasons they mentioned as their motivations for leaving Slovakia and becoming au pairs in the UK were complex, and sometimes apparently idiosyncratic. Dominant themes of economic necessity and the importance of learning English were combined with various personal or cultural issues: One faced unemployment and becoming an au pair was a way to avoid it, someone else came because their life at home felt too boring, another person loved songs on MTV and MTV originated in the UK, someone else broke up with her lover and could not bear staying in the same village, another au pair claimed she came by chance.

It would be tempting to focus only on economic and educational reasons and dismiss the others as too personal or indeed too idiosyncratic and as such unimportant on societal level. Indeed, existing studies (Cox 2006, Hess 2001, 2003, Williams and Baláž 2004) have emphasised the economic dimensions of the au pair migration. Economic inequality among the regions has been recognised as a systemic condition for contemporary paid domestic work (Hondagneu-Sotelo 2001: 19). In particular for au pair employment, analysing data from online au pair agencies, Miloslav Bahna found that demand for paid domestic workers grows with the country's GDP (2006). Also, Rosie Cox argues that au pairs are widely available 'because of the

2   This chapter is the result of my work at the project funded by postdoctoral grant GAČR 13–11062P, 'Paid Childcare and Domestic Work in the Czech Republic and Slovakia'. I am grateful to The Leverhulme Trust Research Project Grant which funded the research *Slovak au pairs and London families: home, material culture and migration*. I conducted ethnographic fieldwork with Slovak au pairs living in London with supplementary interviews by Daniel Miller with host families from October 2004 for 12 months. Research methods included participant observation within a range of different spaces and in-depth interviews with 50 au pairs. Most of the au pair interviewees had come to London for a period of half to one year, usually through arrangements made by specialist au pair agencies. They were from 18 to 31 years old. Only five of them were men. I would like to thank Daniel Miller for his friendship and insights, and Nicolette Makovicky for her encouragement, insights, and editing. I am indeed very grateful to all au pairs participating in this research for their time, trust, openness and friendship.

economic conditions in southern and eastern European countries (and some others) and the currency of the English language throughout the world' (Cox 2006: 27–8). Thus, while West European au pairs are seen as travelling for purposes of cultural tourism and leisure, researchers have commonly explained au pairing as an economic strategy used by East-European women to cope with the difficulties of post-socialist transformation. In this literature, both post-socialist transformation and women's strategies are seen in economic terms: i.e. women opt for au pairing because they are either unemployed or can earn more money as au pairs than as workers in Slovakia. Another economically-based explanation originates from the official definition of au pairing as a type of cultural exchange in that women travel to Britain to learn English, a skill which they can use as a tool of economic advancement back at home (Cox 2006, Hess 2001, 2003, Williams and Baláž 2004). In short, both these interpretations underline structural conditions of migration and employment of domestic workers.

In this chapter I will argue that it is important to take all recorded motivations at face value and try to identify some logic behind apparently diverse reasons to migrate. I suggest that if we want to understand the motivations of the Slovak au pairs for migrating, we need to focus on post-socialist transformation in broader than economic terms and also consider ways in which traditional modes of creating personhood and biographies in the area have been challenged since 1989 (Dunn 2004). Drawing on long-term ethnographic fieldwork on experiences of Slovak au pairs working in London during the years 2004 and 2005, I show how prospective au pairs have come to see and represent their temporary stay in Western countries as necessary for their careers and personal development, thus placing their life stories within a larger liberal discursive framework. Such narratives follow the logic found in neo-liberal interpretations of post/socialism and discourses of neo-liberal governmentality, which emphasise the need for increased responsibility, flexibility, and enterprise from the (post-socialist) neoliberal citizen (Creed 2011, Dunn 2004, Junghans 2001, MacNay 2009, Miller and Rose 2008, Rose 1996).

Such socially (and ideologically) legitimate discourse of self-improvement and entrepreneurial activities, however, conceal a set of rather more complex goals associated with migration. Young people sometimes became au pairs when they did not know how to finish unsatisfying relationships, or when they wanted to leave their parental homes or a boring lifestyle. In these cases conventional narratives of self-improvement helped them to achieve their goals without causing conflict or upsetting their relatives, partners or friends. Furthermore, many young people saw au pairing as a rite of passage, marking and proving their maturity, adulthood and independence.

Earning Money, Learning the Language: An Economic Strategy or Legitimation?

The economic and social difficulties accompanying the post-socialist transformation and differences in salaries between the home and host countries are an obvious point, which is made both by researchers (Cox 2006, Hess 2001,

2003, Williams and Baláž 2004) and by the au pairs themselves. Some au pairs consider au pairing itself as migrant labour, comparable with occupations on the formal labour market. During the period of my fieldwork the minimum pocket money for an au pair was £55 a week, the participants of my research were paid £68 a week on average by their host families. In 2004 the average weekly pocket money for an au pair was approximately the same as an average brutto salary per month in Slovakia, in 2005 it was just slightly less.[3] Furthermore, 33 (66 per cent) of our interviewees complemented their pocket money with side jobs, mostly cleaning and babysitting for other than their host families.[4] Some of my informants explicitly compared their pocket money to their or their parents' salaries in Slovakia, or counted what they could do with the possible savings back home. For example, when Karolína discussed her decision to become an au pair with her friends, among other factors she counted how much time she would need to save enough money to buy a studio with her income in Slovakia and compared this with her expected savings from her prospective au pair stay.

After EU enlargement an au pair visit can also become a stepping stone to other employment in the UK – au pairs do get time and money for learning the language and finding a job. For instance Jarmila could not find a job with her specialisation (party catering) in Eastern Slovakia, so she decided to try to find work abroad. She spoke only a little English and was not sure how to look for such a job in London. Thus she decided to become an au pair instead, in order to learn English and get more information about the country and British labour market. She thought her boyfriend would follow her after six months, by which time she would understand English better and be able to find formal employment for both of them. Anna, who came to London as an au pair for the second time, was explicit in her goals:

> I do this [au pairing] only because it gives me time and money to find a job and
> a nice, inexpensive place, ideally not far from a good language school. And once
> I find it, I will immediately say 'bye bye children, bye bye family' and go after
> my own business.

However, while I met numerous au pairs from Slovakia who fit this interpretation, their motivations were much more complex and could not be reduced to an economic strategy. The fact that several interviewees left jobs with prospects which they were apparently happy with indicates that economic aspects motivations for au pair stays are much more complex. There were, for instance, a PR manager and a web-developer, a hairdresser with her own salon, a police clerk, an optician

---

3   In 2004 the average Slovak salary per month was 15,825Sk (£270, 8) brutto; in 2005 it was 17,274 (£295, 6) (According to Statistical Office of the Slovak Republic, http://portal.statistics.sk/showdoc.do?docid=1702). Rate of exchange on October 1st 2004 (1Sk: £58,432).

4   Though law forbids au pairs to do other paid work, my informants did not consider their side jobs to be illegal.

and a nursery teacher among them. All of these people explicitly stated they did not become au pairs for economic reasons. Similarly, although language figured as an important motivation in interviews, only 27 au pairs (62 per cent of the respondents) actually attended language schools, some of which could be found for free during my research in London. In fact, the people who did attend language schools were not necessarily those who claimed to come to London to learn the language.

Some research participants claimed they came to London by chance, just using an opportunity which had appeared. Often the decision was opportunistic and without much forethought, let alone planning or consideration of any specific (economic) advantages. For example, Martina worked in a pizzeria and she saw quite a few of her friends leaving for Switzerland, and she said to herself: 'what will I do at home? I will go too,' and she became an au pair. Lujza, working in a factory producing PC cables, was shocked when her colleague decided to quit her job and become an au pair:

> I told her: 'you are going abroad? You are going to become an au pair? You are not able to go on your own to Nitra [a local town in the neighbourhood] and you are going to London … If you can go, I can go too'. And she said: 'so why do not you come? Come with me then', and so I did.

Despite having a job she liked and being very happy with the relationship with her fiancé, Paula, a hairdresser with her own salon, became an au pair because she felt bored by her life, and wanted to go abroad. Petra told me she came because she had always loved British songs on MTV. Two research participants were master students and five were PhD students coming for a gap year. As other agents of what Russell King (2002: 99) describes as youth migration, then, au pairs were motivated by a mixture of broader goals, from learning language, travelling, seeking experience, 'excitement', or empowerment within their wider relationships or for 'time off' to think about what they wanted to do with their relationships, careers or lives in general. It is important to emphasise that people who considered relationships or culture (such as MTV or 'experiencing life abroad') as their motivation were not necessarily affluent, nor had higher education. In particular, as above mentioned, Petra was unemployed when she took up her au pair position.

When talking about their reasons for migration the au pairs generally mention the importance of studying the English language, learning new skills and improving their chances for better employment. Economic hardship, the high unemployment rate of young people in Slovakia, and a high symbolic value ascribed to both knowledge of foreign languages and travel abroad appeared to be themes through which au pairing was spoken about in everyday life. And yet, it is apparent that the reasons of learning a language and economic possibilities frequently served to hide far more complex (and perhaps less acceptable) reasons to migrate. Decisions to become an au pair were related also to the complexity of their relationships with parents, romantic partners, or friends and au pairs used their stays in the UK as a means of gaining more freedom or empowerment in these relationships.

For example Barbora, who was working in a book shop, had a relationship with a married man who could not make a decision whether to divorce or not. Barbora decided to leave to London. For her, the au pair stay was a means to show her partner that she could live without him. She also hoped her partner would miss her and would finally realise how much he cared for her. Her partner consequently decided to marry her. Hana, a university student just coming up to graduation, came to London as an au pair because she feared she might end up marrying her boyfriend, whom she did not love anymore. She did not know how to finish the long-term relationship or how to explain this to her partner and both his and her parents. Hana thought that her au pairing would allow her to finish the relationship diplomatically – it would either naturally disappear or she would tell her boyfriend after six months that she had fallen in love with someone else. Paula became an au pair when she found out that her boyfriend had an affair with another woman. She did not want to stay in the small city where they both lived and where too many places were related to their relationship. Their break up was, for her, an opportunity for a deeper life-change. She was 27 and not entirely comfortable with settling down so she saw au pairing as her last chance to start travelling and discovering places she had never been to. Love reasons are not necessary escapist – for example Peter decided he would become an au pair when he missed his girlfriend who had left for the UK a few months before him. He was lonely and was afraid that distance would cause the end of their relationship. Interviews revealed striking readiness to migrate. As Tatiana said in an interview: 'I just wanted to get out' or Ivana: 'I did not have any special reason. I had an opportunity, so I went'. Numerous interviewees mentioned their age as a reason to 'go out' (the word 'out' was also used during the socialist era for abroad, or more often, for hardly accessible West European countries):

ZB: 'Why you decided to become an au pair?'

Janka: 'I wanted to go out. I am young, so I wanted to go out'.

The spontaneity of many decisions to become an au pair, as well as the use of phrases such as to ´go out´ or ´get out´, suggests specific understanding of locality and its position in both history and the global world. For example, when I asked Natália, whom I met at a Czechoslovak party in London, why she decided to become an au pair in the UK, she just asked me, whether I have ever been to Stropkov.[5] No, I have never been to her native town. She said she thought so. I would not have asked her, if I had been there. According to Natália, life in Stropkov stopped. There was no possibility of finding find a good job there, she said, but it was not only the question of getting a job, there was a general feeling

---

5   A small East Slovakian city with approximately 10,000 inhabitants.

of stasis[6] and boredom that bothered her. She felt that nothing was going on and nothing was going to be any different if she had decided to stay there. A similar feeling of stasis, 'backwardness' or boredom also appeared in other interviews. In the next section I will argue that these feelings are related to narratives of transformation.

Dealing with Rupture: Narratives of Transformation[7]

Since the 1990s, media, politicians and economists have commonly depicted the socialist period as a rupture: the era when the 'natural' flow of history and modernity stopped for 40 years. Within this interpretation, the collapse of actually existing socialism is seen as a return to the mainstream of western modernity. Political and economic transformation were often interpreted as a 'return to Europe', the slogan used also by Civic Forum during the first free elections (True 2003: 11). Also nowadays, media and politicians continually compare situation in Slovakia with a 'developed' Europe. For example, most recently, in an on-line discussion about compulsory vaccination in the monthly magazine *Dieťa* [Child], the editor-in-chief appeals to paediatricians to establish practice (in particular informed consent and possibly voluntary vaccination) 'drawing us nearer towards the practices of developed countries of European Union'.[8]

The idea of a 'natural' capitalist development relates to the concept of the 'free market', which is commonly depicted as a 'natural' and impersonal mechanism or means of coordination. As such, it is seen in opposition to the perceived 'artificiality' of centrally-planned and 'constructed' socialist economy. For example, in his book on Czech nationalism Ladislav Holy (1996) quotes Czechoslovak newspapers from the 1990s, arguing that they depicted the market as a symbol of the rational organisation of society or rationality itself: economic reform was often talked about as 'the return of rationality to our society' (Forum, 1990, No. 10); or as 'an experiment in the return to reason' (Lidové Noviny, 11 July, 1990). The introduction of a market economy was a return to 'the normal order' of things (Václav Klaus in Literární noviny, 2 August 1990). (...)The market economy not only operated as a process of natural selection but was itself the result of the process of natural selection (Holy 1996: 153).

---

6   Actually, when speaking about entrepreneurship, the official web page of the city also speaks of stagnation ('characteristic feature of small and middle entrepreneurship in the city is its stasis' (*Stropkov. Úvod – o meste – súčasnosť* at http://www.stropkov.sk/sucasnost1/).

7   I have borrowed the term narratives of transformation from the introduction to this volume written by Nicolette Makovicky.

8   The discussion is available at http://www.dieta.sk/index.php?page=1&type=news&id=11&theme=6&method=main&art=3512)

I believe that the decisions of young Slovaks to become the au pairs in London were articulated in reference to such neo-liberal narratives of socialism and post-socialist transformation. In this respect the Slovak au pair migration can be seen as an analogy of the process of the development of national accounting in post-war France described by Miller and Rose (2008). Miller and Rose suggest that 'governing at distance' operates 'through adopting shared vocabularies, theories and explanations [...] loose and flexible associations may be established between agents across time and space [...] whilst each remains to a greater or lesser extent constitutionally distinct and formally independent' (Miller and Rose 2008: 35). In particular, they illustrate how national accounting was designed as a part of a project of post-war economic reconstruction, which was understood as political modernisation of the country. They argue that one of the mechanisms for its successful instalment was the language: vocabulary framing this process included notions of 'backwardness', 'growth', 'progress' and 'solidarity'. 'It was through this political language that a variety of concrete and micro-level issues were to be thought about and acted upon' (Miller and Rose 2008: 37). In the same way, Slovak au pair migration is also thought and acted in relation to the political language describing a recent Slovak history as a wrong and unnatural path needing a remedy and capitalist market relations as both an antidote and natural and right progress of society.

However, it is important that discourse providing reference points for understanding migration as necessary for personal development is not only linguistic, but permeates also mundane experience with material culture: Numerous anthropological studies of Central and Eastern Europe reveal that western products and life-styles were, in the 1990s, seen as 'normal' in opposition to the socialist or local ones (e.g. Fehérváry 2002, Veenis 1997, 1999). Analysing the history of both material culture and its ideology in GDR Milena Veenis (Veenis 1997, 1999) argues that within socialist ideology, material development was both a mean and measure of progress as well as a tool for creation of (socialist) identity. Because of their superior appearance and quality, unattainable Western consumer goods gradually became the materialisation of unfulfilled promises of socialist utopia. For many inhabitants of GDR they created the place of desires, fantasies and projections and became even more 'real' than local products (Veenis 1997, 1999). Similarly, analysing consumption on a collective farm in Estonia, Sigrid Rausing shows how the Soviet Union, represented in popular Estonian discourse by the Russian minority, was referred to as 'not normal' in contrast to the 'normality' of the West, represented by Finland and Sweden:

> The 'norm' (...) was not used in the meaning of what the norm was, but rather
> in the meaning of what it should have been: what 'normality' would have looked
> like had Estonia's development itself been 'normal', i.e. uninterrupted by the
> Soviet takeover. (Rausing 2002: 131)

Au pairs in particular commonly returned from the UK with several suitcases of clothes considered to be of better quality and/or more fashionable than things they could get in Slovakia. In general, shopping (especially shopping and window shopping for fashion items) was amongst the most favourite free-time activities of the au pairs, who concluded that one either could not get the same stuff in Slovakia, or the same fashion items would arrive there only several years later.

The fact that narratives of transformation can be linked to consumption reinforces the discourse of the socialist era as a rupture and failure through everyday experiences and interpretations of material culture. A consequence of this interpretation is a rather general sense that the natural, real and indeed 'normal' development has been, for a long time, happening elsewhere and one has been left behind. As if it was a race in which one missed 40 years. In the following section I will show why becoming an au pair can become one of the ways in which to deal with this discourse. I will argue that au pairs see mobility and temporary migration as a way to get experience of Western life style and to learn skills associated with Western modernity. Independence, pro-active attitude, individualism, risk-taking, entrepreneurship, ability to choose and flexibility – skills associated with neoliberal personhood (Dunn 2004, MacNay 2009, Miller and Rose 2008, Rose 1996) – are seen as necessary for the personal development of an individual.

Neoliberal Personhood as Rite of Passage

In her monograph about the privatisation and organisation of labour in a Polish factory Elizabeth Dunn (2004) claims that 'transition' from socialism to capitalism involves the creation of a 'different kind of person: one who is active, mobile, and endowed with the ability to choose' (Dunn 2004: 165). Inspired by Miller and Rose's (1990, 2008) Foucauldian[9] notion of (neoliberal) governmentality and enterprising selves, Dunn contends that new personhood is achieved through new (self-)regulatory managerial and marketing techniques, such as audit, accounting, quality control, niche marketing and evaluation of employees. Dunn reveals the links between post-socialism, this new type of personhood, new kinds of governance, and neoliberalism. Indeed, she argues that fundamental changes in Polish economy and society occur exactly through new disciplinary technologies based on self-regulation. Applying audit technologies to people introduces neoliberal governmentality as a new form of disciplinary power in Poland, under the influence of which individuals are forced to regulate themselves as 'free' and self-activating agents (Dunn 2004: 164–5).

While Dunn (2004) does not focus on migration and movement in space, themes of mobility, movement and flexibility re-appear repeatedly within her text. Not only has she recognised 'movement' as a 'key theme' in job interviews she observed in factories, and 'flexibility' and 'activity' as important personality traits

---

9   See, for example, Foucault 2008a, 2008b.

of employees, 'mobility' and 'immobility' codify also capitalism and socialism. Actually, Dunn equals transition from socialism to capitalism with 'transition from an orderly, bounded and rigid system to a fluid, flexible and global one' (Dunn 2004: 74). However, the ethnography of au pair migration provides evidence that the post-socialist transformation of personhood can be achieved – perhaps is even required to take place – through mobility in space.

Indeed, when talking about their reasons for migration, the au pairs generally mentioned the importance of studying the English language, learning new skills and improving their chances for better employment. Anthropologist Jonathan Larson has noted the importance of knowledge of English for understanding the new economic order in Slovakia (2008: 196), a fact also felt and expressed by au pairs, who saw their stays in London as an opportunity to learn English in order to improve their chances on the labour market. For instance, Iveta said:

> I have come here in order to learn the language, as everybody does. I was 25 and I was still living with my parents, and I thought I was too old for that. So I thought I would become and au pair instead. Yes, I have come here to learn the language.

I believe that knowledge of the English language has become an important skill, necessary for success on the Slovak labour market not only because of the Slovak economy's links with foreign investment, but because it proves the labourer's personal characteristics –flexibility and ability to learn new things, agility and also familiarity with 'Western' work practices and life styles.[10] As Larsen's (2002, 2008) ethnography of CV-writing workshops shows, the skills and experiences associated with the West and capitalism have become enormously important on the Slovak labour market. Indeed, he argues that borrowing new styles of curricula vitae from Western business practices instantiates neoliberal models of personhood in the area by teaching pupils to portray themselves as subjects desirable on a capitalist market. Larson thus illustrates how the language of enterprise permeates the vita (participants were supposed and taught to 'sell' and 'advertise' themselves).

And yet, Iveta´s stated motivation for becoming an au pair ´ ... like everybody else ... ´ to learn English, appeared to be a convenient frame for the much more personal and revealing statement that she felt ´too old´ to live with her parents. For the majority of young Slovak au pairs, especially female au pairs, their experience abroad provided a legitimate means for leaving not only moribund education and employment, but gaining independence from their parents. Eighty-two per cent (i.e. 41 out of 50) research participants lived with their parents before becoming au pairs. These women saw the experience of living abroad, learning a new language, and becoming independent and relying only on their own capacities as a lesson in growing up and self-development. For instance, Lenka said:

---

10   Unlike Russian or German, English was hardly taught at primary or high schools during the socialist period and was a new skill associated with post-socialist transformation.

I worked for three years as a nursery teacher in my home town and simply, you know, everything was cared for, I did not have to care for anything. I was staying with my parents, the nursery was at the corner and I did not have any single problem. So I just decided to become independent and prove to myself that I can live without being dependent on my parents. Sure, I wanted also to improve my English and to know a new country. But the main thing was to prove something to myself.

For many females au pairing meant a specific rite of passage, a kind of trial proving adulthood, maturity and independence (see also Búriková and Miller 2010). In the interviews, au pairing was commonly compared to a male rite of passage – military service which in Slovakia was compulsory for men until 2004. For example, when I asked Katka why she decided not to leave when she was unhappy with her working conditions and her treatment by the host family, she said:

> The boys had to go for military service and had to endure it. I just said to myself, if they can go through military, I can go through this. And I will endure it too. I am not a child.

The au pairs also make their stays equivalent with male military service through the medium of material culture. A common decorative element of au pairs' rooms is also found in the rooms of Slovak soldiers: some form of diary, or calendar that au pairs use in effect to count down the period until their next visit home or their return home.[11] Unfortunately, the fact that the au pairs conceptualise their stays as a trial or rite of passage has practical consequences for their common exploitation, as it is one of the main reasons why au pairs remain in situations they find oppressive. They feel it has somehow become a test of their adulthood, and that to go back to their parents, or even mention their unhappiness to their parents, would be a failure in their expectations of self-development.

Au pairing was thus seen as a part of a young person's life cycle before settling down and starting a family. Au pairs often mentioned their mothers, or other older women who suggested that they should leave and enjoy themselves because, once they have a family, they will not be able to travel or spend money freely for themselves. Interestingly, the au pairs interviewed mentioned that, unlike their mothers, their fathers rather tended to oppose their decisions to become au pairs. Elena, in particular, compared being an au pair with a gap year and said she came along for the experience:

> to see the world, grow up and have fun before I settle down. Once I have family and children, I will not be able to do this, and I might have missed such an experience and be unhappy later.

---

11   For more data on au pair's rooms see Búriková (2006a), for more data on the material culture of the Slovak military see Barátová (2006: 33–4).

Figure 8.1   The advent calendar used by an au pair to count down the days left until her visit home

Typically, au pairing was seen as a time when young people could experience certain individualism in their life choices, relationships and consumption. Au pairs often justified their spending on parties, fashion items and fun with a future in which they would have to save money and 'sacrifice' their own desires and needs for the well-being of their families and children. It was against this vision of the future that they saw their present. An au pair stay commonly becomes a time of 'adventure' (see also Jenčová 2007) and of experimenting with possible identities. The vehicles for these experiments were for example buying clothing, social relations, or the realm of sexuality. Indeed, the notion of a more 'exciting life', 'experience' or 'adventure' repeatedly appeared in interviews with female au pairs:

> ZB: 'Why did you become an au pair?'

> Lujza: 'I liked it at university, but I have always wanted to go to England. That has been my dream. And, you know, I am a bit of adventurer, I could not stay it at home. And you must be an adventurer too, otherwise you would not have been here either'.

In short, au pairs both felt and experienced the actual movement to a foreign country as one which involved active choice and risk taking, and perceived mobility (and the ability to be mobile) itself as a desirable trait. To use Dunn's terminology, they saw post-socialist 'bodies' as gaining desired 'flexibility' as much through their actual movement in space, as through education or workplace experience. Migration to and experience with life in ΄Western΄ countries was very important in this quest.

It is not only the ethnography of the au pair experience that shows that the notion of being flexible can be applied to migration. The process of achieving desired (neo-liberal) personal qualities appeared to overlap with understanding of different stages in a young person's life cycle. When Dunn (2004) talks about 'enterprising selves' or 'being flexible', she seems to focus mostly on the sphere of employment (CV, work, job interviews, skills necessary for keeping or getting jobs, personal audit etc.). But for the au pairs becoming 'flexible' depends on growing up and feeling independent from family, relationships or places. They perceived flexibility in a much more fundamental way than exclusively in terms of employment or economic relations. As well as a path to maturity, spending a year abroad was both a way to obtain as well as a way to test or prove desired skills. However, the au pairs expected the loss of this flexibility later in their lives, after becoming wives and mothers. They were comfortable with this perceived loss, but saw their migration as a precondition to acceptance of this loss.

Importantly, this experience of movement is marketable: Williams and Baláž (2004) in particular look at how Slovak au pair returnees try to commodify not only the achieved knowledge of the language, but also their experience abroad per se. Indeed, doing fieldwork in a Northern Slovak village I commonly heard that everybody who was clever and could do something went abroad, 'out' or into the ΄the world', as foreign countries are sometimes called in Northern Slovak villages. To experience mobility and life abroad was conceived of as a proof of one's cleverness and initiative. This expectancy of one's mobility was cross-class: builders and academics were equally expected to prove their qualities through mobility. There are jokes that you cannot find good builders and plumbers in Slovakia nowadays, as everybody who was good at his job has already gone abroad. Similarly, PhD students in anthropology are expected to prove their qualities by getting scholarships abroad and those who do not do so are often implicitly considered as not proactive enough in their academic careers.

The neo-liberal narratives of transformation described above are coupled with the importance of experiences and skills ascribed to the West and capitalism. The result is that traditional models for creation of life projects in the area have been challenged. In particular, a secure life tied within one locality is not only difficult to achieve, such a life is no longer understood as ideal. And yet, most au pairs whom I met in London claimed that after spending some time in the UK they would like to return to Slovakia. It seemed that they felt most comfortable with temporary migration concluded by a successful return home.

Conclusion

The ethnography I have presented in this chapter provides the evidence that the au pairs conceptualise their migration to the UK as a personal development. They do so in two intertwined senses.

Firstly, their stays are a way to create a subject desirable on a capitalist market, in particular an independent, active and flexible individual speaking English. Doing so, the au pairs contribute to the creation of a new type of neoliberal personhood: enterprising selves calculating the profits of their actions and actively projecting themselves and their future (McNay 2009, Rose 1996). I have argued that, in this respect, the au pairs' motivations to migrate should be interpreted with reference to neo-liberal discourse on (post)socialism, especially to the narratives of transformation. This transformation of individual subjects is a part of a larger process of macro-transformation of post-socialist societies (e.g. Dunn 2004). On the other hand, I revealed that au pairs frequently use the very concept of enterprising selves and discourse of self-improvement, learning language and economic advancement in order to conceal other, less acceptable reasons for migration. Doing so, they actively manipulate what seems to be a dominant if not hegemonic concept of neo-liberal personhood for their own purposes.

Secondly, I illustrated how the au pairs simultaneously conceptualise their migration as a rite of passage to adulthood and a life-stage before settling down and starting a family. In their interviews, this route to becoming adult involves gaining independence from their parents, relying on themselves, becoming 'experienced' and being able to endure difficulties. As a period before settling down, their time in London is characterised by certain individualism, enjoying oneself and experimenting with life-style, relationships and consumption. Apparently, there is certain overlap between these characteristics and skills and the qualities of neoliberal personhood and enterprising self (Dunn 2004, MacNay 2009, Miller and Rose 2008, Rose 1996). However, in the case of au pair migration, notions of flexibility and mobility make sense to these young people not because they have undergone some sort of management training or because it is expected in their jobs, but because becoming grown up requires the skills which they see as gained through 'adventure', 'spontaneity', 'mobility' or 'proving' oneself against hardship. In fact, the period of au pairing (the liminal phase) most clearly represents the ideal 'neoliberal self'. While some au pairs saw au pairing as just the start of a more general trend in their lives, others contrasted this time not only with their past, but also with their expected future. They thought that parenthood, fixed employment, mortgage etc. would cause the loss of their flexibility and freedom. Importantly, through the adoption of desirable (and marketable) skills and qualities the transformation on the individual level (process of transition from adolescence to adulthood) merges with transformation on the societal level (transition from socialism into neoliberal capitalism).

References

Anderson, B. et al. 2006. Fair enough? Central and East European migrants in low-wage employment in the UK. [Online]. Available at: http://www.compas.ox.ac.uk/changingstatus [accessed: 1 May 2007].

Anderson, B. 2007. A Very Private Business: Exploring Demand for Migrant Domestic Workers. *European Journal of Women's Studies*, 14(3): 247–64.

Anderson, B. 2009. What's in a name? Immigration controls and subjectivities: The case of au pairs and domestic worker visa holders in the UK. *Subjectivity*, 29: 407–24.

Bahna, M. 2005. Latentná ekonomika kultúrnej výmeny au pair. *Sociológia*, 37(5): 449–74.

Bahna, M. 2006. The Au Pair Employers: Who are They, Whom They Search for and What Do They Await. *Slovak Sociological Review*, 38(3): 245–66.

Barátová, J. 2006. Od "šurovania" po strihanie metra (Život vo vojenskej komunite). *Slovenský národopis*, 54(1): 29–46.

Búriková, Z. 2006a. The Embarrassment of Co-presence: Au pairs and Their Rooms. *Home Cultures*, 3(2): 1–24.

Búriková, Z. 2006b. Prečo majú britské matky au pair a čo sa na tom slovenským au pair nepáči. *Slovenský národopis*, 54(4): 341–56.

Búriková, Z. 2007. Motivácie au pair migrácie zo Slovenska. *Slovenský národopis*, 55(4): 442–56.

Búriková, Z. and Miller D. 2010. *Au Pair*. Cambridge: Polity Press.

Cox, R. 1999. The Role of Ethnicity in Shaping the Domestic Employment Sector in Britain, in J. Henshall Momsen (ed.), *Gender, Migration and Domestic Service*. London, New York: Routledge, pp. 134–47.

Cox, R. 2006. *Language learning and labours of love: the UK au pair scheme and the intersection of productive and reproductive labour*. Paper to the Association of American Geographers Annual Meeting. Chicago, March 2006.

Cox, R. 2007. The Au Pair Body: Sex Object, Sister or Student. *European Journal of Women's Studies*, 14(3): 281–96.

Cox, R. and Narula, R. 2004. Playing Happy Families: Rules and relationships in au pair employing households in London, England. *Gender, Place and Culture*, 10(4): 333–44.

Creed, G. 2011. *Masquerade and Postsocialism. Ritual and Cultural Dispossession in Bulgaria*. Bloomington and Indianapolis: Indiana University Press.

Dunn, E. 2004. *Privatizing Poland. Baby Food, Big Business, and the Remaking of Labour*. Ithaca, NY: Cornell University Press.

Fehérváry, K. 2002. American Kitchens, Luxury Bathrooms, and the Search for a 'Normal' Life in Postsocialist Hungary. *Ethnos*, 67(3): 369–400.

Foucault, M. 2008a. *Security, Territory, Population: Lectures at the Collège de France 1977–1978*. Basingstoke: Palgrave Macmillan.

Foucault, M. 2008b. *The Birth of Biopolitics: Lectures at the Collège de France 1977–1978*. Basingstoke: Plagrave Macmillan.

160 *Neoliberalism, Personhood, and Postsocialism*

Hess, S. 2001. Au- pairstvo: migračná stratégia mladých žien zo Slovenska. *Aspekt* (2–1): 265–71.

Hess, S. 2003. Transmigration of Eastern European Women as Transformation Strategy. [Online]. Available at: URL http://www.illegalisiert.at/migration/women_transmigration260403.htm [accessed: 1 May 2004].

Hess, S. and Puckhaber, A. 2004. 'Big Sisters' are better Domestic Servants?! Comments on Booming Au Pair as business. *Feminist Review*, 77: 65–78.

Holy, L. 1996. *The Little Czech and the Great Czech Nation: National Identity and the Postcommunist Social Transformation*. Cambridge: Cambridge University Press.

Hondagneu-Sotelo, P. 2001. *Doméstica: Immigrant Workers Cleaning and Caring in the Shadows of Affluence*. Berkeley and London: University of California Press.

European Agreement on Au Pair Placement. 24.XI.1969. Strasbourg. [Online]. Available at: http://conventions.coe.int/treaty/en/Treaties/Html/068.htm [accessed: 1 October 2004].

Immigration Directorates' Instructions. 2003. Chapter 4: Permit-free Employment (Short Term) and Training, Section 1: Au Pair Placement. [Online]. Available at: http://www.ind.homeoffice.gov.uk/default.asp?PageId=836 [accessed: 1 October 2004].

Jenčová, I. 2007. Migrácia Ako Dobrodružstvo. *Slovenský Národopis*, 55(4): 457–63.

Junghans, T. 2001. Marketing Selves. Constructing Civil Society and Selfhood in Post-socialist Hungary. *Critique of Anthropology*, 21(4): 383–400.

King, R. 2002. Towards a New Map of European Migration. *International Journal of Population Geography*, (8): 89–106.

Larson, J.L. 2002. Selling Oneself, Selling the Nation: Translating Slovaks for the Eyes of Europe. *The Anthropology of East Europe Review*, 20(20): 37–40.

Larson, J.L. 2008. Ambiguous Transparency: Resumé Fetishism in a Slovak Workshop. *Ethnos*, 73(2), 189–216.

Macdonald, C.L. 2011. *Shadow Mothers: Nannies, Au Pairs and the Micropolitics of Mothering*. Berkeley: University of California Press.

McNay, L. 2009. Self as Enterprise. Dilemmas of Control and Resistance in Foucault's *The Birth of Biopolitics. Theory, Culture & Society*, 26(6): 55–77.

Miller, P. and Rose, N. 1990. Governing economic life. *Economy and Society*, 19(1): 1–31.

Miller, P. and Rose, N. 2008. *Governing the Present. Administering Economic, Social and Personal Life*. Cambridge: Polity Press.

OČKOVANIE – "Džína z fľaše ste už ale vypustili Vy a bude pre to veľmi ťažké obrátiť názor laickej verejnosti na inú stranu. " – DOPLNENÉ O ODPOVEĎ MUDr. Ludmily Elekovej. [Online]. Available at: http://www.dieta.sk/index.php?page=1&type=news&id=11&theme=6&method=main&art=3512 [accessed: 14.3.2012].

Osella, F. and Osella, C. 2000. Migration, Money and Masculinity in Kerala. *The Journal of Royal Anthropological Institute*, 6(1): 117–33.

Priemerná mesačná mzda v hospodárstve SR a indexy miezd v roku 2006. [Online]. Available at: http://portal.statistics.sk/showdoc.do?docid=1702 [accessed: 12 December 2012].

Rausing, S. 2002. Reconstructing the 'Normal', in *Markets and Moralities: Ethnographies of Postsocialism*, edited by R. Mandel and C. Humphrey. Oxford: Berg, pp. 127–42.

Rohde, C. 2011. Biographical constructions of generationality and inter-generationality in processes of au-pair migration. *InterDisciplines*, 2: 105–38.

Rose, N. 1996. *Inventing Our Selves: Psychology, Power, and Personhood.* Cambridge: Cambridge University Press.

Stropkov. Úvod – o meste – súčasnosť. [Online]. Available at: http://www.stropkov.sk/sucasnost1/ [accessed: 14.3.2012].

True, J. 2003. *Gender, Globalization and Postsocialism: The Czech Republic after Communism.* New York: Columbia University Press.

Veenis, M. 1997. Fantastic Things, in S.M. Pearce (ed.), *Experiencing Material Culture in the Western World.* London: Leicester University Press, pp. 154–73.

Veenis, M. 1999. Consumption in East Germany: The Seduction and Betrayal of Things. *Journal of Material Culture*, 4(1): 79–112.

Williams, A.M. and Baláž, V. 2004. From Private to Public Sphere, the Commodification of the Au Pair Experience? Returned Migrants from Slovakia to the UK. *Environment and Planing A*, 36: 1813–33.

Chapter 9

Old Minorities in a New Europe: Enterprising Citizenship at the Polish-Czech Border

Nicolette Makovicky

Introduction

On a hot August day in 2010, I attended the yearly Pastoral Fair (*Jarmak pasterski*) in the small village of Leśna, Southern Silesia, Poland. Amongst the exhibiting craftsmen and women, folk musicians in colourful costumes, and stands with locally-produced smoked cheeses, I spotted a woodcarver sitting quietly behind his stall, smoking a cigarette. Pride of place on his stand was a carved statue of an elderly man and woman riding a donkey, a pitcher of beer balancing on a barrel behind them, and an arrow-shaped sign pointing the way to the European Union (*Unija*) above their heads. Roughly hewn from a log, the squat donkey had a twig for a tail and comically over-sized head and ears. Seated first, the elderly lady held the reigns and a whip, and was painted as though she was wearing local folk costume: a blue, wax-resist print skirt, white blouse with red embroidery, and a lace-trimmed matron cap. Her bare-foot, long-haired, moustachioed husband wore a white shirt and a typical herder's hat. However, what was most striking was that he was holding a large, carved book with words 'Advice for European Union Management' (*Porady unijnego gazdowanio*). The statue represented local perceptions of the ineptitude and wastefulness of European Union officials. However, it was the very traditional medium through which this message was conveyed – woodcarving, the costume-clad figures, and even an apparent allusion to a biblical theme –which caught my attention. By creating a conceptual link between local, Górale vernacular culture and the European project, the carving suggested that the artists saw Highland identity as a key instrument in local negotiations with wider structures of European governance.

Based on on-going fieldwork in Leśna and neighbouring villages in the region of Cieszyn Silesia, this chapter investigates how local actors recruit and use European funding for local socio-economic, cultural, and environmental development programmes. Situated in an overwhelmingly rural area on the Czech-Slovak-Polish border, Cieszyn Silesia has benefited from support from cohesion policy programmes (PHARE, INTERREG) since 1998 and subsidies

Figure 9.1   'Advice for European Union Management'

from the Common Agricultural Policy since 2004. Although none of these
funding schemes are directed a fostering minority identity, in Cieszyn Silesia
they have been instrumental to an exponential increase in cultural cooperation
between Highland (Górale) cultural associations and interest groups within and
beyond the national borders. These connections have led to the emergence of
multiple, conflicting narratives of ethno-historical and geo-political belonging.
And yet, changes in the very architecture of policy-making in preparation for
(and after) European Union accession have inevitably favoured the activities
of certain groups over others. As we shall see below, those who are most
successful in recruiting European money and administrative support from
regional government are those who most strongly associate Góraleness with the
philosophy of 'flexible citizenship' which underpins the European project itself.
Consequently, my focus here diverges from existing examinations of European
Union cultural policy as a political technology productive of European-level
civic identity (i.e. Shore 2000), and considers instead the effect of European

'multi-level governance'[1] on the politics of representation within the region. As Aihwa Ong has argued, the European Union's neoliberal 'articulation between citizenship and the deregulated market' has worked to decouple citizenship from membership of a nation-state, and the disparate affective and legal elements of citizenship from each other (2006: 500). In contemporary Europe, '(u) niversalizing market interests, technologies, and NGOs become articulated with citizenship orders, creating new sites for the making of new claims for resources from state as well as non-state institutions' (2006: 501). In Cieszyn Silesia, Górale identity has itself become one of these 'sites' of claim-making for groups as different as budding agricultural entrepreneurs, civic organizations, and municipal administrators.

In this chapter, I use ethnography to examine the manner in which discourses of 'enterprising citizenship' frame (and limit) the contemporary performance of Górale identity by investigating the effects of models of devolved policy-making on local development projects. Encouraging the use of public-private 'partnerships' between regional government and 'organizational citizens', the principles of European 'multi-level governance' have promoted devolution as democratization. Furthermore, in the post-socialist Polish context this discourse has been informed by a prevailing perception of Communist-era policy-making as a highly centralized, undemocratic, and politically informed mechanism of suppression. Thus, social and cultural policy-reform aimed at building 'sustainable' development in local communities is intimately related to the perceived need to reform (individual and organizational) citizens from 'passive', 'dependent' into 'active', 'enterprising' citizens. Indeed, 'culture' is itself construed as a social and economic panacea for the pains of post-socialist restructuring, and tool for self-emancipation. At the same time, cultural policy has been reconfigured to from an entry-mechanism for actors wishing to join the wider politics of representation. And yet, as I argue in the following, such models of policy-making display a narrow reading of the civic landscape as composed by the associational behaviour of its inhabitants, creating blind spots which disadvantage some local actors and loopholes that are exploited by others. Furthermore, policy reform has also brought with it a discourse of 'partnership' and 'sustainability' which brands certain behaviour as retrograde while rewarding other practices as indicative of admirable 'enterprise', often without considering the limitations of existing infrastructural or fiscal conditions. It thus places administrators of European funding schemes into the role of disciplining agents, seeking to monitor and reform not simply institutional pathways of decision making, but the very conduct of municipal and civic actors. Before considering how contemporary concepts of the Górale self are formed in conjunction with (or resistance to) such disciplining structure,

---

1   In which policy-making competences were increasingly becoming shared between the European Council, Court of Justice, Commission, Parliament, and various subnational actors in the form of European Union regional councils and committees, and lobby-groups, and independent non-governmental associations.

however, I consider the relationship between discourses of culture, identity, and 'enterprising citizenship' in European policy-making at large.

Culture and Enterprise in European Policy-making

Culture and citizenship have long been vehicles for the articulation of competing ideals of European governance. Internal debates within the European Community about culture, citizenship, and identity emerged already in the 1970s, signalling a deepening concern with the need to establish constitutional legitimacy for ever-closer political and economic integration, as well as delineate the relationship of the European Union as a polity and its constituent membership, the European 'people' (Bellamy and Warleigh 2001, Rumford 2003, Shaw 1998). In the 1980s, the European Commission launched bureaucratic attempts to construct a European *demos* using the trappings of nation-building (a new passport, logo, flag and anthem) (Shore 2000, 2004). This promotion of affective citizenship coincided with a general turn towards the notion of 'constitutional patriotism' in the European Commission (Habermas 1992, 1996, 2001), which promised to deliver an ostensibly culturally neutral pan-European identity based on the moral universalism of constitutional principles which could be comfortably twinned with pre-existing, 'nested' regional and national identities. 'Constitutional patriotism', however, fell afoul of the Committee of the Regions. Seeking to maintain the status of subnational entities as 'self-governed polities in control of the common goods of membership and economic development', the Committee supported a more 'culturalist form of citizenship' that linked culture to territory (Delgado-Moreira 2000: 467). Advocating a move towards 'multi-level governance' (Marks et al. 1996, Hooghe and Marks 2001, 2003), the Committee justified cultural initiatives 'in terms of market efficiency, increased economic productivity and also through practical implications for employment, education and the environment' (Delgado-Moreira 2000: 450). 'Cultural aid' became seen as a tool for the 'production of marketable differences in poor regions' (ibid.: 460). The concept of culture as a mitigating force against socio-economic marginalization, then, has long been a core element to European cohesion policy.[2] As such, it has informed the allocation of structural funds which have shaped Poland's pre- and post-European Union accession fiscal and administrative reforms (e.g. PHARE, INTERREG, CAP/ EAFRD).

The post-1989 reform of Polish cultural policy shared this notion that culture, broadly defined, could be a panacea for the pains of post-socialist restructuring. It also embraced 'multi-level governance' as a more efficient and democratic model of policy-making: today, local and regional governments have a decisive role in cultural policy-making, while third sector parties have a limited scope 'as cultural

---

2   The policy of reducing regional inequality among Union member states through the allocation of structural funds.

managers or as agencies to distribute public funds' (Ilczuk et al. 2012). Indeed, the discourse of 'culture as development' has found particularly fertile ground in Poland with the widespread adoption of a community-arts project model under the label of 'cultural animation' (*animacja kultury*) described by Polish cultural theorist Gregorz Godelewski as the 'identification, activation, dynamisation of particular sphere of cultural experience' through the 'creation of the conditions in which people – individuals and groups – are able to realize their needs within the framework of their own culture, discovered or invented' (2002: 64). In practice, the term covers a diverse range of policy reforms and practical interventions in the form of community art, theatre, and social projects, driven by the belief that there is a 'need of cultural and educational interventions in environments of potential marginalization' (Skrzypczak 2003: 70). It advocates the redirection of cultural policy from a prescriptive model towards the task of building local 'social and cultural capital' by turning cultural centres into a 'meeting place between people' (Dunaeva 2013: 27). At the core of the idea of 'cultural animation', then, is an attitude of activity and activism (Kolankiewicz 2002). Indeed, celebrated as a more inclusive, participatory alternative to the politically and creatively stifling cultural policy of the socialist past, 'cultural animation' is often attributed transformative powers: it is a 'democracy-promoting method' and a 'tool of empowerment' which helps 'people undertake responsibility for and take control over their own life' through active participation in communal projects (European Network of Animation 2007).

Promising to cultivate 'activity', 'empowerment', and 'responsibility', *animacja kultury* combines an anthropologically informed conception of culture as practice with a programme for self-reform. It is underpinned by the assumption that the politically informed, centralized cultural policy of Communism was wholly prescriptive and propagandistic by nature and succeeded in producing alienated, passive individuals. Cultural animation, as collective action, thus promises to 're-orient behavioural and conceptual repertoires' in order to 'liberate the entrepreneurial energies and patterns of grass-roots association' which are assumed to have been suppressed by socialism (Junghans 2001: 384). Couched in the language of the 'enterprising self' (Rose 1996), the programme thus remains thoroughly informed by hegemonic discourses in Polish society that have cast marginalized rural populations on the receiving end of the neoliberal structural reforms as 'atomized', 'dependent', and 'over-determined' socialist subjects innately lacking in enterprise and responsibility (Rakowski and Plińska 2010, see also Dunn 2004, Stenning 2005). Yet, it also ties in with the wider rise of neoliberal 'culture talk' within European cultural policy-making during the 1990s and early 2000s. No longer understood as simply a general public good, culture is increasingly conceived of as a resource for social and economic development. This has been accompanied by the breakdown of the 'traditional strict separation between a publicly subsidised non-commercial cultural sector and the cultural industry ... in favour of mixed forms', and paved the way for a 'marketization' of selection criteria for cultural funding towards efficiency, sustainability, and 'value-for-money' (Ellmeier 2011: 7). Furthermore, the dominance of the economic paradigm signals a 'shift from a governance *of* culture to one *through* culture by relaying an array of pressing political concerns from the realm of social and economic policy to that of culture in the sense of artistic expression' (Karaca 2009: 27, emphasis in original). Thus, just as dominant discourses of 'domestic orientalism' (Buchowski 2006) in Polish society currently re-cast the structurally disadvantaged as civilizationally backward, the philosophy of *animacja kultury* presents (local, vernacular) culture as an ideal vehicle for socio-economic betterment through self-expression.

The rise of the discourse of 'entrepreneurial citizenship' in European social policy is already well documented, along with the general re-branding of job insecurity and economic informalization as 'flexibility' and 'micro-enterprise' in the European labour market (Smith 2006: 624). As Peo Hansen has noted that as 'neoconservative and neoliberal forces gained the upper hand' during the 1980s, the European Commission began to adopt an 'increasingly individualized and market-oriented perception of citizenship', which stressed 'notions of active citizenship, volunteerism and charity' in place of a commitment 'to universal and collectively sustained citizenship entitlements' (2000: 145, also Lehning 1997, Mitchell 2006, Shuibne 2010). Extending this line of enquiry, this chapter asks what role 'entrepreneurial citizenship' plays in the formation of ethnic and regional identities in (postsocialist) Europe where culture has only recently become the 'locus of collective rights to self-determination' (Kempney 2005: 355). How are the demands of 'flexibility', 'responsibility', and 'active citizenship' reflected in funding for cultural projects? How do these demands shape local attempts to harness culture as a political asset? And, indeed, what bearing do successful (and failing) projects tell us about the changing performance of Górale minority identity in the area? On one hand, these questions are concerned with changes in the architecture of policy-making I outlined above. As Uta Staiger (2009) observes, the embrace of 'organizational citizens' and (non)governmental 'stakeholders' by European policy-makers has been accompanied by the move away from an ontologically narrow paradigm of culture as identity towards the conception of on culture as a platform for public advocacy and a mechanism for facilitating active citizenship. As we shall see below, this is evident in the formulation and implementation of European structural funding for cultural and cross-border activities initiatives in Cieszyn Silesia, as well as Polish cultural policy at large. On the other hand, these questions relate to vernacular perceptions of identity and agency amongst the Górale inhabitants of the region, and the ways in which they choose to enrol cultural policy and (European) funding streams into their own programmes for local development. As we shall see below, it is through these projects that the universal principles underpinning both European policy-making and models for community development such as *animacja kultury* are confronted with the complex realities of multiple overlapping and conflicting narratives of ethno-historical belonging on the ground. Furthermore, these projects of self-determination challenge prevailing discursive link made between 'enterprising' behaviour and 'sustainable' development, as much as they at times support them.

Being Górale in Cieszyn Silesia: Between Nation-states

Historically and administratively linked, the three communities of Leśna, Karpacz, and Głowno are commonly known as the 'Trójwies' (Triple Village), and are situated high in Carpathian Mountains of Southern Silesia, on the borders with the Czech and Slovak Republics. The inhabitants of the Triple Village proudly claim Górale (Highlander) heritage pointing to a history of transhumant pastoralism, characteristic folkways, traditional costume, and music tradition. For over a century, the local amateur folk troupes *Karpacz* (founded 1901) and *Leśna* (founded 1952) have participated festivals celebrating Górale culture in Poland, Slovakia, and the Czech Republic, as well as local, national, and international festivals of folklore across Europe and beyond. They are called out to dance and sing at every major community and religious event, whether it be the yearly Harvest Festival (*dożynki*) or the inauguration of a new municipal building. Across the Trójwieś, several construction companies specializing in building 'Górale-style' log houses are feeding a new fashion for neo-traditional vernacular architecture, while local folk dress is still considered de rigueur for artisans, musicians, and even organizers of a multitude of local festivals and fairs. Indeed, the performative aspects of Górale identity have become an integral part of the local tourism industry which now supports an ever-growing number of galleries and souvenir shops, 'old-style' inns serving traditional cuisine, and bed-and-breakfast establishments advertising access to bracing mountain trails. However, it is the local dialect, or *gwara*, which is seen as the most significant and lasting legacy of highland culture and paramount to the maintenance of local identities. As Jerzy, a local gallery-owner, explained:

> Our dialect includes a lot of Czech words: German words – or Austrian words from olden times, so we speak 'many languages'. You know, in Karpacz 'się opowiado', in Głowno 'się gwari ', and in Leśna 'się żondzi ‹ [all ‹to speak›], so from those three words you can see that between the villages there are different dialects. And the people in the Żywiec region, they already speak a language characteristic of the region which we villagers call 'Polish'.

Jerzy's statement makes it obvious how even minute differences in vocabulary and pronunciation are instrumental for placing people within a local geography of fragmented, far-flung hamlets, but also how language ties the Trójwieś to regions across the national border and to a culturally diverse past which is seen as at the same time 'traditional' and transnational. His reference to '*Austrian words from olden times*' signalled his belief that the centuries when the area formed part of the Austro-Hungarian Empire as part of the Duchy of Cieszyn Silesia left a lasting legacy on the local, Highland experience. Furthermore, as

Jerzy explained to me, Trójwies traditions bore a deep affinity with a larger family of Górale groups across the Polish and Central European Carpathian mountain ranges. This family resemblance emerged from the historic settlement of the Polish Carpathians by successive waves of Polish, Slovak, Rusyn, and Balkan Vlachs migrating westwards through the Carpathians between the fourteenth and the sixteenth centuries (Ćwiżewicz 2001, Radwańska-Paryska and Paryski 1995). Thus, what distinguished the local Górale from lowland Poles was not simply a set of cultural traditions, but also a vaguely defined element of ethnicity. The belief that the communities of the Trójwieś have a deep cultural and ethnic affinity with fellow Highlanders beyond the national borders has been the impetus for the formation of several civic organizations promoting collaboration and knowledge exchange between historically pastoral communities across the Carpathians and between functioning pastures in highland villages run as businesses by self-styled, professional shepherds. In short, the place of the Trójwieś in the historical territory of Cieszyn Silesia, and within a larger Górale cultural group, is actively asserted through an articulation of difference from the rest of the Polish state and an affinity with the broader (Central European) whole.

In contemporary Leśna, Karpacz, and Głowno, then, people employ shifting and overlapping historical and geopolitical frameworks and reference points to make sense of their world, juggling multiple areas of agency (the state, the market, Europe) with shifting concepts of time and geographical belonging. With their references to ancient migratory routes, imperial powers, and the shifting borders of nation-states, narratives of Górale ethnicity and culture can be seen as a continual exercise in boundary-drawing which serves not only to mark out the parameters of Highland identity, but simultaneously delineates spaces for the exercise of individual agency. Whether they draw their legitimacy from references to the local community, a mythological, transnational Górale past, or the historical geo-political entity of Cieszyn Silesia, these narratives provide alternate space-times or heterotopias for the enactment of individual agency and its interpretation. However, as we see above, they do so only with the support (or despite the resistance) of bureaucratic structures and cultural, political, and economic institutions. The choice of narratives and discourses, and the recruitment of institutions for their support by local actors, has changed dramatically since 1989, allowing for the flourishing of multiple, over-lapping notions of territorial identity which engage with, challenge, or even completely bi-pass the Polish nation state. In the following, I take a closer look at how European Union structural funding in the form of subsidies from the Common Agricultural Policy and cohesion policy (PHARE, INTERREG) have offered local actors (municipalities, civic organizations, entrepreneurs) the opportunity to foster meaningful relations with the Polish Górale minorities within and beyond Polish borders. Paying special attention to the way in which different actors have managed to harness the devolution of European and Polish decision-making processes, I highlight the ways in which they engage with or contest the notions of 'partnership' and 'sustainability' which underpin the desired trait of 'enterprising' behaviour. The contested nature of these concepts was especially clear in relation to projects supported by the *Euroregion Těšínské Slezko-Śląsk Cieszyński* which bridges municipalities along the Polish-Czech borderlands.

Re-inventing Czieszyn Silesia as a 'little homeland'

An integral part of the European Union's Cohesion Policy, cross-border 'Euroregions' have been formed since the 1990s in an attempt to facilitate the flow of capital, labour, and products across national borders, strengthening areas which had previously been peripheral to the development projects of nation-states (Perkmann 2007).[3] Founded in 1998 on the basis of several existing cross-border bi-lateral agreements between Polish and Czech municipalities, the Euroregion Těšínské Slezko-Śląsk Cieszyński was described to me by the Czech general secretary Václav Laštůka as 'an agreement on piece of paper ... between two partners, one Czech partner, us, and a Polish partner'. This agreement brings together municipalities from each side of the Czech-Polish border under the auspices of the Czech partner the Regional Association of territorial cooperation Cieszyn Silesia (*Regionální sdružení* územní *spolupráce Těšínského Slezska*) and the Polish partner Association for the Development of Regional Cooperation "Olza" (*Stowarzyszenia Rozwoju Współpracy Regionalnej "Olza"*), replicating almost perfectly the geo-political boundaries of the nineteenth century Habsburg Duchy of Czieszyn Silesia. His Polish counterpart, Bogdan Kasparek was similarly blunt in his characterization of Euroregions in general as essentially 'artifical' administrative constructs. And yet, both men felt that Czieszyn Silesia was an exception to the rule, building on pre-existing cultural and linguistic affinities between Poles and Czechs on either side of the border. 'History is a very strong element in our collaboration', Kasparek told me. 'The Euroregion Czieszyn Silesia ... as one of the regions which have a certain thread running through their culture, which bring together microregions which were once a whole, is a little less artificial'. Barely half a mile away, across the border with the Czech Republic, Václav Laštůka outlined the confluence of the historical territory of the Duchy and that of today's Euroregion on a map in his office, and told me 'this is an exception, this is *us* ... in other places it is not the case'.

---

3   The term covers a diverse range of institutional structures designed to foster transnational co-operation between local and regional administrative entities, as well as non-governmental and not-for-profit actors across two or more border territories. Euroregions are the implementation agencies for certain European Union programmes and funding streams, but do not in themselves correspond to any pre-existing legislative institutions, or have any independent legislative power. They derive their competencies from the status of their members.

Michael Keating has remarked that regions seeking to extricate themselves from the political and cultural confines of a nation-state often 'call on older, pre-state traditions to support them' (Keating and Hooghe 2005: 272). Writing on the strength of local territorial identity in Czieszyn Silesia, Marian Kempny (2005) calls this tendency 'historical paleoterritorialism', arguing that together with the post-War influx of Poles into Silesia and the existence of a sizeable Polish-speaking minority on the Czech side of the border led inhabitants to regard themselves as belonging to 'their little homeland' (*mała ojczyzna*). Marooned inside Czechoslovakia when the 1920 border with Poland was drawn up along the river Olza, the Poles of the Zaolzie (literally 'behind the Olza') maintained a strong sense of group identity through language-based schooling, publication, and a rich associational life. Today, a high number of the cross-border projects funded by the Euroregion celebrate the communalities of Polish Highland culture on both side of the border. This has generated some criticism of the Euroregion as a vehicle for the promotion and retrenchment of Polish (and Polish Górale) identity: 'In this case, Czechs feel that these are so-called 'Polish-Polish' projects. To which we say, yes, that is true, but the Polish nationals living here are Czech citizens' Laštůka told me. When the conversation moved on to recent attempts at collaborative history-writing, however, his tone became sharper; 'If there are to be any money for Czech-Polish collaboration, then there has to be a mutual equivalence. If it is a Czech or a Pole who writes, he always writes the truth, only that truth always offends'. On the Polish side, however, Bogdan Kasparek, disagreed with Laštůka's opinion that the organization should 'leave history to the historians'. He argued that the issue of the Polish minority was one 'politicians swept under the carpet' in the early days of the Euroregion in favour of 'political correctness', not only alienating Polish groups but giving out the impression that they wanted to preserve minority culture 'principally as a sort of open-air museum, a tourist attraction'.

Behind the celebratory rhetoric of cultural cooperation and communality advertising the Euroregion Těšínské Slezko-Śląsk Cieszyński, then, there lay a Gordian knot of historical ethnic and national tensions which remain unresolved to this day. The fact that many of the so-called 'Polish-Polish' projects which did meet with approval revolved around boosting tourism through the support of vernacular culture may have contributed to Kasparek's contrite observation about the commercialization of Polish minority culture. The municipal cultural centre (*Gminny Ośrodek Kultury*) in Karpacz was responsible for initiating a series of programmes of this kind under the titles Promotion of Górale Folk Art on the Polish-Czech-Slovak Triangle (*Promocja góralskiej twórczośi ludowej na trójsztyku polsko-czesko-slowackiem*) and Górale Traditions on the Polish-Czech-Slovak Triangle (*Góralskie Tradicie na trójsztyku polsko-czseko-slowackiem*). Aimed at supporting and marketing local artisans, the programmes were run together with a Czech partner organization promoting Górale culture and tourism in the Zaolzie, and funded by a grant from the Euroregion's Fund for Micro-projects. Katarzyna, a young employee at the Karpacz GOK, described the project as allowing artisans from both sides of the border to tap into a growing number of folkloric events in the Polish-Czech borderlands in order to 'together show off the shared Czech-Slovak-Polish (Górale) culture'. In essence, the programme consisted in organizing and coordinating the invitation and participation of artisans to fairs and festivals where they could 'exhibit their wares, show them off, and sell them'. 'The aim is to create a lasting collaboration to enable them to promote themselves as one', Katarzyna told me. This wish to create an enduring network of contacts for the commercial support of local artisans, however, also appeared motivated by the perceived need to re-awaken and strengthen the image of the Polish Górale minority south of the border. Claiming that the interest in Górale culture had been 'extinguished a bit' by half a century of assimilation with majority Czech culture, Katarzyna saw one major goal of the project as providing the social and financial capital for the few existing Górale artisans from the Czech side to 'work within the majority culture which is on the Czech side', while giving Polish Górale artisans the possibility to 'penetrate not only our region, but beyond it'.

Euroregions have all too often been defeated by irreconcilable 'institutional, cultural or operational difficulties', remaining 'a technocrat's construct with little relevance in the real world' (Herschell 2011: 154–162). Yet, listening to Katarzyna speak about their efforts to promote 'shared Czech-Slovak-Polish culture', it became clear that the Euroregion's rhetoric of transnational, cross-border cooperation was the subject of constant re-interpretation and renegotiation by applicants and administrators on both sides of the border. Although Katarzyna, Vaclav, and Bogdan all operated with a notion of Cieszyn Silesia as a 'little homeland' and the foundation of a particular historically constituted regional identity, the perspective from the Trójwieś did not correspond to that I heard in the offices of Euroregion administration itself. Rather than as a meeting place of two national traditions, projects like the *Promotion of Górale Folk Art* and *Górale Traditions* re-invented the Euroregion of Czieszyn Silesia as the historical territory of a single cultural group – the Cieszyn or Silesian Górale. Sentiments of regional belonging, then, became synonymous with Góraleness, turning Euroregion funding into a vehicle for the promotion of minority identity. Causing palpable tensions between the Euroeregion's coordinating partners, this question of minority identity was largely wrought through the denominations of nationality and citizenship by Vaclav Laštůka and Bogdan Kasparek. Their own discussions of the Euroregion's historical roots in the pre-1918 Duchy of Cieszyn Silesia were dominated by ethno-linguistic classifications: the minority population in the Czech Zaolzie were thought of as predominantly Polish (rather than Górale) leading projects promoting Highland vernacular culture to be labelled 'Polish-Polish' projects, while narratives of a separate Górale cultural and ethnic identity were entirely lost on the Polish. Indeed the Habermasian aspects of Laštůka's attempts at downplaying the importance of minority 'Polish-Polish' projects by pointing out that the Poles of the Zaolzie were in fact Czech citizens appeared to indicate his wish to prevent any accusations of partisanship. Kasparek, for his part, appeared to interpret this unwillingness to engage in a proper dialogue with

Polish minority civic associations as undermining the principles of cross-border dialogue itself.

The latent conflict surrounding the role and status of minority identity, then, appeared to be intimately associated with attempts to shore up the integrity of the Euroregion project itself. Aware of criticisms of administrative incompetence and nepotism levelled at neighbouring collaborations on the Polish-German border, Laštůka was keen to stress that the organization was not in the business of 'buying cooperation for European (Union) money' (see Kramsch and Hooper 2004, Leibenath et al. 2008). Indeed, as we shall see below, both men appeared to be more worried about allocating funding to projects which would maintain long-term sustainable growth, than attempting to divide it along historical or ethno-cultural lines. As members of the Euroregion's steering committee, they oversaw the allocation of the so-called Fund for Mikro-projects (*Fundusz Mikroprojektów*) aimed at fostering the 'development of interpersonal relations along the border, educational, social, and cultural initiatives' (SRiWR "Olza" 2010: 17). Initiated in 1999, the *Fundusz Mikroprojektów* taps into a funding stream for Czech-Polish cooperation allocated under the National Regional Policy Framework with means from the European Regional Development Fund (until 2004 PHARE CBC, then INTTERREG III A and INTERREG IV A) and is the main source of financial support for cultural projects by participating municipalities, institutions, and civic organizations. Yet, just as the concept of Cieszyn Silesia as 'little Homeland' differed widely depending on the perspective of the speaker, the definitions of 'partnership' and 'sustainability' outlined by European directives were an issue of ongoing contention and negotiation between all three parties. Those managing the allocation of funds fretted about the correct way to administer benchmarks, while applicants from the Trójwieś lamented the mismatch between fundamental aspects of the funding criteria clashed with the realities of a tight fiscal environment.

Animating Culture in the Trójwieś

'Funding should not be given on the principle "give me money and I'll think about what to do with them"', Vaclav Laštůka told me. Speaking to me in his offices on a summer afternoon in 2011, he was eager to emphasize that only applicants with feasible project proposals were supported by the Czech side of the cross-border partnership. According to Laštůka, the partnership was occasionally hampered by the reluctance of his Polish partners to agree on hard and fast criteria (*'Czech rules'*) for their evaluation. Filtering tensions between the Czech and Polish sides of the partnership through national stereotypes, he explained – partly in jest – that while Czechs often erred on the side of caution, Poles had a tendency to make 'impulsive' decisions with the expectation that the parameters for funding could be renegotiated at a later date. Bogdan Kasparek, for his part, remained of the opinion that long-term sustainability could be fostered by a certain amount of flexibility in the interpretation and application of funding criteria. Describing Poland as a relatively poor funding environment, told me that 'we cannot do everything by the book'. 'We often find that someone comes to us for a consultation', he continued, 'and says, for example, 'I would like to build an amphitheatre', help me to write it so I can access the money' (*wyciągnąć pieniądze* – literally 'pull out the money'). This amphitheatre was brainchild of the mayor of the village of Jasienica, who – Kasparek suspected – was aiming to boost his chances for re-election. Pointing out that Jasienica already ran cross-border projects with the Czech village of Petřvald, he told the mayor 'Good, but then go to your Czech partner and create an agenda. An agenda for collaboration. Include what you want, but we have to justify the infrastructure by showing it is necessary in order for you to intensify your cooperation'. Aiming to align the goals of the applicant with those of the organization at large, in short, Kasparek presented the allocation of funds as conditional upon the partners committing themselves to participation in the transnational network which made up the institution itself. Having eventually gained support from the Fund for Micro-projects, Kasparek noted with satisfaction that the Mayor's project had initiated cultural activities (a Czech-Polish amateur theatre festival, regular folkloric performances by amateur tropes from Slovakia, Poland and the Czech Republic, and a cross-border Harvest Festival) which continued long after the funding itself had dried up.

By making evidence of active collaboration the foremost criteria for gaining access to funding, Kasparek appeared just as keen to ensure the feasibility and long-term impact of any funded projects as did his Czech partner. However, unlike Laštůka, Kasparek appeared to consider the content of the project less important than its ability to foster creativity, collaboration and momentum. Not only did his evaluation of a successful project seem to draw from fundamentally similar principles to those found in the prevailing Polish discourse of 'cultural animation', but the narrative of the mayor and his amphitheatre also came across as a morality tale. Arriving for pragmatic advice on how to 'pull out the money' from European Funding streams, the mayor of Jasienica seemed to understand the European project simply as an alternative source of income for the municipality 'from above' (*z góry*). By insisting that they worked together to re-shape the project into a form acceptable to both parties, Kasparek appeared to be keen to distance himself from the mayor's perception of 'partnership' as a type of privileged access to insider information (or even, to funding itself). Rather, his efforts to shift the discourse from one of 'pulling out' money 'form above' to an 'agenda for collaboration' with a Czech partner reflected a move towards a wider use of 'partnership' discourse in development policy coupling the idea of 'solidarity or equality while also meeting neoliberal demand for contract, responsibility and self-interest that fits with the new business environment' (Dahl 2001: 13). Thus, Kasperka positioned himself not simply as a gatekeeper to European funding, but also a disciplining agent who set about transforming the mayor from a passive recipient of financial aid to a responsible, 'entrepreneurial' citizen working on behalf of his community.

Kasperka did acknowledge, however, that certain aspects of the European Union directives governing the allocation of structural funding were unsuited to the local fiscal environment. The fact that European funding was released only after activities had ceased and accounts had been settled, he told me, was often an insurmountable obstacle for municipalities and local civic organizations. In fact, when I visited the Trójwieś the following November, just as the fiscal year was drawing to a close, precisely this question of cash-flow appeared to weigh particularly heavily on Katarzyna's mind. The two projects Promotion of Górale Folk Art and Górale Traditions, she told me, had caused financial problems for the municipality. In order to finance the programme, it had taken out a loan which it was now struggling to repay due to the late receipt of the promised European funding. 'Well, we submitted the accounts last year in December', she explained, 'and it was not until recently that we received a part of the money. And not yet all of it. Sometimes you wait 2 or 3 years for the money, and that is a problem for institutions and organizations like us'. As a result, they were unable to commit to any new projects. Rather than risking further debt, Katarzyna and her colleagues told me they preferred to apply for funds from the Visegrad Foundation, or national programmes, which supplied funding 'quickly' and upfront (*z góry*– literally 'from above'). Admitting that such programmes were run along 'old principles', she ruefully commented they were 'better principles'. Indeed, despite their willingness to fund projects up front, neither the Visegrad foundation nor funding streams available from the Ministry of Culture remained immune to new criteria of fiscal efficiency and sustainability. Speaking about national funding streams, Katarzyna lamented: 'In the beginning, it was simple, very concrete ... you write what you wanted to do, how many months, what you wanted to buy, what it cost, and it was all good. And now it is set out according to Union rules, and you have to write the same, but put the emphasis on the future ... but what will be in the future is hard to say'.

Katarzyna's positive evaluation of 'old' principles of funding *z góra* indicated she felt that the 'new' funding regime represented a significant curtailment of her agency by decoupling the receipt and allocation of funds from the on-going social responsibilities and financial constraints of the municipality. Contrary to the mayor of Jasienica, she did not see funding received 'from above' as a financial bonus to be used at the municipality's discretion, but as a tool of fiscal prudence which allowed the financing and implementation of local projects on the ground. Indeed, her comments indicated that the move from the funding of concrete projects 'from above' on the basis of their content, to the retroactive provision of financial support for cross-border partnerships, was failing to cater for the interests of the local population. For all their efforts, activities such as the Promotion of Górale Folk Art and Górale Traditions had had little impact on the ground: 'Broadly speaking, our people (*ludzie nasi*) ... are not used to exhibitions. This is a village, here life is understood differently, here life is practical ... So our people come if invite them individually, call them (on the phone), sometimes several times, asking them to come'. Despite the feverish activity which pervaded the work of the Karpacz GOK, she told me that she felt cultural life in the municipality was suffering from a lack of funding.

Presumably referring to European funding, she acknowledged that 'some things are easier to do. It is easier to set up a partnership, but certain things seem to have become much more difficult'. Arranging and funding activities for the local youth had proved to be most challenging. Indeed, while they arranged plenty of activities for young people, such as judo, football, breakdance class, and music and craft lessons based in local vernacular culture, Katarzyna recalled her own childhood as one where the municipality had held more promise for the young; 'for example, there used to be a cinema in Karpacz, and there is none now. In Leśna, there was a House of Culture during communist times and there was a youth club. So in some ways, things are worse, mainly there doesn't seem to be money for culture'.

Katrzyna's laments present a potent critique of not only the de-centralized nature of Polish cultural policy, but the notion of culture as 'activism' which underpins the push for further devolution. In contrast to the discourse of cultural animation which presented the infrastructure of Communist social cultural policy as a mechanism of alienation, she portrayed the Leśna House of Culture, the Karpacz cinema, and the Youth Club as precisely the 'meeting places between people' which they now seek to achieve. As such, her comments revealed a crucial weakness in their emancipatory rhetoric of not just *cultural animation*, but policy-reform at large, which encourages marginalized populations to use existing resources to create 'social and cultural capital' without taking adequate measure of the very real limitations created by funding parameters, the fiscal environment, and local traditions of collective action. She highlighted the fact that the parameters of 'sustainability' – defined by Kasperka as precisely the accretion of social capital which secured continued partnership – not only elevated directed self-expression into a self-evident virtue by discounting the importance of project content, but also tended to fail to recognize the value of pre-existing social capital. Indeed, at the heart of Katarzyna's critique lay the observation that partnerships and collaborations between municipalities and/or civic organizations did not automatically foster social capital or create an environment of activism amongst the population if financial support was simultaneously withdrawn from the social infrastructure which had underpinned the community collective for half a century. Rather, partnerships brought together interested parties around a well-defined goal – in this case, the commercial production of arts and crafts – often drawing together a limited number of social actors (artisans, entrepreneurs, civil servants) who acted as both administrators and recipients of funding.

In the last section I trace the formation of one of these 'communities of interest' (Mosse 2005: 16) around a European Union funded bio-diversity programme aimed at facilitating the return of commercially viable pastoral agriculture to the Polish Highlands. Just like the 'paleoterritorialism' which characterizes cultural projects funded through the Euroregion Cieszyn Silesia, this project is intimately related to an imagined geography of a Górale homeland as occupying much of Central Europe.

Carpathian Partnerships: Reviving Pastoral Culture

'What do you mean "Sir"? I always tell everyone, that you should not make a lord out of a Góral (*nie zrobić pana z górala*). The gentlemen are down in the cities' Adam – Karpacz's self-styled headman – admonished me mid-way through my first meeting with him on a warm September evening in 2010. Wishing to be polite, I had addressed him using the conventional Polish *Pan* (Mister, or Sir), instead of the more informal ty, but he cringed visibly and asked me to address him by name, or using a local term, such as ujcu ('uncle'). A father of two in his late thirties, Adam is one of a growing number of rural entrepreneurs across the Polish Carpathians which have become involved in reviving local, historical forms of transhumant pastoralism and cheese-making. Describing himself as a reformed rebel who had spent the decade after 1989 admiring what he termed 'Western culture', Adam told me that he felt local traditions of pastoralism were 'definitely encoded somewhere in our DNA'. Growing up, he had witnessed how Górale music, dance, and even costume were cultivated, but later came to the conclusion that 'something was missing': sheep. Adam painstakingly reconstructed Karpacz's pastoral tradition by seeking out older members of the community, and making several trips to the Polish Tatras to learn from communities which had retained a greater knowledge of grazing and cheese-making. Today, the milk for Adam's cheeses is supplied by over 200 sheep owned by 19 different local families. They graze on local pasture-land from April to September, under the watchful eyes of several shepherds. While some of his products are sold locally to tourists, Adam sells cheese wholesale through a producers' co-operative, and supplies restaurants within and beyond Poland.

Speaking to Adam throughout that summer; however, it quickly became clear that he aimed to more than start a business by reintroducing pastoralism to the hills surrounding the village. 'When the source is polluted', he told me poetically, 'then the river is dirty. You have to clean the source, to create the conditions for the return to it'. Lamenting the system of subsistence farming which had persisted throughout the later twentieth century, he blamed the Communist regime for 'intentionally doing everything to break down' pastoral traditions in the area. Adam saw Poland's move towards market democracy in the early 1990s, and especially the country's entry into the European Union, as facilitating real changes in attitudes to pastoral agriculture. He singled out the regional government of Silesia (*Wojewódstwo Śląskie*) as a particular ally, praising the lengths local officials had gone to match the needs of budding pastoralists with the requirements of the European Union's Common Agricultural Policy. Referring to the imperfect fit between the CAP's programme of subsidies for farmers according to the land-area managed, and the communally-based nature of local pastoral traditions, Adam said: 'Well, you see that is the whole problem ... you see all countries which have signed the Policy are banned from providing subsidies for livestock. [...] All the money goes through surcharges on agricultural land, but it is possible for them to pay a subsidy for servicing livestock'. This funding was accessed through the construction of a regional bio-diversity programme *Owca Plus 2010–2014* (literally 'Sheep Plus') which could tap into the CAP's second pillar of funding, the European Agricultural Fund for Rural Development Fund. This multipronged initiative aimed not only to re-introduce pastoralism in the region, but also the 'cultivation of cultural identity connected to pastoralism, the promotion of traditional vernacular culture, and the development of crafts and manufacture of products sheep and goats' (*Owca Plus* 2009: 32). It thus fell well within the EAFRD's remit of supporting the 'restructuring, development and innovation' in rural areas (Nori and Germini 2011: 3).

Adam's role in the project was to act as consultant and partner in the implementation of the development if the programme's overall strategy. Like other EAFRD programmes, Owca Plus was run using the LEADER approach aimed at the 'implementation of local development strategies through public-private partnerships called "local action groups"' (EAFRD 2012). This meant that *Owca Plus* became a potent vehicle from which to launch several new 'action groups' on Górale cultural diversity and bio-diversity such as *Karapty Naszym Domem* (from 2010), *Karpaty Łączą* (from 2012–5) and *Fundacja Paterstwo Transhumance* (from 2012). On paper and on-line, the implementation of the *Owca Plus* had apparently led to the emergence of a plethora of new 'local action groups' and mutual partnerships between these groups and other municipal, regional, and transnational (non)governmental actors. It appeared to signal the emergence of 'active citizenship' amongst villagers and reflect a blossoming of a lively civic culture in the region. In practice, however, it was Adam and his colleague Łukasz who were instrumental in constructing this intricate network of civic associations and working groups – either directly as initiators and de-facto leaders, or through their membership of the producers' cooperative. Indeed, when I spoke to Adam about Owca Plus, he appeared to read these activities primarily through the lens of his business, characterizing it as 'a sort of scheme (*kombinacja*), through which we can divert (money) into our industry in a legal manner'. And yet, together with Łukasz, Adam instrumentalized the very same working relations with fellow interest groups and producers in Romania and the Ukraine to organize the so-called Carpathian Sheep Transhumance 2013 (*Redyk karpacki 2013*): a 3-month migration of 300 sheep the entire length of the Carpathian mountains from Brasov in Romania, across the Ukraine, Slovakia, Poland, and ending in the Czech Republic. Reconstructing the 'historical transhumance of the Vlach shepherds', the project's declared aim was to support the 'sustainable development' of (erstwhile) pastoral communities by bringing together NGOs, local government, media and commercial sponsors with an interest in promoting 'the cultural and ecological values' of the Carpathians (*Redyk Karpacki* 2013).

The *Redyk Karpacki*, in other words, was nothing less than a spectacular transnational performance of a particular concept of authentic Górale cultural identity. As founders of the local chapter of the Polish Association of Highlanders (*Związek Podhalan*), both Adam and Łukasz felt the Górale were not simply 'inhabitants of the mountains', but Highlanders – that is, those who 'refer to pastoral culture' and 'build their identity on the base and source of a way of life that was being created across the Carpathians'. Identifying fellow Górale groups in the Czech and Slovak borderlands, as well as Ukranian Lemkos (Rusyns) and Romanian Hutsul groups as their cultural brethren, Adam and Łukasz found little interest in territorially bound notions of selfhood like those offered by European Union funded programmes of transnational dialogue. Rather, they equated Highland culture with a somewhat romanticized of liberty and mobility: waxing lyrical over plate of smoked sheep's cheese and a bottle of homemade raspberry brandy one evening, Adam told me that 'a Górale isn't a person connected to a certain place, he is person on the road. Because the shepherd is a person always in motion. The most characteristic thing about a Górale is his need for freedom'. Chiming in, Łukasz added that this was a 'very modern mentality' as suited to the realities of contemporary global society as it had been to the hardships of the past: 'For example, the fact our homeland is not in one concrete place, but spread across the widely understood world, in which a person migrates. And you could say, a contemporary person is one that migrates, for he migrates for work, for education, and often he emigrates'. Rooted in transhumant pastoralism, then, Adam and Łukasz saw Górale culture as providing the blue-print for successful agency in a united Europe (and a globalizing world). Indeed, there was a striking affinity between their conception of a de-territorialized mobility as the core of a truly Górale spirit and Ong's notion of the 'flexible citizen' who embraces 'flexibility, migration, and relocations' and sees them as 'practices to strive for rather than stability' (1999: 19).

The construction of *Owca Plus* and the *Redyk Karpacki* as avenues for the successful performance of Górale identity illustrates its profound interdependency with wider structures of governance. The move towards public-private consultation facilitated the formation of a 'community of interest' around the question of bio-diversity, while simultaneously allowing the idea of Górale identity as rooted in pastoral agriculture itself to become a rallying point for a group of entrepreneurs interested in attracting subsidies from the CAP. Having successfully recruited regional policy-maker and European funding for their activities, Adam, Łukasz, and their colleagues promoted a Górale self which reflected their specialist (business) interests and which co-existed with other local discourses on Highland culture. Yet, their success also highlights the manner in which policy-makers' reliance on 'organizational citizens' has created its own silences and omissions. Recruited by regional policy-makers, the partnerships established under the umbrella of Owca Plus brought together interested parties around a well-defined goal, Adam, Łukasz, and their associates gained a privileged position from which their particular narrative of identity could be turned into a political (and financial) asset. Observing a similar dynamic in European Union policy-making at large, Chris Shore argues that the privileged position of 'organizational citizens' reflects a 'form of neoliberal governmentality that is actually undermining democratic government and promoting a politics of exclusion' by recasting policy-making as 'essentially 'technical' or 'organizational' matters to be decided on the basis of scientific and technical expertise rather than public debate' (2011: 287–9). As we saw in the case of the mayor of Jasienica, and even Katarzyna and the Karpacz GOK, claims to such technical expertise in Cieszyn Silesia are highly contested amongst public institutions and civic organizations. However, if models of policy-making and the performance of identity are also intimately linked in the region, this suggests that these changes in decision-making also promote the view of Górale cultural identity itself as the preserve of experts – be they shepherds, municipal cultural administrators, or the heads of regional development agencies.

Conclusions

In this chapter, I have been concerned with uncovering the way in which pre-accession policy-reform and post-accession European Union funding for transnational cooperation have delivered new frameworks for the definition and performance of what it means to be a Highlander on the Polish-Czech-Slovak border. Classical anthropological theory tells us that ethnic and territorial identities are relational, relying on the maintenance of difference vis-à-vis a social, historical or religious 'Others' (Barth 1969). In the case of the Polish Górale, this 'Other' has historically taken the form of the economic and bureaucratic structures of the socialist and post-socialist Polish nation-state (Pine 1998, 2003, 2007). Yet, as the comic statue of the Górale *dziadek* (grandfather) riding to Brussels to deliver to the European Commission his advice for their management of the Union, European structures of governance are now seen by people in Cieszyn Silesia as trumping those of the Polish nation state. In fact, the European project has become the vehicle for the promotion of multiple, overlapping narratives of territorial belonging which re-imagine ever larger slices of the Central and Eastern European Carpathian mountain ranges as 'Górale country'. Such shifts in the scalar dimensions of such imagined geographies, however, signal a more profound redefinition of the terms by which are encouraged to conceive of their own agency and act in Polish (and European) society: rather than the centralized and highly politicized cultural policy of the Communist past, European models of devolved policy-making ('multi-level governance') which stress civic activism now set the parameters for cultural practices and performances from pastoral agriculture and artisanship, to the performance of local folklore. Indeed, they form a new set of ideals for good governance while promising to turn 'passive', marginalized citizens into ideal 'active' and 'enterprising' citizens.

One of the consequences of this shift has been the emergence of 'communities of interest' which have gained privileged access of certain groups to financial and administrative support. The emphasis on public-private partnerships and engagement with 'organizational citizens' worked to the advantage of actors like Adam and his colleagues, who could not only claim the status of 'stakeholders', but learned to display an associational behaviour legible to regional government. However, while Adam and Łukasz gladly embraced discourses of 'partnership' and 'sustainability', others contested it. Katarzyna, working within the more legally and fiscally restricted parameters of the local municipality, portrayed the funding of partnerships as insufficient support of the bread-and-butter activities of everyday community building in the Trójwieś, while criticizing the expectation of 'sustainable' outcomes as unrealistic. Her criticisms highlighted the degree to which the emancipatory rhetoric of 'activation' in policy reform ignored the limitations created by funding parameters, the fiscal environment, and local traditions of collective action, and failed to recognize the value of pre-existing institutional infrastructure. The activities which she would have liked to see funded were all too easily classified as the result of a 'passifying' Communist cultural policy funded 'from above'. Indeed, as we saw in the case of the mayor from Jasienica, however, it was precisely the expression of a preference for funding 'from above' (*z góry*) which marked actors out for criticism from those administering European funds. Worried about accusations of cronyism, or appearing to 'buying cooperation for European money', Bogdan Kasparek and Václav Laštůka took upon themselves the role of disciplining agents who would monitor and reform the conduct of municipal and civic actors who displayed a lack of 'responsible' activism. Indeed, precisely the case of the mayor of Jasienica illustrates the tautological relationship between the categories of 'partnership' and 'sustainability' themselves: by making the criteria for gaining access evidence of active collaboration, Laštůka and Kasparek committed partners to the transnational network which made up the Euroregion itself, giving them further access to funding for continued cooperation. As in the case of *Owca Plus*, this ostensibly open model of funding ended up generating its own 'community of interest'. Ironically, then, the parameters set up to ensure the funding of 'enterprising citizenship' in Cieszyn Silesia appear to be instrumental in reinforcing the split between a small subset of highly active and engaged actors, and a large majority who have neither the means nor the connections to claim the status of 'stakeholder'.

References

Bellamy, R. and A. Warleigh. 2001. *Citizenship and Governance in the European Union*. London and New York: Continuum.

Ćwiżewicz, K. 2001. *Musical Rites of Entertainment among Gorale of the Polish Tatra Mountains*. London: University of London.

Dahl, G. 2001. *Responsibility and Partnership in Swedish Aid Discourse*. Discussion Paper 9. Uppsala: Nordiska Afrikainstitutet.

Delgado-Moreira, J. 2002. Cohesion and Citizenship in EU Cultural Policy, *Journal of Common Market Studies*, 38(3): 449–70.

Buchowski, M. 2006. The Spectre of Orientalism in Europe: From Exotic Other to Stigmatized Brother. *Anthropological Quarterly*, 79(3): 463–82.

Dunaeva, V. 2013. Miejsce animacji kulturalnej w działaności polskich i rosyjskich lokalnych ośrodków kultury po przelomie ustrojowym (na wybranych przykładach). *Adeptus*, 1/2013: 26–40.

Dunn, E. 2004. *Privatizing Poland. Baby Food, Big Business, and the Remaking of Labour*. Ithaca, NY: Cornell University Press.

Ellmeier, A. 2003. Cultural entrepreneurialism: on the changing relationship between the arts, culture and employment. *International Journal of Cultural Policy*, 9(1): 3–16.

European Network of Animation. www.enoa.ro.

Godelewski, G. 2002. Animacja I Antropologia. In G. Godelewsk, I. Kurz, A. Mencwel and M. Wójtowski *Animacja Kultury. Doświadczenie i przyszłość*. Warsaw: Instytut Kultury Polskiej UW, pp. 56–70.

Habermas, J. 1992. Citizenship and nationality. Some reflections on the future of Europe. *Praxis International*, 12(1): 1–19.

Habermas, J. 1996. The European Nation State. Its achievements and limitations. On the past and future of sovereignty and citizenship. *Ratio Juris*, 9(2): 125–37.

Habermas, J. 2001. *The Postnational Constellation: Political Essays*. Cambridge, MA: MIT Press.

Hansen, P. 2000 "European citizenship", or Where Neoliberalism Meets Ethnoculturalism. *European Societies*, 2(2): 139–65.

Herschell, T. 2011. *Borders in Post-socialist Europe: Territory, Scale, Society*. Farnham: Ashgate.

Hooghe, L. and G. Marks. 2001. *Multi-level Governance and the European Union*. London: Rowman and Littlefield.

Hooghe, L. and G. Marks. 2003. Unravelling the Central State, but How? Types of Multi-level Governance. *American Political Science Review*, 97(2): 233–43.

Keating, M. and L. Hooghe. 2005. By-passing the Nation-state? Regions and the EU Policy Process, in J. Richardson (ed.), *European Union: Power and Policy-making*. London and New York: Routledge.

Ilczuk, D., Nowak, M. and E. Bender. 2012. Country Profile: Poland. Compendium of Cultural Policies and Trends in Europe. Council of Europe/ERIcarts. www.culturalpolicies.net.

Junghans, T. 2001. Marketing Selves. Constructing Civil Society and Selfhood in Post-socialist Hungary. *Critique of Anthropology*, 21(4): 383–400.

Karaca, B. 2009. Governance of or through culture? Cultural Policy and the politics of culture in Europe. *Focaal – European Journal of Anthropology*, 55/2009: 27–40.

Kempney, M. 2005. 'Nation-building as Communist 'Rational Planning Strategy' Subverted by Local Narratives'. *Polish Sociological Review*, 4(152): 349–65.

Kramsch, O. and B. Hooper. 2004. *Cross-border Governance in the European Union*. London and New York: Routledge.

Lehning, P. 1997. *Citizenship, Democracy and Justice in the New Europe*. London: Routledge.

Leibenath, M., Knippshild, R. and E. Korcelli-Olejniczak. 2008. *Cross-border Governance and Sustainable Spatial Development. Mind the Gaps!* Berlin: Springer.

Marks, G., Hooghe, L. and Blank, K. 1996. European Integration from the 1980s: State-Centric v. Multi-level Governance. *Journal of Common Market Studies*, 34(3): 341–78.

Mitchell, K. 2006. Neoliberal governmentality in the European Union: education, teaching and technologies of citizenship, *Environment and Planning D: Society and Space*, 24: 389–407.

Mosse, D.2005. Global Governance and the Ethnography of International Aid, in D. Mosse and D. Lewis (eds), *The Aid Effect: Giving and Governing in International Development*. London: Pluto Press, pp. 1–36.

Nori, S. and M. Germini. 2011. The Common Agricultural Policy vis-à-vis European Pastoralists: principles and practices. *Pastoralism: Research, Policy and Practice*, 1: 27.

Ong, A. 2006. Mutations in Citizenship. *Theory Culture Society*, 23(2–3): 499–505.

Perkmann, M. 2007. Construction of New Territorial Scales: A Framework and Case Study of the EUREGIO Cross-border Region. *Regional Studies*, 41(2): 253–66.

Program aktywizacje gospodarczej oraz zachowania dziedzictwa kulturowego Beskidów I Jury Krakowsko-Częstochowskiej *Owca Plus* na lata 2010–2014. Katowice. 2009.

Radwańska-Paryska, Z. and W. Paryski. 1995. *Wielka Encyclopedia Tatrzańska*. Poronin: Wydawnictwo Gorskie.

Rakowski, T. and V. Plińska. 2010. Etnografia jako działanie społeczne/animacja kultury. *Prace Etnograficzne* 38/2010: 85–93.

Rose, N. 1996. *Inventing Our Selves. Psychology, Power, and Personhood*. Cambridge: Cambridge University Press.

Rumford, C. 2003. European Civil Society or Transnational Social Space? Conceptions of Society in Discourses of EU Citizenship, Governance, and the Democratic Deficit: An Emerging Agenda. *European Journal of Social Theory*, 6(1): 25–43.

Shaw, J. 1998. The Interpretation of European Union Citizenship. *The Modern Law Review*, 61(3): 293–317.

Shore, C. 2000. *Building Europe. The Cultural Politics of the European Union*. London and New York: Routledge.

Shore, C. 2004. Whither European Citizenship? Eros and Civilization Revisited. *European Journal of Social Theory*, 7(1): 27–44.

Shuibhne, N. 2010. The Resilience of EU Market Citizenship. *Common Market Law Review*, 47(6): 1597–1628.

Skrzypczak, B. 2003. Dokąd zmierza dom kultury? in B. Skrzypczak, S. Mołda (eds), *Ośrodek kultury I aktywności lokalnej w poszukiwaniu modelu instytucji społecznościowej*. Warsawa: Stowarzyszenie Centrum Wsierania Aktywności Lokalnej CAL.

Smith, G. 2006. When 'the logic of capital is the real which lurks in the background'. Programme and Practice in European 'Regional Economies'. *Current Anthropology*, 47(4): 621–39.

Staiger, U. 2009. New Agendas? Culture and Citizenship in EU policy. *International Journal of Cultural Policy*, 15(1): 1–16.

Stenning, A. 2005. Where is the Post-socialist Working Class? Working-Class Lives in Spaces of (Post-)Socialism. *Sociology*, 39(5): 983–99.

Stowarzyszenie rozwoju i współpracy regionalnej "Olza". Sprawozdanie z działalności stowarzyszenia rozwoju i współpracy regionalnej "Olza" – Polskiej strony Euroregionu Śląsk Cieszynski-Tešinské Slezsko (1998–2010).

Afterword

Elias talks to Hayek (and learns from Marx and Foucault): Reflections on Neoliberalism, Postsocialism and Personhood

Don Kalb

I

Let me start with an anecdote that circulated among anthropologists and sociologists in the Netherlands while I was a student in the early eighties. At some point in the roaring 1970s, the great sociologist Norbert Elias, living in Amsterdam at the time, was sitting in a tram opposite a young man. On the guy's T-shirt was written in bold letters: "I am Independent". Elias, in his seventies, said: "Excuse me Sir, but that slogan is not correct: You are not *In*dependent, You are *Inter*dependent".

The story captures in a nutshell some of the well known philosophical problems associated with the core assumptions of neoliberalism. Nevertheless, in the next part of that exchange, excluded from the anecdote, Elias may well have graciously admitted that, while everyone *was* indeed *inter*dependent, some thought that they ought to be less interdependent than others and could get away with it. To magnify those claims of exception and their material consequences, neoliberalism began its world ascendency, unperturbed by the inadequacy of its rather juvenile philosophical positions.

In the 1970s, Elias was a world famous scholar enjoying the interest of many younger disciples in the booming sociology, anthropology, and history departments of the Western world. There was a fast growing and lively section in the International Sociological Association called 'Figurational Sociology' that was dedicated to discussing and extending Elias' sociology. His popularity was due among others to the fundamentally relational character of his approach.[1] This relational approach promised a transformation and revitalization of the social sciences, which many believed were in a deep crisis. Elias resolutely rejected the reification of 'societies' into things. This was a recurrent problem in the structuralist and functionalist theories of the time, but also in some of the more mechanical Marxisms. He also refuted the opposite idea, which saw separate and independent individuals as the basic building blocks of society. Such individualist notions

---

1   See for the overall approach in particular, Elias 2000, 2005, 2009 (these are reprintings).

were embodied in the rational actor approaches promoted by methodological individualists, dominant in positivist sociologies as well as in the disciplines of economics and psychology (in different ways). Society versus the individual and vice versa was a false polarity, Elias insisted. Instead, he focused on the 'social figurations that people formed with each other'. Such 'figurational' forms had ontological priority over 'individuals' and 'societies', Elias argued. In Elias's work, these figurations were organized around work, neighbourhoods, political associations, modes of rule, and ritual forms such as court and sporting societies. They added up, as it were, into more large-scale and complex 'configurations', another word for 'societies' or 'civilizations', which could be seen as 'chains of social interdependence' based in complex relational balances of power between the various groupings of actors. These configurations were always shifting over time and differentiating over space as human agency acted within and against these relational power balances between people, which were both the cause, the medium and the outcome of such dynamic forms. They were thereby perpetually set in motion, never in stasis, and were dynamic without any preconceived or intentional direction. It was the contingent dynamism of these relational power balances that produced histories and history simultaneously, at entangled micro and macro scales. Such histories, for Elias, encapsulated 'socio-genesis' as well as 'psycho-genesis'. Elias thus critiqued the synchronic mode in which much social science operated, and rejected its snapshots. It was these dynamic relational histories – histories in which persons as well as their social networks and the wider societies of which they were a part were made and unmade – that social research should discover and describe.[2]

At the time, his work was one of the most audible clarion calls against reductionist individualism and reifications of the social order. It was far from alone in being so. Elias's work shared this spirit with the new streams in Anglo-Marxism: E.P. Thompson's (1965, 1980) rejection of abstract structuralism, economic reductionism and positivism in historiography, for example; or the cultural Marxism of Raymond Williams (1971, 1977, 2005) and Stuart Hall (e.g. 1978, 2006). Compared to Marxist authors, however, Elias was much less interested in labour, class and social production as the key mechanisms of social interdependence in capitalist societies. The 'new social history', British cultural studies, and the new Marxian anthropologies were more interested in urban working classes and Third World peasants, respectively, and focused on the relational forces and class inequalities of capitalism and imperialism (for example, Wolf 1982), foci that were of minor interest to the more bourgeois tainted figurational sociologists. Indeed, Elias was hardly interested in ideas about capital and capitalism, and tended to believe that post-feudal social developments

---

2   Both Eric Wolf and Charles Tilly were much inspired by Elias's general approach, with the latter increasingly using the notion of 'relational explanation' as an alternative to 'structuralist' and 'individualist' explanations, see for example, Tilly 1998, 2001a, 2002b. See also Kalb 1997; Emirbayer 1997; Rebel 2010.

necessarily led to an equalization of classes of people. His 'civilizing process' was another term for the embourgeoisement of society.

The interest of social researchers in Norbert Elias's work faded rapidly in the later 1980s. In retrospect it now seems that it was squeezed between the new (post)structuralist tendencies in academic social theory on the one hand, and an increasingly dominant neoliberalism in wider society and politics on the other. New, verbose structuralisms were promoted by Anthony Giddens (1986) and Pierre Bourdieu (1977), who both made ritual bows to Elias while trying to reach for his more psycho-genetic and micro-sociological subtleties without truly matching him. It was Michel Foucault who then usurped the more historical and 'psycho-genetic' interests expressed in Elias's work while shifting the vocabulary from 'civilizational processes' to 'disciplinary processes' (see for example, 2010). Foucault's disciplinary thesis was the ideological opposite of Elias' embourgeoisement thesis, while based in not dissimilar empirical observations and data. He thereby articulated a much more cynical idea of the constructivist powers around the bourgeois state than Elias was ready for. Elias saw the modern state very much in the light of his experience of the collapse of the monopoly on violence during the European civil wars of the early twentieth century, with Nazism as its outcome. For Elias, the modern state remained the ultimate expression and guarantor of the peaceful social interaction that was made possible by post-feudal developments in the division of labour and power. The post-feudal state regulated and monopolized the use of violence. It instilled and enforced 'self-control' in people. However, it did so almost as an expression of bourgeois civilizational development itself: self-control was both the necessary precondition for as well as the outcome of the emergence of large-scale complex state societies. For Foucault, in contrast, the state was a post-human panopticon that identified, isolated, and repressed 'non-productive' human desires and imposed modern 'productivist' governmentality on its subjects through various 'technologies of rule'. It was among other this Left critical theory of the state that turned Foucault into a guru for the emergent postmodern field of cultural studies and made him a strong early voice in the analysis and critique of neoliberalism (2010 (1978)).

It was perhaps above all Elias's silence on labour, class and capitalism that left 'figurational sociology' ill prepared for the coming neoliberalizations of human societies. Neoliberalism after 1980 simply did not accord with Elias's deeply relational vision of human social forms in which so much was interdependent. Moreover, neoliberalism's material consequences squarely refuted Elias' optimistic belief in the historical connection between the 'lengthening of chains of social interdependence' and the levelling of power differences, privileges, and inequalities. The now increasingly dominant Hayekian (2010 (1944)) mythologies of individualism, rational actors, and profit maximization – all seen as innate human norms – left Elias's figurational sociology by the wayside as too complex, too historical, too soft, and too socially democratic. New class polarizations also made his basic historical vision obsolete or at least inadequately specified. Capitalists and their neoliberal supporters in state administrations began the reversal of the equalizing of class relationships that Elias had identified as the key long-term trend in Western societies. While capital globalized and added so many new populations to its web of production and extraction, it disentangled itself from its twentieth-century interdependence on national societies and citizen-workers, who themselves remained perfectly dependent on it. Neoliberalism, by aggressively picturing the self-interested individual as the basis of both social life and of all sound economics, offered itself openly as an ally for the resurrection of capitalist dominance in the 1970s and 1980s (Harvey 2005). It went on to occupy the state bit by bit, driving back all those 'artificial' interventions in the natural freedom of the individual – including the freedom of individual corporations and capitals – that the postwar system had erected in order to prevent crises and collapses such as those of the 1930s (for recent overviews see Peck 2012, Stedman Jones 2012).

However intellectually naïve and socially immature, the 'I am Independent' of the young person in Amsterdam was thus vindicated by history, though not in the rebellious left-hedonistic sense that he might have wished. The neoliberal individual came in Hobbesian, Lockean, and Smithian forms. Paul Lafargue's (1883) 'right to laziness' was not part of it. And it came indeed in quintessentially Foucauldian modes: as a state-driven, imposed, and institutionally incentivized neoliberal project of productivist governmentality and market making. No surprise that Marx and Foucault gradually became so closely aligned in the academic analysis and critique of neoliberalization, despite the spontaneous *humeurs* of their promoters.[3]

II

Imposed governmentality? That is not how neoliberalism saw itself, as Makovicky emphasizes in the introduction to this book. The "propensity to barter" was, as in Adam Smith, seen as natural and innate. Individual profit maximization and opportunity seeking were perceived as a fundamental human motivation, a primary social phenomenon, and the source of all progress. Greed was a force for good in society through the "hidden hand of the market" which delivered a steady 'trickle down' of wealth. In contrast, the state and social collectivities were seen as secondary and – except for kinship and a narrowly defined 'civil society' – artificial. Their tendency to encroach on liberties was seen as *the* force for evil, the key enemy of happiness, progress, and civilized life. Such obstacles for progress were perpetually thrown up by corrupt groups of 'social insiders', and were a perennial moral and social cancer that would always tend toward hypertrophy and catastrophe if liberals were not steadily on guard.

This is why recent critical work on neoliberalism stresses the proselytizing aspects of the creed. According to the proponents of this creed, the goal was

---

3   See the two recent key debates in anthropology on neoliberalism in *Focaal* 2008, *Social Anthropology* 2012/13.

never reached, purity was always threatened by 'distortions' and 'biases', and vigilantes should always be ready to blow the whistle. The devil hides by definition in the details. Neoliberalism thus tends towards sectarianism even when it is dominant. The sect is clustered around some visible high priests and think tank mouthpieces, but is mainly composed of grey experts in state bureaucracies, advisory organs, consultancies, universities and of course, banks and employer organizations, who duly advocate and impose 'normality'. Sectarianism aligns by nature with technocratic bodies that are sheltered from democratic meddling. Neoliberal technocracy has become both a global and a local mammoth force, if need be commanded by top bankers themselves. And then there are the media organizations, these days often owned by a handful of profit driven transnational corporations, largely dedicated to neoliberal politics, with some moral qualms here or there over its excesses of greed.

Postsocialist Central and Eastern Europe has seen a great deal of this sectarian proselytizing combined with technocratic dictates. Makovicky rightly quotes Leszek Balcerowicz, the first finance minister of the democratic Polish state and later governor of the Central Bank of Poland. Balcerowicz has often been seen as one of the most unerring 'reformers' in CEE. People who knew him personally have often noted that he was driven by something close to religious zeal. The principled neoliberal monetarism that Balcerowicz advocated and implemented through institutions sheltered from the influence of the public, such as the Central Bank of Poland, was based as much on an idea of redemption as on expert economic insight. At a commemorative conference in Vienna in 1999 I heard him literally say that socialism had served to "crowd out conscience", a creative collusion of Christian and market language of course, but also an outright moral condemnation of the newly sovereign Polish people in whose name he was supposed to govern the economy (see Kalb 2002).

III

Balcerowicz was an example, and no exception. There is a peculiarly defining generative tension, a foundational syndrome perhaps, in postsocialist Central European politics. The empirical core of this syndrome is about trust. Not the timeless lack of trust that postsocialist CEE citizens are said to feel against all forms of centralized rule. That observation merely echoes the facile complaints of its elites. It is the other way around: the issue emerges from the lack of trust that postsocialist rulers, technocrats and opinion makers have felt for their citizens right from the very start of democratization, and even before it. The new elites were profoundly suspicious of the popular attitudes in their nations, which were supposed to have been deeply formed by socialism. The spontaneous, but not 'natural' (sic!), inclinations of their postsocialist compatriots could never be trusted, despite the obvious fact that these same citizens had just clearly rejected state socialism – a state socialism that was the fundamental other of neoliberalism.

And despite the fact, that they had democratically put these same new leaderships in control of their newly sovereign (people said) states. From the very first weeks of 'democratic rule' CEE governing elites began an assault on the supposed 'claiming behaviour' and 'learned helplessness' of their citizens. Citizens responded in kind, partly by the informal practices they knew, partly by withdrawing largely from formal democratic politics and forcing almost every new government out after each electoral period. It was the somewhat paranoid unfolding of this peculiar generative syndrome that has defined CEE political culture in the first 25 years after the fall of the Wall. It is perhaps the very definition of postsocialism.[4]

This unfolding, it bears repeating, took place against a dramatic background of collapsing employment, escalating inequalities, income stagnation for many, and massive outmigration of the young and capable. Ideologically it was all wrapped up in a common and sovereign desire to 'return to Europe', amid close-up monitoring by the EU, the IMF, and the World Bank. To fathom the material context of hope and delusion one only needs to refer to the learned prognosis of Adam Przeworski in 1991, who feared, against the more dominant optimistic predictions, that it could well take 25 years for CEE to 'catch up' with Western Europe economically (1991). An incredibly optimistic pessimism, we now know, after some more learning.

Buchowski (2006), for example, has shown how the media in Poland indulged in the 're-orientalization' of workers and peasants, as they were not deemed suitable for that commonly desired 'return to Europe', in contrast to those who believed themselves to be among the new Polish 'middle classes'. Polish sociologists like Sztompka (1993) and Szaczi (see Kalb 2002), openly doubted the 'civilizational competences' of their co-nationals. Romanian political scientist Tismaneanu (2009, orig. 1999) warned incessantly of the totalitarian populist impulses of less educated Romanians. These were not marginal critics. They were highly influential academics in the respective countries. In such a climate of public opinion, neoliberal policy-makers felt reaffirmed and doubled up their organized distrust of the people. In the first decade after 1989 this distrust was particularly intense in places such as Poland, where dissidence had nurtured circles of technocrats who came equipped with their own readings of Hayek and other neoliberal intellectuals. Such experts had sometimes served at the World Bank or had received grants to Western think tanks. Neoliberal zeal was even more characteristic of the Baltic countries, in particular Estonia and Latvia, where neoliberalism had been magnified into a national identity project against formerly Soviet and now Russian imperialists. Annist's chapter in this book gives a good sense of the mythological excesses. After 2000, neoliberal proselytizing spread to the Balkans and Romania and took on new forms. Romanian 'anticommunism' came close to being an official state ideology, as conservative elites tried to deflect popular disaffection with neoliberal outcomes by criminalizing the whole communist past and condemning any Left political alternatives to neoliberal rule, as Florin Poenaru has shown

4   My approach builds on Kalb 2000, 2002, 2005, 2009, 2011, 2012.

(Poenaru 2013). 'Democrats' in Serbia, meanwhile, did not hesitate to deny the democratic credentials of populations that failed to applaud the destruction of their local economies by state policies of privatization and liberalization (Vetta 2011). Recently, I overheard a Belgrade-based psychologist wonder in earnest whether her university department had 'a right to survive' if it was not going to make a profit. Neoliberal zeal was one form of appearance of the 'foundational syndrome' of postsocialist capitalist states in Central Europe, outright 're-orientalization' and 'othering' of victimized populations a more dramatic instance of the same.

That partly explains why the relationship between neoliberalism and personhood in postsocialism, the title of this collection, remains an urgent issue. The new neoliberal governing classes in CEE geared whole state narratives – 'transition narratives' as Makovicky calls them – plus associated forms of institutional design, supported by official public opinion, toward a popular educational project that hoped to save their newly independent countries and citizens from their pasts and from their spontaneous but unnatural selves. The project was indeed about 'modal personality engineering'. Governing classes began with warning against 'dissimulation' and 'claiming behaviour'. By the end of the decade they were openly fearing what they believed were the as yet subterranean but accumulating forces of a crypto 'totalitarian' populism that might soon surface. Since 2005 they have been in almost open panic as populism almost everywhere in CEE threatens neoliberal political business-as-usual.

While Foucauldian perspectives on neoliberalism have proliferated globally, it is perhaps in Central and Eastern Europe that they have found their most natural habitat. Here was a whole new state-making, managerial cum capitalist project born under the very sign of neoliberalism right at the moment of its global victory. And initially there truly seemed to be little counter-talk around. Neoliberalizations elsewhere were always forced to align themselves with other and prior public forces and traditions, whether social democrat, Christian, conservative, Confucian, socialist, statist or whatever. Elsewhere neoliberalism would therefore always subsist as an impure assemblage. But in CEE the major non-neoliberal patrimony with which neoliberalism could have been forced to align, socialism, had been forcefully (r)ejected as part of the act of re-gaining sovereignty. Socialism had become the absolute other of the newly independent nation-states, in some cases even its quasi-constitutionalized other. Here then was what seemed like a natural 'blank slate' for the neoliberals. The Central European lands appeared like a fertile soil, cleaned of all the roots of neoliberalism's main historical opponent.

That is, except for its people. While popularly railing against state socialism, they had been fed and nurtured exclusively by it. Here were newly sovereign nation states whose democratic elites suspected their citizens of being their own cultural fifth column, in fact their own sovereign undoing. Non-neoliberal counter-forces were therefore always 'absent-present', imagined as a dormant ghost that could unexpectedly rise out of the bottle or as a silent force corrupting the moral project from within. Suspicion and zeal were each other's flipside, the forceful re-engineering of the 'modal personality' its chief concern.

III

Makovicky (Introduction) points out that the ideas of 'flexibility' and 'self-direction' played key roles in this popular education project. Had not state-socialism gone under because of its rigidities, its lack of flexibility? Were state socialist societies not 'command economies' where units acted on dictates from above rather than on market signals from below and had they not therefore failed to become 'self-directed'? Had not a totalitarian party state prevented people from being 'self-directed' in the public and private sphere, and had it not made them dependent on paternalist handouts? Neoliberalism suggested that each and every person ought to be a small flexible accumulation unit, nurturing and counting her/his assets and deploying them efficiently for optimal and accountable gain in dynamic environments.

The year 1989 saw some impulses toward radical democracy and worker self-management in CEE (Kalb 2009), but before long it was this particular neoliberal vision of market-oriented individuals that swallowed it all, certainly so as a mythological theme and partly so as a guide for institutional design and incentives. If you refused to act as a surplus generating unit, you were apparently unable to take responsibility for yourself. You could therefore be expected to throw yourself back into the arms of the state at any moment, and ask for favours and care in exchange for dumb obedience. You were then a proven *Homo Sovieticus* and a serious liability for the newly sovereign society, whose scripted aim it was to restore the Central European middle classes to the position of glory they once presumably held. The latest dramatic instantiation of this discursive figure reappeared during the purportedly 'middle class' demonstrations in Sofia in the late spring and summer of 2013. People said that the old 'socialist' alliance between mafia, oligarchs and the poor corrupts the nation and holds a whole 'productive' society back from achieving prosperity and happiness. The virtuous and deserving and the *lumpen* and the undeserving were unambiguously identified in such narratives. This was not the only circulating narrative in Sofia, but it was an important one, in the articulation of which established intellectuals and media played a less than 'horizontalist' role.[5]

Elizabeth Dunn's ethnography of a privatized enterprise in Southeastern Poland is probably the anthropological *locus classicus* for the study of neoliberalism and personhood in postsocialism, and an inspiration for Makovicky and her authors in this book (Dunn 2004). Dunn began from the assumption that such flexible neoliberal persons were first of all formed on the workshop floor of a market driven capitalist firm. The book studies the myriad mechanisms on the shopfloor and in the organization of the baby-food plant, which was bought up by an American firm that were to produce these 'flexible', 'self-directed' workers who are keen to be

---

5   I was in Sofia from 19–22 July, and involved in a workshop with (among others) local researchers who gave me a wealth of details about the ongoing protest wave during several discussions, thanks among others to Mariya Ivancheva.

'market players'. Dunn shows that Polish workers can indeed be fervently playing this game. Foucauldian neoliberal governmentality seemed to be happening and rather more smoothly than the *homo sovieticus* story implied.

However, her study also captured the tension between neoliberalism and its absent/present other in CEE as it was crystallizing out in the late 1990s/early 2000s. During interviews at homes of befriended workers, it became clear that people kept their own distinct narratives about capitalism and markets. They certainly did not want state socialism back, Dunn concluded. But in their hybrid language of social Catholicism mixed with socialist traditions, her informants did express a rather different moral economy, one that unambiguously continued to privilege use values over surplus values. There was little doubting that in private conversations her interlocutors seemed to appreciate social solidarity and public welfare more than individualist success, at least as a social norm. Dunn surmised that postsocialist workers had provocative counterpoints to offer to Western neoliberalism.

In my own research on Polish workers (2009) this insight is vindicated and is followed up further. Coming just a bit later in time than Dunn's project and being more focused on union activists, it shows how this hybrid critical sensibility came to align itself over time(and in the absence of a credible leftist alternative) in some cases with the organicist neo-nationalism of the Polish Right. In Poland, a right wing bloc emerged in the 2000s with strong support from some labour segments, favouring national values and national accumulation and rejecting the endless circulation and surplus extraction of transnational capitalism as bad for Poles. Similar populist processes had been happening elsewhere in CEE, with Hungary being something like the Right wing avant-garde (but less the outlier it is often made out to be) (Kalb and Halmai 2011). However, these Right wing processes in response to neoliberalizations were also happening in Western Europe, Northern Europe, and Southern Europe, as well as in the US. They were quite universal in the old industrial world in fact, while taking contingent and diverse forms in different places. They therefore seemed to be associated just as much with the dispossessions and disenfranchisements of class under neoliberal capitalism as such as with the subdued voices of a particular Central European past – nationalist as well as state-socialist – even though such local histories did of course inform the symbols and narratives that were being used (ibid.).

The chapters in this book do not go into such shifting political processes of subject articulation in response to neoliberal capitalism and forms of 'personhood' over time. They generally interrogate neoliberalism 'at work' on its own turf. They show that, like Dunn's workers, white collar workers in banks and consultancies in Romania, Slovak au-pairs in London, construction contractors in Romania, and 'ethno-entrepreneurs' in the Carpathians are fully capable of endorsing the flexibility and 'self direction' that neoliberalism cherishes. Further, they show that people from Central Europe are frequently accepting (temporary) migration as a matter-of-fact part of their social reproduction (Sekerakova-Burikova, Umbres); are working very long hours for low pay (Chelcea, Petrovici); are often living with little or no leisure or holiday time, and without much job security or social security (Chelcea, Petrovici); and find it close to impossible of having a professional career as a woman with children (Petrovici). They in fact show, but do not say so explicitly, how fragile or illusory 'middle class' aspirations in postsocialism are. This seems one silent but very big theme of the book. And they show, once more, that the elite and Western prejudices about rigidity and a lack of self-motivation were always just that, prejudices.

The case studies also demonstrate the subtle discursive distances that people articulate *vis-à-vis* core neoliberal assumptions, even though one sometimes needs a deeper look to be able to see this. It comes out very effectively in Sekerakova-Burikova's chapter. Slovak au-pairs would in the first encounter conveniently reiterate neoliberalism's story of going where the action is, in the West of course, 'earning money', having 'success', 'climbing up'. But on closer scrutiny their choices often seem to be driven by the more encompassing wish to see something of the world, meet people, make friends, and speak languages. Interestingly, their mothers are generally encouraging their daughters to do so. Is this an effort to protect them against marrying at a young age with a local guy and becoming a young mother in an environment of stagnation and decline? It seems so. Their fathers meanwhile are reluctant to see them leave, perhaps for the obverse reason. In any case: the horizons and processes of choice of these itinerant girls from the Slovakian provinces far exceed the neoliberal imagination. And in doing so they express the deeply relational processes of social becoming that Elias was interested in.

Chelchea's middle-level Romanian bank managers, too, seem well aware of how little they are actually able to enjoy the secure social status and related pleasure and leisure that bank clerks in socialism were used to. And though failing to find the collective leverage for organizing against their employer or for openly speaking up, they refuse to obey the bank's official rule that individually negotiated compensation packages are not to be communicated and discussed with colleagues. They know perfectly well that this would only enhance the banks' ability to play them off against each other and manipulate them. Umbres' fascinating construction entrepreneur in Romania has been trained in building enterprises in the west and aspires to a superior quality of work, design and materials. No lack of flexibility and self-direction in his case. Nevertheless he knows perfectly well that he needs to embed himself in local Romanian networks, gain local trust and reputation, and attune costs to the shifting and not always transparent ability of customers to pay. If neoliberalism cherishes clear contracts, the survival of this successful entrepreneur depends on leaving prices and payments open for as long as needed. Hamilton's small entrepreneurs in Halle, in the former GDR, are just as '*Wessie*' as any western entrepreneur when it comes to self-initiative and flexible agency on markets. But within the local context of a sharp *Wessie/Ossie* debate in Germany (slowly subsiding I guess), they prefer to emphasize a sense of local social responsibility, a style said to be characteristic of what nowadays is called the *Wossie* type of entrepreneur.

In all these cases, Eliassian social relations, situated social interdependencies and networks explain what people do and how they seem to think. I would call this 'relational realism'. As Elias emphasized, two idols must be avoided. The one is a reification of society, as in 'Central European culture' or 'postsocialism', big spatiotemporal container concepts which are then by themselves supposed to explain particular forms of thought and behaviour among the subjects of our research. Reification of society is closely associated with cultural essentialism. Such static and nominalist macro-container concepts cannot grasp the specificities, differentiations, and dynamism inherent to these 'real-life' situated cases and can only serve to contextualize them cursorily at the broadest possible level. The other is methodological individualism. Neoliberalism's preferred rational actor only helps to explain the most obvious. In rational actor-analyses the unexplained rest is then often once more relegated to essentialist culture explanations. The two bipolar idols are in fact closely connected. The authors in this book show how the methodological alternative of relational realism can be deployed through fieldwork and to what sort of close-up discoveries this can lead.

IV

However, these chapters also ring a bell about possible trouble with two of the key terms of this collection: neoliberalism and personhood. I will thus end with some of the troubling sounds that I'm hearing, starting with the idea of the person. As implied above, the people studied in the chapters of this book are complex, divided and ambiguous persons, reflecting the nature of the environments in which they live. They speak not always with a clear voice, nor probably always with a steady voice. They are aware that global media, governmental elites, and employers are continuously making demands on them as persons, as do their families, friends, and wider personal networks. The clue for a relationally realist approach is to acknowledge that all these different forces may be pulling in partly different directions and confront persons with not always easily reconcilable claims, obligations, and ultimate goals. This is indeed what all chapters succeed in demonstrating. The chapters are about the paradoxes and contradictions of living a life in severely neoliberalized social contexts against the backdrop of a state-socialist past and an insecure peripheral capitalist presence.

My point is that these paradoxes and contradictions are both intimate and large-scale, and that they are utterly real. Anthropology has had its 'Culture and Personality' school in the 1930–50s, where whole cultures were assumed to produce particular modal personality types, such as among the different native American tribes (Benedict 1993, orig. 1933). These approaches were later rejected as overly idealist explanations of human behaviour and sentiments. Some of this 'culture and personality' impulse was taken up again by Clifford Geertz (1973) in the 1970s, and this was certainly part of his great success. It also clearly lingers on in anthropology as a sort of default approach to everything, if only because it is what the wider public often expects us to do. Several key works on neoliberalism also liberally make use of notions of the person and personhood, such as the Anglo-Foucauldian authors Emily Martin (2007) and Nikolas Rose (Miller and Rose 2008), both cited by Makovicky. But does '*the* person' not somehow presume exactly the bipolarity of society and the individual, culture and the person, that Elias and other relational realists were critiquing? Does the notion of '*the* person' not depend on a strong idea of '*the* culture' – indeed once more as a reified and static abstraction? Is this not also how neoliberalism sometimes emerges in the work of for example Martin and Rose: as a strong encapsulating universe from which there is little escape or relief? In her introduction, Makovicky points out that even these 'big cultural' theorists of neoliberalism have been forced to acknowledge the myriad ways in which persons under neoliberalism are *also* a bit dependent on actors other than neoliberal administrations. In other words: that the relationship between neoliberalizing administrations and their clients or subjects is never the only relationship that helps to constitute them as persons.

I would prefer to see neoliberalism not as a culture that produces a particular personhood but as a hegemony that exerts specific pressures and sets certain limits on the possible paths of personal becoming.[6] Hegemony, in this vision, is not a cultural consensus but a structured field of social relations of dominance. In that hegemonic field, the dominant never totally dominate, because they cannot control and monopolize all the relational resources and practices that actors maintain, nor oversee all the claims that subjects are making on each other. Nor do they control, in a literal sense, subjectivities. What they will do their utmost to keep control over, under neoliberal capitalism, is the generation and extraction of surplus value. They will also try to use all bureaucratic apparatuses at their disposal to make people obey the accumulation imperative, will see few reasons to compensate those who fail to compensate themselves, and will try to manage cognitive and ideological processes in society so that anger will be channelled into manageable forms of protest and resistance. They will often succeed in this hegemonic project, given the massive resources they can command, and given the very limited means of independent survival most common people have access to. But how much they will succeed is an open question, as is also illustrated by the chapters in this book. And whatever success they will have is rarely explained by popular consensus about and support for their rule.

Neoliberalism, as we know, has a tendency to be omnipresent and omnivorous (Clarke 2008). Since its discovery as a linking-concept among critics of corporate globalization and welfare state retrenchment in the late 1990s its meanings have constantly expanded and more links have been added. It is now seen as simultaneously an ideological program; a set of governmental tools and instruments; the governmentalities, rationalities, and subjectivities emerging from the use of those tools and the ritualizations of the ideology; the alignments it

---

6   For this view of hegemony in anthropology see among others Roseberry 1994; Kalb 1997; Crehan 2002.

makes with institutional traditions with a different origin, as in 'neoliberal ngo's and neoliberal human rights'; a convenient stand in for capitalism; and a period-concept marking out the properties that distinguishes our era from other periods, in particular the preceding world era of state socialism in Eurasia, welfare statism in the West, and developmental-statism in the South. To further compound this complexity, it has become the archetypal multi-scalar concept, conjoining global structures and processes with regional and national level ones and all the way down to the intimate properties of personhood and sociality. In short, if you want to say a lot by saying nothing these days, use the N-word as much as possible.

This is not to imply that we could or should do without it, as yet, but it does suggest that we should try to use the term judiciously, sparely, and sharply. I am not convinced by Larson's suggestion, for example, that the Anglo-Saxon template for writing a *curriculum vitae* is by definition neoliberal, unless, that is, Anglo-Saxon professional culture or bio-culture as a whole is seen as thoroughly neoliberal, which for me stretches the term too far. I certainly see what Larson is out at, but I am not sure that we are not losing more than we are gaining with such a stretching strategy. If Miller and Rose write that neoliberalism comprises "a new ethic of the active, choosing, responsible, autonomous individual ... " (see Makovicky's Introduction), I wonder whether those epithets were not in fact the timeless properties by which the West as a whole has always tried to distinguish itself from the East (and the rest) since the rise of Athens. We could even add 'rational' to that list, or 'manly', and of course democratic. There is also a close resemblance to how Protestantism distanced itself discursively from Catholicism. These are also typically classical liberal notions, rather than necessarily neoliberal ones. Similar problems of precision occur with the notion of 'audit culture'. Auditing seems to be a property of all good Weberian bureaucracies as they monitor their sub-departments and subject populations. It is the precise use and the contents of the audit that matters under neoliberalism, not the audit itself. What about 'enterprising selves', 'flexibility', 'initiative, action, and agency' (Makovicky's Introduction)? Again there seems a much older Western, protestant, liberal, and mercantile pedigree here. We almost seem at the point where we would begin to equate the sheer human capacity to count with neoliberalism as such.

The rule seems to be that all the individual separate items associated with neoliberalism, in particular the tools and instruments of governance, but also quite a few of the key ideological terms, become only truly neoliberal in the context of, yes, neoliberalism. It is then the whole assemblage of neoliberalism as historical context, the totality, to use an old word, which ultimately defines the material properties of its parts, and not the other way around. This of course underlines neoliberal's continuing importance as a period concept defining an era of (global) capitalism. Which is in fact a definition in terms of a particular sort of hegemony in the sense defined above.

I am therefore tempted to isolate as the crucially defining property of neoliberalism not any of its advertised symbols such as the market and the individual etc., but rather that major feature of its material social reality that its mouthpieces have constantly been seeking to obscure: this is, predictably, class, class interest, and the new capitalist class polarizations (see also Kalb 2012, 2014). The underside of 'the market', 'privatization', 'liberalization' etc. has indeed been dispossession and disenfranchisement, precariatization and informalization, including of course increased mobility and migration. While most chapters assume the informalization and precariatization as a backdrop, it is mainly in the chapters by Annist and Makovicky that disenfranchisement and dispossession appear. Makovicky shows how utterly inadequately EU subsidiarity compensates for the full package of modern industrial modernity that state socialism had offered in the small town landscapes of the Carpathians. These are now stagnating places with collapsing employment and declining public services, left alone by public bureaucracies to largely fend for themselves. This is so notwithstanding the ability of some people to stay and prosper, for example in the ethno-art sector or the eco-agricultural sector that the EU has affiliated itself to. Annist takes this further and comes closer to the skin of what it means to be dispossessed by state imposed neoliberalizations in the former kolkhoz landscapes of the Baltics. The older former kolkhoz workers who have not found the means to leave for better shores are, after 20 years of public abandonment, even left dispossessed of each other, as sacrificed people refuse to become associated with their co-victims of neoliberalism. Personhood and markets? It is the new class formations that may provide the 'real' clue to the structure of life under neoliberalism, I suspect. Social reproduction has become precarious, fragile and tense. People, seriously impoverished or hanging on in style, cling to older ideals of 'community' and the 'nation', or to the agonistic symbol of 'the middle class' that was once offered as the promise for all at the 'end of transition'.

References

Benedict, R. 1993 [1933]. *Patterns of Culture.* Boston: Houghton-Mifflin.
Bourdieu, P. 1977. *Outline of a Theory of Practice.* Cambridge: Cambridge University Press.
Buchowski, M. 2006. The Specter of Orientalism in Europe: From Exotic Other to Stigmatized Brother. *Anthropological Quarterly,* 79(3): 463–82.
Clarke, J. 2008. Living with/in and without neo-liberalism. *Focaal – European Journal of Anthropology,* 51: 135–47.
Crehan, K. 2002. *Gramsci, Culture and Anthropology. An Introductory Text.* London: Pluto Press.
Dunn, E. 2004. *Privatizing Poland: Baby Food, Big Business, and the Remaking of Labor.* Ithaca: Cornell University Press.
Elias, N. 2000. *The Civilizing Process.* London: Wiley-Blackwell.
Elias, N. 2005. *The Court Society.* Dublin: University College Dublin Press.
Elias, N. 2009. *Was Ist Soziologie?* Frankfurt: Juventa Verlag.

Emirbayer, M. 1997. Manifesto for a Relational Sociology. *American Journal of Sociology*, 103(2): 281–317.

Foucault, M. 2010. *The Birth of Biopolitics*. Oxford: Palgrave Macmillan.

Geertz, C. 1973. *The Interpretation of Cultures*. New York: Basic Books.

Giddens, A. 1986. *The Constitution of Society: Outline of the Theory of Structuration*. London: Polity Press.

Hall, S. et al. 1978. *Policing the Crisis: Mugging, the State and Law and Order*. London: Palgrave Macmillan.

Hall, S. et al. 2006. *Resistance Through Rituals: Youth Subcultures in Post-War Britain*. London: Routledge.

Harvey, D. 2005. *A Brief History of Neoliberalism*. Oxford: Oxford University Press.

Hayek, F.A. 2010. *The Road to Serfdom*. London: Routledge.

Kalb, D. 1997. *Expanding Class: Power and Everyday Politics in Industrial Communities, The Netherlands 1850–1950*. Durham, NC: Duke University Press.

Kalb, D. 2000. Localizing Flows: Power, Paths, Institutions, and Networks, in D. Kalb, M. van der Land; R. Staring et al. (eds), *The Ends of Globalization: Bringing Society Back In*. Lanham: Rowman and Littlefield, 1–32.

Kalb, D. 2002. Afterword: Globalism and Postsocialist prospects, in C.H. Hann (ed.), *Postsocialism: Ideals, Ideologies and Practices in Eurasia*. London: Routledge, pp. 317–35.

Kalb, D. 2005. From Flows to Violence: Politics and Knowledge in the Debates on Globalization and Empire. *Anthropological Theory*, 5(2): 176–204.

Kalb, D. 2009. Conversations with a Polish populist: Tracing hidden histories of globalization, class, and dispossession in postsocialism (and beyond). *American Ethnologist*, 36(2): 207–23.

Kalb, D. 2011. Introduction: Headlines of Nation, Subtexts of Class: Working Class Populism and the Return of the Repressed in Neoliberal Europe, in D. Kalb and G. Halmai (eds), *Headlines of Nation, Subtexts of Class: Working Class Populism and the Return of the Repressed in Neoliberal Europe*. Oxford and New York: Berghahn Books, 1–63.

Kalb, D and Halmai, G. 2011. *Headlines of Nation, Subtexts of Class: Working Class Populism and the Return of the Repressed in Neoliberal Europe*. Oxford and New York: Berghahn Books.

Kalb, D. 2012. Thinking about neoliberalism as if the crisis was actually happening. *Social Anthropology*, 20(3): 318–30.

Kalb, D. 2014. (forthcoming). Class and the new anthropological holism, in J. Carrier and D. Kalb (eds), *Anthropologies of Class*.

Lafargue, P. 1883. *The Right To Be Lazy and Other Studies*. Chicago: Charles Kerr and Co.

Martin, E. 2007. *Bipolar Expeditions. Mania and Depression in American Culture*. Princeton: Princeton University Press.

Miller, P. and N. Rose. 2008. *Governing the Present: Administering Economic, Social and Personal Life*. Cambridge: Polity Press.

Peck, J. 2012. *Constructions of Neoliberal Reason*. Oxford: Oxford University Press.

Poenaru, F. 2012. Budapest: Unpublished Dissertation CEU.

Przeworski, A. 1991. *Democracy and the Market: Political and Economic Reforms in Eastern Europe and Latin America*. Cambridge: Cambridge University Press.

Rebel, H. 2010. *When Women Held the Dragon's Tongue and other Essays in Historical Anthropology*. Oxford and New York: Berghahn Books.

Roseberry, W. 1994. Hegemony and the Language of Contention, in G.M. Joseph and D. Nugent (eds), *Everyday Forms of State Formation: Revolution and Negotiation of Rule in Modern Mexico*. Durham, NC: Duke University Press.

Stedman Jones, D. 2012. *Masters of the Universe*. Princeton: Princeton University Press.

Sztompka, P. 1993. Civilizational Incompetence: The Trap of Post Communist Societies. *Zeitschrift für Soziologie*, 22(2): 85–95.

Thompson, E.P. 1965. *The Making of the English Working Class*. New York: Vintage.

Thompson, E.P. 1980. *The Poverty of Theory and other Essays*. New York: Monthly Review Press.

Tismaneanu, V. 2009. *Fantasies of Salvation: Democracy, Nationalism, and Myth in Post-Communist Europe*. Princeton: Princeton University Press.

Tilly, C. 1998. *Durable Inequality*. Berkeley: University of California Press.

Tilly, C. 2001a. Introduction: Anthropology confronts Inequality. *Anthropological Theory*, 1(3): 299–306.

Tilly, C. 2001b. Relational Origins of Inequality. *Anthropological Theory*, 1(3): 355–72.

Vetta, T. 2011. Nationalism is Back! Radikali and Privatization in Serbia, in D. Kalb and G. Halmai (eds), *Headlines of Nation, Subtexts of Class: Working Class Populism and the Return of the Repressed in Neoliberal Europe*. Oxford and New York: Berghahn Books, 37–56.

Williams, R. 1971. *Culture and Society, 1780–1950*. London: Penguin.

Williams, R. 1977. *Marxism and Literature*. Oxford: Oxford Paperbacks.

Williams, R. 2005. *Culture and Materialism*. London: Verso.

Wolf, E. 1982. *Europe and the People without History*. Berkeley: University of California Press.

Index